The Search for Justice

CW00551890

The Search for Justice

Lawyers in the Civil Rights Revolution, 1950–1975

PETER CHARLES HOFFER

The University of Chicago Press
Chicago and London

The University of Chicago Press, Chicago 60637
The University of Chicago Press, Ltd., London
© 2019 by Peter Charles Hoffer
All rights reserved. No part of this book may be used or reproduced in any manner
whatsoever without written permission, except in the case of brief quotations in
critical articles and reviews. For more information, contact the University of
Chicago Press, 1427 E. 60th St., Chicago, IL 60637.
Published 2019
Printed in the United States of America

28 27 26 25 24 23 22 21 20 19   1 2 3 4 5

ISBN-13: 978-0-226-61428-1 (cloth)
ISBN-13: 978-0-226-61431-1 (paper)
ISBN-13: 978-0-226-61445-8 (e-book)
DOI: https://doi.org/10.7208/chicago/9780226614458.001.0001

Library of Congress Cataloging-in-Publication Data

Names: Hoffer, Peter Charles, 1944– author.
Title: The search for justice: lawyers in the civil rights revolution, 1950–1975 /
    Peter Charles Hoffer.
Description: Chicago; London: The University of Chicago Press, 2019. | Includes
    bibliographical references and index.
Identifiers: LCCN 2018035644 | ISBN 9780226614281 (cloth: alk. paper) |
    ISBN 9780226614311 (pbk: alk. paper) | ISBN 9780226614458 (e-book)
Subjects: LCSH: Civil rights lawyers—United States—History—20th century. |
    Law—United States—History—20th century. | Civil rights—United States—
    History—20th century. | Segregation in education—Law and legislation—
    United States. | United States—History—1945–
Classification: LCC KF299.C48 H64 2019 | DDC 340.092/273—dc23
LC record available at https://lccn.loc.gov/2018035644

♾ This paper meets the requirements of ANSI/NISO Z39.48–1992 (Permanence of Paper).

Contents

Preface vii

Introduction: Lawyering in the Civil Rights Era 1

Prologue: The Long Night of Jim Crow 14

1 The Road to *Sweatt v. Painter* 25

2 *Brown v. Board of Education* 52

3 Making the Case for Segregation 85

4 They Had a Dream 122

5 Whose Victory? Whose Defeat? 151

6 Legal Academics and Civil Rights Lawyering 167

**Conclusion: Politics or Law? Legacies of Lawyering
in the Civil Rights Era** 189

Index 197

Preface

This is my fourth book in a series on the role of law, lawyers, and legal practice in American political life. The first argued that law and lawyers were central to the American experience and needed to be added to the standard account of our history. The next two books tracked the lawyers through the American Revolution and the Civil War, respectively. The present work concludes that series with the study of lawyering in the Civil Rights Era. I believe that these are the three critical moments when lawyers and lawyering altered the course of our history.

A more conventional version of similar arguments focuses not on the lawyers but on "publican" moments in American constitutionalism, when lawyers, among others, refashioned the formal structures of our government. Those moments included the drafting of the federal Constitution, followed by the adoption of the Bill of Rights; the crafting of the Reconstruction Amendments; and the shifting of governmental functions during the New Deal. To be sure, lawyers played key roles in all of these, but the first two could not have occurred without the lawyering of the Revolution and the Civil War, respectively, and we now realize that the changes in federal government operation during the New Deal were not so profound as their supporters and their critics said at the time. The Civil Rights Era introduced far more lasting reconfigurations of our laws than occurred in the New Deal.

Nothing of the work I have described above is definitive. None of it, I venture to say, was meant to be definitive. Mine and others' are interpretive essays intended to raise as many important questions as they answer. One contribution they make to the literature on American history cannot be questioned, however. Lawyers on both sides of the Revolution, secession and the Civil War, and civil rights litigation played absolutely crucial parts, at critical times, in making our history.

This book could certainly have been two or three times its present size. There are so many remarkable stories within the larger story of civil rights litigation from 1950 to 1975, and so many remarkable people who lived those stories, that it seems almost unfair to write as concisely as I have tried to do. I suppose that is true of every history book. I have one precedent on my side, however. Once upon a time, oral argument before the first sessions of the Supreme Court of the United States had no time limit. Leather-lunged counsel like Daniel Webster could and did go on for hours. Written briefs could be any length. Eventually, the Court limited oral argument to an hour for each side. Written briefs for the principal parties according to Rule 32 of the Federal Rules of Appellate Procedure may not exceed thirty pages in length. The result is more concise presentation. I think that choosing to say only what is important is a worthy goal for academics as well.

Acknowledgments are the easiest parts of a book to write. N. E. H. Hull, Michael Klarman, Robert Pratt, Christopher Schmidt, and Mark Tushnet agreed to read the manuscript for the author. Two anonymous readers for the Press were generous and helpful. Chuck Myers, my editor at Chicago, took the manuscript and under capacious wings carried it to safety like the eagle in *The Return of the King*. Copy editor Erin DeWitt ensured that the manuscript landed perfectly intact. I am deeply grateful to all of them. Remaining errors are my own. Parts of this book are derived from *The Federal Courts: An Essential History*; it was a collaborative effort, though the present author wrote the parts herein reproduced. Thanks for reading the manuscript also go to Clare Cushman, Daniel Ernst, Paul Finkelman, Daniel Holt, Laura Kalman, Paul Kens, Jake Kobrick, Jon Lurie, Edward Purcell, Bruce Ragsdale, Michael Wells, Russell Wheeler, William Wiecek, the Hon. J. Harvie Wilkinson, and of course to my coauthors, N. E. H. Hull and Williamjames Hull Hoffer.

Lawyering in the Civil Rights Era

The Civil Rights Era was a time of simmering unrest in American political and social life. Although scenes of turbulence played out in the mass media, the real crisis was one of self-reflection. If the turmoil was comparatively law-abiding compared to upheavals like the American Revolution and the Civil War, the challenge for law and lawyers of the Civil Rights Era was in some ways as profound as it was in the Revolutionary Era of 1761–76 and the Civil War Era of 1861–65. At issue was the future of social and political relations among the races. Lawyers demonstrated the power of law to define what was at stake; to resolve competing concepts of order and equality; and in the end to hold out the promise of a new and better nation. As Burke Marshall, head of the Civil Rights Division of the Department of Justice under presidents John F. Kennedy and Lyndon Baines Johnson, put it, some years later: "The subject matter of the civil rights and the bringing to bear the processes of the law on that, you know, is a matter of great interest—at least, it seemed to me to be obvious at the time; I suppose it wasn't obvious to everyone, but it seemed to be obvious at the time—1961, that that was going to be the most interesting lawyers' work going on in the country. And for many lawyers, it was."[1]

---

1. On the Revolutionary lawyers, see Peter Charles Hoffer and Williamjames Hull Hoffer, "A Clamor of Lawyers": The Legal Profession in the American Revolution (Ithaca, NY: Cornell University Press, 2018), and on the Civil War lawyers, see Peter Charles Hoffer, Uncivil Warriors: The Lawyers' Civil War (New York: Oxford University Press, 2018). Burke Marshall, oral history, Johnson Presidential Library, October 28, 1968, 1–2.

This is as good a place as any to say that "civil rights lawyering" is itself a contested term. While the trend among historians of race is to reach back into the nineteenth century to begin the story of racial injustice and the search for justice, Christopher Schmidt argues that legal historians might best focus on what he calls "an alternative approach to the history of civil rights, one

My offering here is an interpretive essay on the role of the lawyers and lawyering of the Civil Rights Era, roughly defined as 1950–75, focusing on issues of school segregation. School desegregation was the "archetypical" civil rights issue of this period. The emphasis on equality in educational opportunity tracks that of the Legal and Educational Defense Fund (LDF) of the National Association for the Advancement of Colored People (NAACP). Even in this narrower scope of civil rights, the book is not intended to be an exhaustive recounting of cases, people, and places, as many fine works on the subject have covered that ground. Instead, it is a subjective argument about the way in which the methods of lawyers *acting as lawyers* structured the story.[2]

Who were the crucial participants in this tectonic shift of law? The Legal Defense and Educational Fund of the NAACP, alongside local NAACP counsel, brought lawsuits and carried on appeals for over twenty years in state and federal courts. Although lawyering in American was adopting a corporate model, NAACP lawyers had little interest in progressing up the ladder of corporate law practice. Instead, they were the avatars of another kind of lawyering—public interest law. The very founding document of the LDF called on its lawyers to represent worthy causes gratuitously. Support would come from contributions to the LDF as it pursued this objective.[3]

---

focused on what I call the *constrained tradition* of civil rights. This history places the evolving, contested, but historically particularized legal concept of civil rights at the center of inquiry" (italics in original). This focus is particularly important for a tale about lawyers and lawyering. Schmidt continues that "much of the force of the term was in its usefulness differentiating civil rights from other legal claims or strategies targeting racial inequality. Considered in its historical context, the civil rights label has been a tool of exclusion as well as inclusion. This important history gets lost when historians insist that civil rights should be understood to include the very racial justice claims that historical actors understood the term to exclude." See Schmidt, "Legal History and the Problem of the Long Civil Rights Movement," *Law and Social Inquiry* 41 (2016): 1083. My reading of Schmidt's distinction is that it is not only permissible but useful to narrow the focus of a book on civil rights lawyering to the period 1950–75.

2. "Archetypal": Tomiko Brown-Nagin, "The Long Resistance and Historical Memory" (paper presented at the Annual Meeting of the American Society for Legal History, Las Vegas, NV, October 27, 2017).

3. Patricia Sullivan, *Lift Every Voice: The NAACP and the Making of the Civil Rights Movement* (New York: New Press, 2009), 161, 298; Mark V. Tushnet, *The NAACP's Legal Strategy against Segregated Education, 1925–1950* (Chapel Hill: University of North Carolina Press, 1987), 156–58. Public interest lawyering heretofore was limited to working for the government. With the advent of civil rights public interest lawyering, that paradigm shifted dramatically. The inheritors of the new model—counsel for political dissidents, for example—sought individual rather than societal remedies, however. See Robert Borosage et al., "The New Public Interest Lawyers," *Yale Law Journal* 79 (1970): 1069–152.

Sometimes overlooked but always present in this story were three other groups of lawyers. The first comprised members of the bar who defended the regime of Jim Crow explicitly or implicitly. Some of these men sat in the United States Congress and there crafted a series of virtual briefs for white southern traditions and states' rights. Among them, Richard Russell of Georgia, Strom Thurmond of South Carolina, Allen Ellender of Mississippi, and Price Daniel of Texas are well known to every student of twentieth-century American political history. Others, who did not attain national office, like John Patterson of Alabama and J. Lindsay Almond of Virginia, were important men in their time, though they may not be as well known today. Many were politicians and owed office to white constituencies that believed in Jim Crow. Some defended blacks in court; a few saw the injustice of segregation; but in the main they spoke for separation of the races.[4]

The third group of lawyers who belong in the civil rights story were those who sat on the state and federal benches and heard civil rights cases. Sometimes they were amenable to the new claims, and sometimes they were not. It was common practice to appoint federal judges from the region whose courts they were to hold. Thus, southern men heard challenges to Jim Crow. They had grown up with segregation, and even if they thought it wrong, they might not see it as an aberration of law or society. Although federal judicial office is appointive—the president nominates, the Senate confirms, and then the president signs the commission—the judges also have constituencies. Rarely did presidents nominate candidates from the opposing party; the Senate sometimes refused to confirm; and even once on the bench, the judges were judged by the lawyers who practiced in their courts and by the communities in which they sat.[5]

The last group of lawyers who were present throughout this story but played their part largely near its end and, for most of them, at some distance from the fray were law professors. Civil rights lawyering had always found

4. On the southern bar, including the members who sat in the Congress during the *Brown* era, see John Kyle Day, *The Southern Manifesto: Massive Resistance and the Fight to Preserve Segregation* (Jackson: University of Mississippi Press, 2014); and Jack W. Peltason, *Fifty-Eight Lonely Men: Southern Federal Judges and School Desegregation* (Urbana: University of Illinois Press, 1971); for some exceptions, see Sarah Hart Brown, *Standing against Dragons: Three Southern Lawyers in an Era of Fear* (Baton Rouge: Louisiana State University Press, 2000), 103–4 (defense of Willie McGee).

5. On the federal judiciary in this period, see Peter Charles Hoffer, Williamjames Hull Hoffer, and N. E. H. Hull, *The Federal Courts: An Essential History* (New York: Oxford University Press, 2016), 281–366.

friends and critics in legal academe. Not only were Charles Hamilton Houston and others from Howard University School of Law key players, young Harvard Law School professor Felix Frankfurter among others acted as consultants. Thurgood Marshall at the LDF had cultivated support from legal academe, and his use of professors from it and other disciplines in litigation had established bridges between higher and professional education and courtrooms. After *Brown*, the volume of law school professors' writings on civil rights exploded. "Legal scholars spent considerable effort analyzing and justifying," or in some cases criticizing, the reasoning of the courts. In classrooms and in public forums, the law professors shaped the meaning and assessed the impact of Civil Rights Era lawyering.[6]

It is the interaction of these four groups over the quarter century 1950–75 that is the subject of this book.

The nature of that interaction cannot be understood without some sense of the important role that lawyers played in the post–World War II period. After the war, lawyering had become big business—big not only because millions of dollars were at stake in anti-trust, patent, and other lawsuits, but in the sense that the major law firms now employed hundreds of lawyers, where once they had been much smaller partnerships. The reason was a revision of federal procedure in 1938, shifting from presenting the case at trial to much more extensive pretrial evidence gathering (so-called discovery) and management of cases. The young attorneys who gathered that evidence served law firms as associates, hoping, after a period of apprenticeship, to become partners in the firm. As a result, mega-firms appeared, with hundreds of lawyers in offices all over the country. Hourly fees grew, especially for clients of the major law firms. Class-action lawsuits, particularly for products liability, brought dozens of law firms together with thousands of clients harmed by the products. The fate of major industries came to depend on the quality of lawyering on both sides of these cases. Some, like tobacco products liability, spanned decades and led to congressional action.[7]

At the same time, the importance of law schools and law professors in American public life also grew. Law schools became more self-consciously

6. Risa L. Goluboff, *The Lost Promise of Civil Rights* (Cambridge, MA: Harvard University Press, 2007), 263. HeinOnline lists 89 law review articles and notes with "Civil Rights" in the title between 1900 and 1952. In the period 1953 to 2016, that number rises to 3,656.

7. On the rise of the mega law firms and the impact of the Federal Rules of Civil Procedure, see Stephen N. Subrin, Martha L. Minow, and Mark S. Brodin, *Civil Procedure: Doctrine, Practice, and Context*, 5th ed. (Frederick, MD: Aspen, 2016), chap. 4.

professional, expanding the size of their faculties and their student bodies, admitting women and minority candidates, forming associations among themselves like the Association of American Law Schools, and reaching out to leading practitioners and jurists in the American Law Institute. Even raising the standards for admission, one way in which established law schools tried to squeeze out night-school and part-time school competition, could not stem the rising number of schools and the diversification of newly minted lawyers. At the start of the century, there were only fourteen thousand law students; by mid-century, the first-year law schools' class was larger. The University of Michigan Law School was the largest in the country in 1900; it had nine full-time and two part-time professors. By 1950 its faculty had doubled. In 1960 there were thirty-nine full-time teachers, and by 1970 there were forty-eight. Another gauge of the growing importance of the legal academy was the geometric rise in law professors' salaries, from levels approximating other professors', to heights matching those of medical school and business school teachers. Law professors occupied key positions in the New Deal federal government and continued during and after World War II to staff regulatory agencies and the courts. Numbers of law school professors were appointed to the highest federal bench, including Supreme Court justices Felix Frankfurter, William O. Douglas, Wiley Rutledge, and Harlan Fiske Stone.[8]

The line between the public and the private in law, long established and long respected, was blurred in these years. In theory, private wrongs were the business of the courts. Public wrongs were the business of the legislative branch. Courts looked backward to harms; legislatures looked forward to general policies. That was the orthodoxy at least. In civil rights cases, righting individual harm required changes in general policy. Civil rights lawsuits

8. Lawrence M. Friedman, *American Law in the Twentieth Century* (New York: Simon and Schuster, 2001), 36–39; Jerold Auerbach, *Unequal Justice: Lawyers and Social Change in Modern America* (New York: Oxford University Press, 1977), 102–29; Robert Stevens, *Law School: Legal Education in America from the 1850s to the 1980s* (Chapel Hill: University of North Carolina Press, 1983), 172–80, 206–7; Peter Charles Hoffer, Williamjames Hull Hoffer, and N. E. H. Hull, *The Supreme Court: An Essential History* (Lawrence: University Press of Kansas, 2006), 221, 267, 268, 285; Brian Z. Tamanaha, *Failing Law Schools* (Chicago: University of Chicago Press, 2012), 46–47; "The Law School Faculty," Michigan Law, University of Michigan, https://www.law.umich .edu/historyandtraditions/faculty/Pages/default.aspx; American Bar Association, "First Year and Total J.D. Enrollment by Gender, 1947–2011," https://www.americanbar.org/content/dam/aba /administrative/legal_education_and_admissions_to_the_bar/statistics/jd_enrollment_1yr_total _gender.authcheckdam.pdf.

looked to the future and asked courts to sit as miniature legislatures, something that judges (at first) were reluctant to do. The story of civil rights lawyering can thus be written as the way in which courts were persuaded to manage remedies for future harms on a large scale. In the course of this evolution
of lawyers' and judges' roles, sometimes called the rise of public interest lawyering, all four groups were brought into continuous contact. But not all four
of them had the same view of their roles.[9]

Public interest lawyering is ordinarily about "win-win" outcomes. That is,
the ideal result of the litigation is improvement in the standard of living for
all the parties. This was not precisely true of the LDF campaign. The lawyers
and their clients might argue that the end of Jim Crow would be a blessing for
both blacks and whites, but the thrust of the campaign lay in achieving equal
rights for black people. As LDF leader Thurgood Marshall told a conference
of the NAACP in 1944, "All of the statutes, both federal and state, which protect the individual rights of Americans are important to Negroes as well as
other citizens. Many of these provisions are, however, of particular significance to Negroes because of the fact that in many instances these statutes are
the only protection to which Negroes can look for redress." There was thus
a sense of relentlessness in the drive for the end of forced segregation, for a
single lost case was a throwback to a time when victories for civil rights were
few and far between.[10]

By contrast, defenders of Jim Crow and opponents of desegregation looked
backward, sometimes as far as the founding generation, and sometimes only
as far as the antebellum "Old Constitution" of states' rights and limited fed-

9. Morton Horwitz, *The Transformation of American Law, 1870–1960: The Crisis of Legal Orthodoxy* (New York: Oxford University Press, 1992), 11, 51. I am not sure where to put the following disclaimer, but I suppose this note is as good a place as any. There were lawyers aplenty,
indeed a growing number of them as the 1960s progressed, in the various departments of the
federal government who played a role in the desegregation story. Notable members of the Department of Justice and the Solicitor General's office included Herbert Brownell, J. Lee Rankin,
Simon Sobeloff, Philip Elman, John Doar, and Burke Marshall. But the roles they played were
inseparable from the larger story of executive action. In other words, one cannot understand
their lawyering without a thorough analysis of the Eisenhower, Kennedy, and Johnson adminis-
trations. To do that would take this book on a tour of presidential politics far beyond its present
boundaries.

10. Thurgood Marshall, "The Legal Attack to Secure Civil Rights," NAACP Wartime Conference, 1944, in *Thurgood Marshall: His Speeches, Writings, Arguments, Opinions, and Reminiscences*, ed. Mark V. Tushnet (Chicago: Chicago Review Press, 2001), 90. On public interest lawyering, see, e.g., Martha Minow, "Political Lawyering: An Introduction," *Harvard Civil Rights–Civil
Liberties Law Review* 31 (1996): 287–96; and, generally, Alan K. Chen and Scott L. Cummings, *Public Interest Lawyering: A Contemporary Perspective* (New York: Aspen, 2013).

eral government. These were the "constitutional principles" to which they adhered and which they espoused, at least in public discourse. They were also
conservative sociologists of law, contending that law must embody and protect existing social relationships, including Jim Crow. This conservatism grew
in part from a sense of isolation—that the South was still under siege and that
any breach in the wall of Jim Crow would bring a flood of unwanted change.
In interviews and memoirs of southern pro-segregation lawyers' "conservative point of view," many of them came across to the interviewer as honest
and able counsel, arguing as best they could for their constituents. The more
radical of these, without the cautions and canon that law school and practice impose, were far less reasonable, though perhaps franker in their expressions. Their references to feared outcomes of desegregation like mongrelization, unreal and hysterical in light of dispassionate observation, were not mere
hyperbole.[11]

For the federal judges who heard these cases, precedent, particularly
prior decisions on point from the U.S. Supreme Court, seemed to predeter-
mine the outcome. Under the rule of recognition key to all Anglo-American
courts, decisions by higher (appellate) courts were precedent for new cases on
point—but in the 1940s the case law, once so clearly supportive of Jim Crow,
was beginning to change. Before the war, the federal courts had blocked some
forms of discrimination in housing, employment, and travel on public accommodations. Still, against this rising tide stood the embankment of *Plessy v.
Ferguson* (1896) and its progeny. Precedent thus seemed to lay on the side of
the segregationists. Added to this, the judicial temperament was supposed to
be conservative in one sense—cautious in what judges were supposed to do
and in particular unwilling to act as a legislative body or to make rules for
cases not before the court. The LDF lawyers and some of the judges did make
the interpretive leap, however, and on it the edifice of modern civil rights
would rest.[12]

11. Conservative point of view: John E. Batchelor, *Race and Education in North Carolina:
From Segregation to Desegregation* (Baton Rouge: Louisiana State University Press, 2016), ix;
mongrelization: Jane Dailey, "Is Marriage a Civil Right? The Politics of Intimacy in the Jim Crow
Era," in *The Folly of Jim Crow: Rethinking the Segregated South*, ed. Stephanie Cole and Natalie J.
Ring (College Station: Texas A&M University Press, 2012), 198–99. On the Old Constitution and
southern antebellum thinking, see Hoffer, *Uncivil Warriors*, 2, 3, 166, 180.

12. Did the lawsuits and the decisions of courts, hence the work of the lawyers, really matter?
Surely, "the efficacy of court decisions depends on many social and political factors." Litigation
often fails to help those most in need, for they have the least access to lawyers and courts. Courts
of equity issuing injunctions largely depend on the good faith of parties. When parties resist
or obstruct, courts must rely on other branches of government for enforcement. When courts
overreach, as in *Dred Scott v. Sandford* (1857), they may do more harm than good to the public

The role of the law professors was more subtle. For the most part, they were commentators on the litigation, sometimes with the aid of hindsight, always with a primary concern with pedagogy. Insofar as that pedagogy elevated doctrine above practice, the law professors' contribution was more concerned with getting the law right than with outcomes for the parties. But this, too, had a feedback effect on the litigation, as we will see.

*

From the outset, I wondered if it were possible to tell this story without taking sides on it. In most historical accounts, the struggle for civil rights for minorities is a morality play, with good and evil occupying opposite sides of the courtroom. Can there be a more neutral or at least sensitive narrative? On the one hand, lawyers are trained to argue whichever side of the case they are employed to argue, and historians are trained to seek neutrality if not objectivity in their accounts. But must one credit the sincerity of the defenders of the regime of segregation? Or judges who find nothing wrong with Jim Crow?[13]

The lawyers of the Civil Rights Era grew to adulthood in a nation divided by high walls of segregation. On one side were the local lawyers and New York– and D.C.–based counsel of the LDF who fought to tear down those walls along with local lawyers, almost all of them African Americans, who represented victims of Jim Crow. On the other side were the counsel for segregated state governments. The differences between the two groups was striking. The most visible was race. With a few exceptions, the LDF and the local legal affiliates of the NAACP were African American men. With no exceptions, their segregationist opponents were white men. One could hardly have drawn a more visible contrast.

---

weal. But even the most severe critics of the civil rights litigation's efficacy would concede that it inspired the conscience of right-thinking men and women and led blacks and whites to seek legal solutions to social problems. In this sense, even those who opposed civil rights, when they found themselves in court, had to abandon the most violent of older anti–civil rights tactics. This musing based on Michael J. Klarman, *From Jim Crow to Civil Rights: The Supreme Court and the Struggle for Racial Equality* (New York: Oxford University Press, 2004), 462–64.

13. Historians who work in primary source materials tend to credit the sincerity, if not the objectivity or even the knowledgeability, of the authors of those sources. True, sometimes a public speaker or memo writer will outright lie, but less often will the author of a diary, a private letter, or some other writing meant for limited circulation intentionally mislead. Historians are trained nevertheless to weigh the credibility and the motives of such writings, treating them as evidence rather than as confessions. Bigots may be sincere in their bigotry, a fact that may make more liberal-minded scholars cringe, but a fact nonetheless.

Moreover, the lawyers who opposed segregation were not politicians. That is, they were not elected officials who spoke in an official capacity. Some would, in time, take seats on the bench, but they were rarely motivated by the exigencies of electoral politics. Overwhelmingly, their opponents in court were political figures who owed their place in government to a white, pro-segregation electorate. Thus, they were not free agents in the sense that the LDF counsel were. Whatever reservations they had about the justice of segregation, their written briefs and their arguments in court, their presentations in public, and their testimony in legislative chambers conformed to the beliefs of the most ardent of their voters. The reason was simple if appalling; come election time, they often found that they had to adhere to pro-segregationist rhetoric or lose out to competitors for office who were even more antipathetic to civil rights.

A final difference: the LDF lawyers were often first-generation professionals, rising to public prominence in the course of their assault on segregation. The defenders of Jim Crow were a more varied lot; some came from the aristocracy of the robe in the South, but others had come from hardscrabble backgrounds, and one can see in their lawyering for the cause something of the animus they felt for their better-off comrades.

One can understand, if sympathy is out of the question, why white southern lawyers who became politicians would feel the necessity of supporting Jim Crow. Some did it out of personal commitment to the idea that forced separation of the races by law was good for both peoples. Others were simply following the prejudices of their white constituents. A few liberals on race, like Alabama attorney general Richmond Flowers, learned that empathy with the wrong shade of underdog would cost them reelection. His condescension for civil rights leaders and ideas slowly evolved into an appreciation of the moral and legal side of the issues, for which he found himself demagogued out of office.[14]

Sometimes members of the federal bench expressed their personal belief that segregation existed for and promoted the good of both races. Though sitting behind a bench raised above and apart from the rest of the southern federal courtroom, those who grew up with segregation were sometimes hard-pressed to envision a world without it. Judge John J. Parker of North

14. John Hayman, *Bitter Harvest: Richmond Flowers and the Civil Rights Revolution* (Montgomery, AL: NewSouth, 1996), 123; Klarman, *Jim Crow*, 407; Anne Permaloff and Carl Grafton, *Political Power in Alabama: The More Things Change . . .* (Athens: University of Georgia Press, 2008), 168.

Carolina and the Court of Appeals for the Fourth Circuit was one of these. As Parker, in 1920 a Republican running for the governorship in Democratic North Carolina, sarcastically conceded, "How could we do it without you, Mr. Nigger?" Or consider the case of federal district court judge T. Whitfield Davidson of Texas. Born and bred in the land of cotton and Jim Crow, feisty and conservative, from the bench he lectured Thurgood Marshall on how slavery brought the master and the bondsman together in common goodwill; that emancipation was "an interruption" in that often sentimental relationship; and in civil rights cases, "the Supreme Court frequently writes the law as it thinks it ought to have been or ought to be, setting aside the rule of precedent." Not every defender of Jim Crow based their view on such overtly racialist views. Sam J. Ervin Jr. was proud that he spent "twenty years in the Senate fighting unrelentingly for the principle of government fidelity to the Constitution" and against the "foolish idea that all of the things that seem to be evil can be cured by the federal government." "Activist Supreme Court justices" were high on his list of reprobates for that "unrestrained exercise of judicial power."[15]

On the other hand, one is sorely tempted to find heroes and villains in the usual places. That is how Robert L. Carter, Thurgood Marshall's lieutenant and a superb lawyer in his own right, tells it. From his own experience, he had learned that, although a lawyer, "I was as vulnerable to destruction through racial discrimination as the poorest and most unlettered black person." He resolved "to fight to remove the barriers of racial discrimination under which blacks were forced to live. . . . This struggle became central to my professional life." A later generation of civil rights lawyers recognized the signal contribution of the LDF to this struggle. Young Julius Chambers, finishing his law degree at the top of his class at Chapel Hill in 1962, was inspired by Thurgood Marshall. "He was an impressive guy," Chambers recalled. "I knew what he

---

15. Parker, quoted in Glenda Gilmore, "False Friends and Avowed Enemies," in *Jumpin' Jim Crow: Southern Politics from the Civil War to Civil Rights*, ed. Glenda Gilmore, Jane Dailey, and Bryant Simon (Princeton, NJ: Princeton University Press, 2000), 221; T. Whitfield Davidson, *The Memoirs of Judge T. Whitfield Davidson* (Waco, TX: Texian Press, 1972), 107; Sam Ervin Jr., *Preserving the Constitution: The Autobiography of Senator Sam J. Ervin Jr.* (Charlottesville, VA: Michie, 1984), ix, x, 181. One wonders if Ervin was being entirely honest, with himself if not with his readers. For one historian, Logan Sawyer III, Ervin's view of the Constitution was acquired only after he entered the U.S. Senate and had to formulate a jurisprudential critique of *Brown* in the service of the Southern Caucus's "Manifesto." Sawyer, "Originalism from the Soft Strategy to the New Right" (paper presented at the Annual Meeting of the American Society for Legal History, Las Vegas, NV, October 28, 2017).

had been doing, so I was using him as a kind of role model." By the second half of the 1960s, Chambers and his law partners were the face of the LDF in North Carolina.[16]

For every Carter, Chambers, and Marshall who served on the LDF, there were dozens of local black lawyers who handled the civil and criminal legal needs of black communities. They faced the evils of Jim Crow every day in and out of court. Although they were not full-time civil rights lawyers, they were the backbone of the NAACP, and they worked with clients to bring cases to the LDF and joined in the litigation. One, from my own adopted state of Georgia, may serve as an exemplar for all of them. Donald Hollowell shared the experiences of many of these lawyers, serving his country in World War II and returning to his native soil to find prejudice and discrimination waiting. In the practice of law, he found a way to make a living and to make a difference for his community. While most of his clients had to be rescued from the clutches of a Jim Crow criminal system, Hollowell helped integrate the University of Georgia and worked on other civil rights cases. Hollowell's gift lay not in the elucidation of constitutional theory so much as in the caring and practical ways he won a fair hearing for his clients. As one of the beneficiaries of those efforts concluded of him and his peers, "'Hollowell and these others advanced justice and freedom. They really helped make democracy real . . . by chipping away, cases by case, plaintiff by plaintiff, school by school, to knock down this evil system of institutionalized legalized racial separation.'"[17]

Yet for all the large and small injustices of Jim Crow in the law, on both sides of the courtroom aisle these were lawyers, and lawyers are accustomed to playing by rules. Some are laid down by bar associations to which they belong, others by the courts in which they practice. Some are less formal than others, but just as compelling. Civility is one of them. The irony, then, is that when courtrooms had segregated seating for spectators (and some state lower courts segregated counsel until the Supreme Court, in *Johnson v. Virginia*

16. Jack Greenberg, *Crusaders in the Courts: How a Dedicated Band of Lawyers Fought for the Civil Rights Revolution* (New York: Basic, 1994), 291; Robert L. Carter, *A Matter of Law: A Memoir of Struggle in the Cause of Equal Rights* (New York: New Press, 2005), 53; Julius L. Chambers, quoted in Richard A. Rosen and Joseph Mosnier, *Julius Chambers: A Life in the Legal Struggle for Civil Rights* (Chapel Hill: University of North Carolina Press, 2016), 45, 122–41.

17. Maurice C. Daniel, *Saving the Soul of Georgia: Donald L. Hollowell and the Struggle for Civil Rights* (Athens: University of Georgia Press, 2013), 67–89, 167; Julian Bond, quoted in ibid., 205.

[1963], barred the practice), there was no hard-and-fast rule requiring segregated seating for lawyers in federal courts. When, for example, Thurgood
Marshall—representing the black parents and children of Clarendon County,
South Carolina's segregated schools—sat across the Supreme Court bar rail-
ing from John W. Davis, formerly a presidential candidate now chosen by
South Carolina governor James Byrnes to defend the state's mandatory separation of the races, the two men traded humorous stories and other courtesies
before and after they sparred in oral argument. Davis was a die-hard believer
in the inferiority of the black man, and Marshall rightly did not trust Davis
or Byrnes, himself a former Supreme Court justice, "yet when presented with
a black man in the shape of a lawyer, Davis put on a display of public racial
egalitarianism that he would have found impossible to maintain in another
setting." Marshall was reciprocally accommodating. Davis was the first man
to congratulate Marshall on his victory in *Briggs v. Elliott*, decided along with
Brown v. Board of Education.[18]

★

In litigation, each side alternates in bearing the burden of proof. I have chosen
to take seriously the legal arguments and regard the players as lawyers seeking to win through acceptable legal methods. The chapters here follow that
formula. The first introduces the civil rights lawyers' team and brings them
to court to argue against segregated professional and graduate schools. The
second chapter tracks the lawyers in the "school cases," including the judges
who upheld segregation. Chapter 3 follows the southern lawyers' push back,
in court and in Congress. Chapter 4 takes the story and the people through

18. Kenneth Walter Mack, *Representing the Race: The Creation of the Civil Rights Lawyer*
(Cambridge, MA: Harvard University Press, 2102), 235; Johnson v. Virginia, 373 U.S. 61, 62 (1963)
(per curiam): "The petitioner, a Negro, was seated in the Traffic Court in a section reserved for
whites, and when requested to move by the bailiff, refused to do so. The judge then summoned
the petitioner to the bench and instructed him to be seated in the right-hand section of the
courtroom, the section reserved for Negroes. The petitioner moved back in front of the counsel
table and remained standing with his arms folded, stating that he preferred standing and indi-
cating that he would not comply with the judge's order. Upon refusal to obey the judge's further
direction to be seated, the petitioner was arrested for contempt. At no time did he behave in a
boisterous or abusive manner, and there was no disorder in the courtroom. The State, in its Brief
in Opposition filed in this Court, concedes that in the section of the Richmond Traffic Court
reserved for spectators, seating space 'is assigned on the basis of racial designation, the seats on
one side of the aisle being for use of Negro citizens and the seats on the other side being for the
use of white citizens.' . . . Such a conviction cannot stand, for it is no longer open to question that
a State may not constitutionally require segregation of public facilities."

the 1960s. A fifth chapter asks who won and who lost, in light of white flight, and discusses the appearance of new doctrines like freedom of association. Chapter 6 explores the legal academics' contribution to the story. The conclusion examines the political and legal legacies of the civil rights lawyering, including the later careers of the leading counsel.

The Long Night of Jim Crow

This is a story about race and the law, and the lawyers who took a leading role in defending and dismantling the regime of Jim Crow. It begins at the end of the Civil War. During slavery times, there was no Jim Crow. Whites and blacks worked alongside one another in the fields and mills. The social controls of the South's "peculiar institution" were rooted in law and imposed rigorously, though individual slaves might be valued, and most slaves found ways to negotiate space and time for themselves and their loved ones in the interstices of the law. For in the law of slavery, the slave was property, a commodity in the stream of commerce. He or she had no rights "which the white man was bound to respect," according to Chief Justice Roger Taney's dictum in *Dred Scott v. Sandford* (1857).[1]

1. Dred Scott v. Sandford, 60 U.S. 393, 407 (1857) (Taney, C.J.). On slave law: Thomas D. Morris, *Southern Slavery and the Law, 1619–1860* (Chapel Hill: University of North Carolina Press, 1996), 42 (the "idea of property is the key"); Polly J. Price, *Property Rights: Rights and Liberties under the Law* (Santa Barbara, CA: ABC-CLIO, 2003), 61–62 (chattel slavery in America was a form of personal property). Michael O'Brien, *Conjectures of Order: Intellectual Life and the American South, 1810–1860*, 2 vols. (Chapel Hill: University of North Carolina Press, 2004), 1: 247, finds that slavery was hardly a central theme in southern intellectual thinking in the last years before the war. More important were science, nature, the environment, and modernity, though the latter was a "deeply implicated" modernity "in an idiosyncratic version mostly based on slavery" (17).

What is race? Biologically, it has little significance. As ancestry, it embodies culture and attitude. If we go back far enough in time and place, we are all mixed race and one race—*Homo sapiens sapiens*. As a matter of law in the following pages, it is almost synonymous with color, and "white" and "black" become proxies of an entire range of disfiguring distinctions. To win their suit against racial discrimination in *Mendez v. Westminster* (1947), plaintiff Mexican American parents argued that their children were "white." Philippa Strum, *Mendez v. Westminster: School*

At the end of the Civil War, the Thirteenth Amendment, the Civil Rights Acts, the Enforcement Acts, and the Fourteenth and Fifteenth Amendments of the period 1865–75 were supposed by their enactors to overturn Taney's facile and demeaning racialist doctrine. A regime of legal equality, if not social intercourse, was the aim of these congressional reformers. The dream of Reconstruction died hard. Instead of equality, versions of the two "Mississippi Plans" based first on the open use of force and then on the legal disenfranchisement of the newly freedmen left them in peril of their lives. Hooded violence, coupled with growing northern indifference to the plight of the former slaves, aided and abetted by the determination of former Confederate leaders to regain their lost status, led to the "Redemption" of the former Confederate states. Largely left to themselves in power, the white redeemers assayed the erection of the wall of segregation. The Redeemers replaced the social and economic inequalities of slavery with another legal regime, given the name Jim Crow (after the blackface minstrels of the antebellum years).[2]

Although the color line was early and forcibly drawn in the reconstructed states, jurors and judges did not always turn their backs on black litigants. In fact, when blacks came before the southern bench and pleaded their rights as property holders, workers, and parents, more often than not the courts honored their claims. Even when freedmen sued white defendants or appealed to state upper courts, they won as often as they lost. The most successful tactic was to plead that they had been duped because they could not read or understand the law by unscrupulous whites who should, according to the code of honor and white supremacy, have behaved better. Hiring a white lawyer helped too. As one Mississippi Supreme Court judge told fellow members of the state bar association in 1923, "We like to have the respect of the colored people, and every lawyer, in my experience, had stood for a square deal before the law for the colored race . . . in the last ditch, the colored man has only one friend, and that is his lawyer." And perhaps Justice J. B. Holden really believed what he said—the statistics tend to support his argument. Litigants who sued to gain equal rights or made equal rights arguments fared far worse, lawyer

Desegregation and Mexican American Rights (Lawrence: University Press of Kansas, 2010), 3, 9–10, 63–64; Mark Brilliant, *The Color of America Has Changed: How Racial Diversity Has Shaped Civil Rights Reform in California, 1943–1978* (New York: Oxford University Press, 2010), 60.

2. C. Vann Woodward, *The Origins of the New South, 1877–1913* (Baton Rouge: Louisiana State University Press, 1981), 80, 321–25; Eric Foner, *Reconstruction: America's Unfinished Revolution, 1863–1877* (New York: Harper, 1988), 587–88; Edward Ayers, *The Promise of the New South: Life after Reconstruction* (New York: Oxford University Press, 1992), 136; Osha Gray Davidson, *Best of Enemies: Race and Redemption in the New South* (Chapel Hill: University of North Carolina Press, 2007), 73.

or no, than litigants in property and tort suits, and this disparity went all the way back to the end of Reconstruction.[3]

With a few exceptions concerning the Fifteenth Amendment, Congress and the federal courts threw in the towel when the broad commitment to equality under the federal Constitution was challenged, and in a series of Supreme Court cases, states were permitted to install all manner of demeaning Jim Crow rules. For example, the Civil Rights Act of 1875 provided that public accommodations could not be denied to paying customers on the basis of their race. In the *Civil Rights Cases* (1883), the majority of the Court struck down the public accommodations section of the act as outside of the power of Congress under the fifth clause of the Fourteenth Amendment. In vain did Justice John Marshall Harlan dissent, "I cannot resist the conclusion that the substance and spirit of the recent amendments of the Constitution have been sacrificed by a subtle and ingenious verbal criticism. . . . If, then, exemption from discrimination, in respect of civil rights, is a new constitutional right, secured by the grant of State citizenship to colored citizens of the United States—and I do not see how this can now be questioned—why may not the nation, by means of its own legislation of a primary direct character, guard, protect and enforce that right? It is a right and privilege which the nation conferred." Among these were subterfuges to deny blacks a place in the polling booth, the jury box, and the seats of government. In defense of these, white leaders insisted that black people preferred their own accommodations, churches, and public spaces, although any visitor to the post-Reconstruction South would see how inferior the accommodations allowed black citizens were. Moreover, for some white southern lawyers, "God almighty drew the color line and it cannot be obliterated."[4]

In 1892, plaintiff Homer Plessy and counselor Albion Tourgée tested Louisiana's version of this racialist ideology. Two years earlier, the state had passed a railroad car segregation law. Plessy was selected by a committee of his fellow Afro-Creoles because he could "pass" for white, and they arranged for the conductor and a detective to detain and then arrest Plessy after he bought his first-class ticket and refused to switch to the black car. It was a "test case." The committee lost their case in the Louisiana courts (where John Ferguson was a

---

3. Melissa Milewski, *Litigating across the Color Line: Civil Cases between Black and White Southerners from the End of Slavery to Civil Rights* (New York: Oxford University Press, 2018), 52–77, 177, 179, quotation on 175.

4. Civil Rights Act of 1875, 18 Stat. 335–337 (also known as the Force Act); U.S. v. Stanley (Civil Rights Cases), 109 U.S. 1, 26, 50 (1883) (Harlan, J.).

trial court judge) but appealed to the Supreme Court on Thirteenth Amendment and Fourteenth Amendment grounds.[5]

Tourgée, a civil rights advocate and former Reconstruction agent in North Carolina, former U.S. solicitor general Samuel F. Phillips (who had represented the government in the *Civil Rights Cases* ten years earlier), and local counsel James C. Walker argued that the Louisiana Separate Car Act violated the Reconstruction Amendments as well as the common law of common carriers, but the Court was not impressed. Justice Henry Billings Brown wrote for the majority of the Court, dismissing both constitutional and common-law grounds for the lawsuit, then continued to explain the social basis for segregation. There was no need for this passage in the opinion; it was not the basis for denying the appeal as a matter of law. As such, it was just as much dicta as Chief Justice Taney's remarks about black citizenship in *Dred Scott*. But Brown thought it had to be in the opinion to refute Harlan's expected dissent. "The object of the amendment was undoubtedly to enforce the absolute equality of the two races before the law, but in the nature of things it could not have been intended to abolish distinctions based upon color, or to enforce social, as distinguished from political equality, or a commingling of the two races upon terms unsatisfactory to either." A law that limited where a person of one color could sit on a train and did not so restrain a person of another color did not disparage, harm, or make any assertion about the first person. "If this be so, it is not by reason of anything found in the act, but solely because the colored race chooses to put that construction upon it. . . . We think the enforced separation of the races, as applied to the internal commerce of the State, neither abridges the privileges or immunities of the colored man, deprives him of his property without due process of law, nor denies him the equal protection of the laws, within the meaning of the Fourteenth Amendment."[6]

The long-established usages of discrimination presumed that segregation was part of a natural order, and Justice Brown continued, "If the two races are to meet upon terms of social equality, it must be the result of natural affinities, a mutual appreciation of each other's merits and a voluntary consent

---

5. The story of the plaintiffs and their counsel is told in Williamjames Hull Hoffer, *Plessy v. Ferguson: Race and Inequality in Jim Crow America* (Lawrence: University Press of Kansas, 2011), 8–68.

6. 163 U.S. 537, 544, 551 (1896) (Brown, J.); George Frederickson, *White Supremacy: A Comparative Study of American and South African History* (New York: Oxford University Press, 1981), 197–98.

of individuals." The alternative, that "social prejudices may be overcome by legislation, and that equal rights" could be "secured to the negro . . . by an enforced commingling of the two races" was a social impossibility more than a legal one. "Legislation is powerless to eradicate racial instincts or to abolish distinctions based upon physical differences, and the attempt to do so can only result in accentuating the difficulties of the present situation. . . . If one race be lower to the other socially, the Constitution of the United States cannot put them upon the same plane." Equal but separate, Brown found, did not violate the Thirteenth or the Fourteenth Amendments.[7]

John Marshall Harlan's dissent in *Plessy* echoed his dissent in the *Civil Rights Cases*: "In respect of civil rights, common to all citizens, the Constitution of the United States does not, I think, permit any public authority to know the race of those entitled to be protected in the enjoyment of such rights. . . . I deny that any legislative body or judicial tribunal may have regard to the race of citizens when the civil rights of those citizens are involved. Indeed, such legislation, as that here in question, is inconsistent not only with that equality of rights which pertains to citizenship, National and State, but with the personal liberty enjoyed by every one within the United States." The federal laws, "if enforced according to their true intent and meaning, will protect all the civil rights that pertain to freedom and citizenship. . . . These notable additions to the fundamental law were welcomed by the friends of liberty throughout the world. They removed the race line from our governmental systems." Harlan concluded: "Our Constitution is color-blind, and neither knows nor tolerates classes among citizens. In respect of civil rights, all citizens are equal before the law." Ironically, it was Harlan's dissent that introduced the term "separate but equal," regarded as a perverse reading of the intent of the framers and a distortion of the reality of discrimination.[8]

Justice Brown was not a southerner. He was a New Englander, from a good family, well-educated and -bred. He practiced law in Detroit, Michigan, and was not tarred with pro-segregationist politics. Harlan was a southerner and had grown up in Kentucky owning slaves before he chose to fight for the Union and supported Reconstruction. Their respective views did not represent anything like well-entrenched regionalism. Instead, Harlan's voice on the Court was like Jeremiah's in the wilderness. Brown's views were conventional expressions of the white supremacist ideology of the period.[9]

7. 163 U.S. at 551–552 (Brown, J.).

8. 163 U.S. at 555, 559 (Harlan, J.).

9. Thomas C. Mackey, "Henry Billings Brown," in *The Supreme Court Justices: A Biographical Dictionary*, ed. Melvin Urofsky (New York: Routledge, 2015), 68–69 (Brown shared the views

In the Progressive Era, cases like *Plessy* piled up on federal dockets. What prevented the courts from intervening in the most egregious of these was a sense that the courts could not do what Congress refused to attempt—to impose a national regime of equal law on a recalcitrant region of the nation. No case better illustrated this than the appeal of Pink Franklin. In *Franklin v. State of South Carolina* (1910), the first of the NAACP cases, the Supreme Court deferred to local juries and state courts. Pink Franklin was a share-cropper who refused to plow a field until later in the day. A constable, acting under a South Carolina law that made such refusals criminal, burst without warning or warrant into Franklin's home, and Franklin killed the constable. The all-white trial jury found Franklin guilty of murder, even though key pieces of evidence were withheld from Franklin's defense counsel. The Supreme Court was not about to oversee every criminal trial in which a claim of racial discrimination was made. "The States have the right to administer their own laws for the prosecution of crime, and the jurisdiction of this court extends only to the reversal of such state proceedings where fundamental rights secured by the Federal law have been denied by the proceedings in the state courts," Justice William R. Day concluded. Franklin was executed.[10]

Were federal courts to return to the Reconstruction enforcement acts' regime, they would be inundated with challenges to racialist state court decisions. There was no constitutional reason for federal courts to interfere with state courts in criminal cases, Day concluded. His narrow view of "fundamental rights" implied that for him and the majority of the justices, the Fourteenth Amendment's Due Process and Equal Protection Clauses did not "incorporate" (that is, impose on the states) the guarantees of the Fourth, Fifth, and Sixth Amendments. Where Congress had acted, however, there were grounds for the federal courts to intervene in state criminal prosecutions, as the peonage cases, discussed below, revealed.[11]

The Franklin case had introduced a new player in the field—the National Association for the Advancement of Colored People. Organized by a multi-racial elite cadre of reformers a year earlier, the NAACP set out to remedy

---

of northern white, educated, upper-middle-class conservatives); Linda Przybyszewski, *The Republic according to John Marshall Harlan* (Chapel Hill: University of North Carolina Press, 1999), 63–65 (slavery was an aberration), 71–72 (America's mission was not racist).

10. Franklin v. South Carolina, 218 U.S. 161, 164–165, 168 (1910) (Day, J.).

11. The "incorporation doctrine" is the subject of a good deal of academic and jurisprudential scholarship. Compare Akhil Reed Amar, *The Bill of Rights: Creation and Reconstruction* (New Haven, CT: Yale University Press, 2008), 222–23, defending broad incorporation, with Robert Bork, *The Tempting of America: The Political Seduction of the Law* (New York: Simon and Schuster, 1990), 93–94, stressing the dangers of too loose incorporation.

disparities in economic opportunities for African Americans and to lobby for anti-lynching legislation in Congress. Its purpose at first was thus not litigation relief, but it soon became apparent that the organization had a role in the courts. Among the founders was the New York lawyer Arthur B. Spingarn and Boston lawyer Moorfield Storey. Storey was named the first president, reflecting his distinguished legal and civil rights credentials. He had been the president of the American Bar Association.[12]

The NAACP leadership recognized that there was some hope for racial justice in the courts through resuscitation of Reconstruction Era legislation. For example, Franklin had relied on the Habeas Corpus Act of 1867, a fact that the NAACP recognized as it followed the case. The statute tilted the federal-state judicial relationship, allowing for removal of an individual in the custody of the state to the federal court issuing the "great writ." The act was a product of the Reconstruction Congress at its high tide, based on the assumption that southern state courts would use the vagrancy statutes of the first "black codes" to effectually re-enslave the freedmen. The "peonage statute" of 1867 similarly brought the federal government into the arena of civil rights enforcement. The NAACP took an interest in the laws against peonage, although cases were brought by the Department of Justice rather than by private individuals, and the NAACP did not keep extensive files on the subject until the 1920s.[13]

Points of light for civil rights reformers were cases under the peonage act like *Bailey v. Alabama* (1911). In it, the Court refused to admit the extent or nature of state-sponsored or state-allowed oppression of minorities. Instead, the majority found technical grounds to invalidate discriminatory laws, albeit without exploring the racial nature of the discrimination. At the beginning of the 1900s, to insure that its white planters had a ready supply of cheap black labor, Alabama made it criminal for a farmworker to receive an advance for labor under a contract and either fail to perform the labor or fail to continue to labor for the period of time stated in the contract. Failure to complete the contract subjected the laborer to a term of forced labor. The only individuals convicted under the statute were black men. Conviction turned a free labor relationship into peonage—a form of labor barred by the Peonage Abolition Act of 1867. In fact, the sponsors of the act in Congress foresaw the re-enslavement

12. Gilbert Jones, *Freedom's Sword: The NAACP and the Struggle against Racism in America, 1909–1969* (New York: Routledge, 2004), 11–13.

13. Federal Peonage Abolition Act of 1867, 14 Stat. 546; Richard Hofstadter, *Age of Reform: From Bryan to F.D.R.* (New York: Knopf, 1955), 61, 77–78, 182; Goluboff, *Lost Promise*, 177.

of black agricultural workers through statutes like Alabama's. The Alabama law also included an instruction that judges were to give to the jury that non-performance of the agreed-upon labor was presumptive evidence of the intention to defraud, in effect making the defendant guilty until proven innocent: "The refusal of any person who enters into such contract to perform such act or service, or refund such money, or pay for such property, without just cause, shall be prima facie evidence of the intent to . . . defraud . . . his employer." This 1907 addition to the 1903 criminal statute closed any avenue the laborer had to escape conviction. Because many of these so-called contracts were verbal and the only witnesses were the (black) laborer and the (white) boss, the evidentiary burden the new law placed on the laborer was almost insurmountable. Not surprisingly, all white juries routinely found the accused guilty. Alabama had found its way back to the "black codes" that the state legislature had passed in 1865.[14]

Alonzo Bailey was a black farm laborer caught in the web of debt and dependence that the Alabama law wove. He sought a writ of habeas corpus in federal court to free him from his incarceration under the state statute. The state's attorney general explained in oral argument before the Supreme Court why Bailey should not be granted the get-out-of-jail card. "The statute was to punish fraudulent practices and not mere failure to pay a debt. . . . [I]f a rule of evidence which excludes the defendant from testifying as to his motives has the effect of making the rule of evidence prescribed by the statute a conclusive rule, it is due to the particular facts and not to the statute itself." He added that Alabama did not violate federal law against peonage, because the Alabama law did not mention peonage.[15]

Justice Charles Evans Hughes's opinion for the majority turned on the Alabama trial court's instructions. Ordinarily, it was the burden of the state to produce such evidence. Alabama simply took the word of the employer, the person who would directly benefit from the conviction. Hughes also noted the penalty for conviction was forced labor for a term far longer than would repay the advance. The labor was due to a private individual—the employer—even though the offense was against the state (as in all criminal cases). So the

14. Bailey v. Alabama, 219 U.S. 219 (1911); Aviam Soifer, "Federal Protection, Paternalism, and the Virtually Forgotten Prohibition of Voluntary Peonage," *Columbia Law Review* 112 (2012): 1607–39; Robert J. Steinfeld, *The Invention of Free Labor: The Employment Relation in English and American Law and Culture, 1350–1870* (Chapel Hill: University of North Carolina Press, 1991), 183–84; 219 U.S. at 228 (quoting the Alabama statute).

15. 219 U.S. at 228 (Hughes, J.). Here and after material adapted from Hoffer, Hoffer, and Hull, *Supreme Court*, 204–5.

state, in effect, had reduced a free laborer to a peon working for a private employer. "It is not permitted to accomplish the same result" by changing the criminal law to make the defendant in such cases guilty until proven innocent, then exclude all evidence of his innocence.[16]

Storey was lead counsel in another one of the few victories for civil rights in the Court. In *Buchanan v. Warley* (1917), a typical Jim Crow residential law in Louisville, Kentucky, offered as its justification "to prevent conflict and ill feeling between the white and colored races in the City of Louisville, and to preserve the public peace and promote the general welfare by making reasonable provisions requiring, as far as practicable, the use of separate blocks for residences, places of abode and places of assembly by white and colored people respectively." Justice Day, following Storey's brief, concluded: "This ordinance prevents the occupancy of a lot in the City of Louisville by a person of color in a block where the greater number of residences are occupied by white persons; where such a majority exists, colored persons are excluded. This interdiction is based wholly upon color—simply that and nothing more." Day was not so interested in the color of the owners, however, as in the right of the sellers. "In effect, premises situated, as are those in question, in the so-called white block are effectively debarred from sale to persons of color." The legal basis was the police power of the state, a term of art covering a multitude of moral and economic regulations. These were permissible under the Fourteenth Amendment's Due Process Clause, according to *Lochner v. New York* (1904), if the state, or its local departments, could show that they were necessary to the health and welfare of the general population. Day doubted that. "This drastic measure is sought to be justified under the authority of the State in the exercise of the police power. It is said such legislation tends to promote the public peace by preventing racial conflicts; that it tends to maintain racial purity; that it prevents the deterioration of property owned and occupied by white people, which deterioration, it is contended, is sure to follow the occupancy of adjacent premises by persons of color." But here, "[the Fourteenth Amendment] was designed to assure to the colored race the enjoyment of all the civil rights that, under the law, are enjoyed by white persons, and to give to that race the protection of the general government in that enjoyment whenever it should be denied by the States."

Day recognized the doctrine of separate but equal to apply to many of these discriminatory ordinances, but here it destroyed the rights of a property

16. 219 U.S. at 236, 244 (1911) (Hughes, J.).

holder. Day made no attempt to apply his finding in any wider context, nor to strike at the racial basis of the discrimination, for

> the question now presented makes it pertinent to enquire into the constitu-
> tional right of the white man to sell his property to a colored man, having in
> view the legal status of the purchaser and occupant. . . . As we have seen, this
> court has held laws valid which separated the races on the basis of equal ac-
> commodations in public conveyances, and courts of high authority have held
> enactments lawful which provide for separation in the public schools of white
> and colored pupils where equal privileges are given. But, in view of the rights
> secured by the Fourteenth Amendment to the Federal Constitution, such leg-
> islation must have its limitations, and cannot be sustained where the exercise
> of authority exceeds the restraints of the Constitution. We think these limita-
> tions are exceeded in laws and ordinances of the character now before us.

Despite the limited nature of Day's reasoning, Storey, the NAACP, and the black property owners had won a victory, and the basis of that victory was the Due Process Clause of the Fourteenth Amendment. In passing, it should be noted that John W. Davis, a leading New York corporate lawyer and soon to be the Democratic nominee for the White House, writing as U.S. solicitor general, joined Storey on the brief. Davis would play a crucial role some years later in another civil rights case.[17]

The NAACP did not always take the lead. In *Guinn v. United States* (1915), for example, the U.S. Department of Justice, with an amicus brief by the NAACP, challenged an Oklahoma constitutional provision for a "grandfather clause." The high court struck down the Oklahoma version of the grandfather clause, which automatically bypassed the literacy test for those men whose grand-fathers had cast votes in prior elections. Oklahoma was not a state when slavery ruled the land, so the clause did not operate to summarily disenfranchise the children or grandchildren of slaves (hence violating the Thirteenth Amend-ment), but by placing the defining date—1867—before the ratification of the Fifteenth Amendment, the state conspired to deny its black citizens the same access to the voting booth as its white citizens. John W. Davis, the U.S. solici-tor general, argued for the Department of Justice against the state—his official

---

17. Buchanan v. Warley, 245 U.S. 60, 70, 74, 79, 84 (1917) (Day, J.); Gloria J. Browne-Marshall, *The Voting Rights War: The NAACP and the Ongoing Struggle for Justice* (Lanham, MD: Row-man and Littlefield, 2016), 53–54; David Delaney, *Race, Place, and the Law, 1836–1948* (Austin: University of Texas Press, 1998), 202n30 (Davis joined in the brief). Other cases that protected the property rights of white sellers included Harmon v. Tyler, 273 U.S. 668 (1927) and City of Richmond v. Deans, 37 F.2d 712 (4th Cir. 1930).

task, but one ironic in light of his later defense of segregated schools in *Briggs v. Elliott* (1951). His point was a simple one: "The necessary effect and opera-tion of the Grandfather Clause is to exclude practically all illiterate negroes and practically no illiterate white men, and from this its unconstitutional pur-pose may legitimately be inferred." The Court agreed, in an opinion by Chief Justice Edward Douglass White, himself a former Confederate soldier and thereafter a staunch defender of Jim Crow: the grandfather clause "re-creates and perpetuates the very conditions which the Amendment was intended to destroy. From this it is urged that no legitimate discretion could have entered into the fixing of such standard which involved only the determination to di-rectly set at naught or by indirection avoid the commands of the Amendment." Strange bedfellows these, Davis, White, and civil rights.[18]

Victories like *Buchanan v. Warley* and *Guinn v. United States* were few and far between, however, until a second set of new players joined in the contest. These were Charles Hamilton Houston and the young lions of his law school at Howard University. Houston was a Harvard Law School–educated, Wash-ington, D.C., lawyer, who became the dean at Howard in 1929. Thereafter he worked assiduously to bring Jim Crow cases to court, and just as hard to re-cruit able young law students to join in the effort. In July 1935, he joined forces with the NAACP national office in New York City, acting as "special counsel" to the organization. The aim was to fulfill the grudging promise of *Plessy*—to make separate but equal a fiscal and institutional reality (or, if states found equal funding an insuperable fiscal burden, to end segregation altogether). Behind that goal was a larger one—to make the two Americas into a whole.[19]

As his health declined, Houston passed the baton to his able student Thur-good Marshall. The legal committee of the NAACP morphed into the Legal and Educational Defense Fund, protecting the tax-exempt status of the parent group. Marshall's legal team, with the financial support of ordinary African Americans and white liberal groups committed to their cause, sought to engi-neer a legal revolution—step-by-step.[20]

18. Guinn v. U.S., 238 U.S. 347, 360 (1915) (White, C.J.); Susan Carle, *Defining the Struggle: National Organizing for Racial Justice* (New York: Oxford University Press, 2011), 284–85.

19. Genna Rae McNeil, *Groundwork: Charles Hamilton Houston and the Struggle for Civil Rights* (Philadelphia: University of Pennsylvania Press, 1983), 82–83, 131–33; Tushnet, *The NAACP's Legal Strategy*, 15, 29, 157–58.

20. Tushnet, *The NAACP's Legal Strategy*, 47–48; McNeil, *Groundwork*, 151–93.

The Road to *Sweatt v. Painter*

Even if the end of World War II war seemed a triumph of liberty and human dignity over tyranny, a good war for a good cause, the ideals of the Atlantic Charter of 1941—freedom from fear and want—for which Americans fought abroad, remained elusive on the home front. The challenge lay ahead to keep the nation safe from its foreign enemies while guaranteeing equal protection of law and civil liberty for all its people. In the face of a second Red Scare and the persistence of Jim Crow regimes, post–World War II federal courtrooms became legal battlegrounds. One of the many challenges for the lawyers of the day was the growing demand for minority rights.[1]

The front lines of this battle were the state and federal courts, for Congress and state legislatures had long refused to face the smoldering issues of Jim Crow. The judges of these courts not only reflected the attitudes of the time and of their own regions, they were also political figures. State judges were elected officials. Federal judges were appointed and confirmed by the chief executive and the U.S. Senate. Political ideologies and partisan affiliations thus found their way into the courtroom.[2]

1. David M. Kennedy, *Freedom from Fear: The American People in Depression and War, 1929–1945* (New York: Oxford University Press, 1999), 853. The "Four Points" were elucidated in President Franklin D. Roosevelt's January 6, 1941, State of the Union address.

2. On the politics of courts and courts as political institutions, see David W. Neubauer and Stephen S. Meinhold, *Judicial Process: Law, Courts, and Politics in the United States*, 5th ed. (Boston: Wadsworth, 2010), 13–15; Henry J. Abraham, *Justices, Presidents, and Senators: A History of U.S. Supreme Court Appointments from Washington to Bush II*, 5th ed. (Lanham, MD: Rowman and Littlefield, 2007), 163–96; and Sheldon Goldman, *Picking Federal Judges: Lower Court Selection from Roosevelt through Reagan* (New Haven, CT: Yale University Press, 1997), 65–197. On the refusal of Congress and the states to legislate against Jim Crow, see Klarman, *Jim Crow*, 168–69;

One might surmise that because federal judges were not popularly elected, they would be above the mob clamoring for Jim Crow. Most as lawyers had little to do with civil rights questions, however. When they came on the bench in these years, that situation changed. Thus they brought to their decisions a wealth of local experience but little direct contact with civil rights. The result was that they viewed the civil rights lawsuits in light of their experience with other matters, including their family's and neighbor's values, rather than in the context of post-WWII national attitudes. What resulted was a good deal of unconscious, and some conscious, resistance to the idea of genuine legal equality. Certainly, most did not see the courts as the place to impose that equality.

At the same time, the culture of the United States was changing profoundly, and these changes had a direct impact on judging. Before World War II, one could say that the country was a collectivity of distinct localities. After the war, the culture of the nation was becoming more homogenous and less local. By the early 1950s, over 50 percent of American households had at least one television set. Television was knitting the nation together in a way that local newspapers and radio stations did not. Television was national. In this sense, the continuing localism of the newly named lower federal judiciary was a throwback to an earlier time. Perhaps that was not wholly accidental. President Harry S. Truman wrote to one judge that "the appointment of federal judges is the most important thing that I do," and Truman's own career was a throwback to an earlier time of small-town politics. One got ahead through personal service and reciprocal favors, but Truman's judges did not violate the unwritten rule that a federal judge must come from or live in the region where he would sit. As a later president under fire for appointing judges to the South whose views were, to say the least, not wholly supportive of civil rights conceded, "I think that the men who have been appointed to judgeships in the South, sharing perhaps as they do, the general outlook of the South, have done a remarkable job in fulfilling their oath of office." The author meant the white outlook of course. Given that the author of this somewhat backhanded compliment, John F. Kennedy, recognized that many of these judges were reluctant partners in the civil rights movement, his qualification was more telling than his affirmation.[3]

and James C. Cobb, *The South and America since World War II* (New York: Oxford University Press, 2011), 14–15, 34.

3. James L. Baughman, "Television Comes to America, 1947–1957," *Illinois History*, March 1993 http://www.lib.niu.edu/1993/1po/ihy930341.html; Truman to William M. Byrne, October 19,

Federal judges are appointed by the president and confirmed by the Senate. Truman's "Fair Deal" program included a genuine effort to advance the cause of civil rights, and he took executive steps in that direction, including the beginning of the desegregation of the armed services. Among other steps was the recess appointment on October 14, 1949, of William H. Hastie to the Court of Appeals for the Third Circuit, the first non-white judge named to a life-tenure federal judgeship. To be sure, there was a partisan back story. Hastie had helped swing black votes for Truman during the 1948 campaign. With the Senate back in session, Truman nominated him in January 1950 and had to press hard for confirmation. Hastie's distinguished career helped. An Amherst College and Harvard Law School graduate, Hastie had left private practice in D.C. to serve as an assistant solicitor in the U.S. Department of the Interior (1933–37), a territorial judge in the Virgin Islands (1937–39), and as governor of the Virgin Islands from 1946 to 1949. He had also served as dean of Howard University's school of law from 1939 to 1946. Although a single judgeship hardly signaled the end of racial discrimination, it was a first step that civil rights advocates noticed and applauded.[4]

But Truman filled southern federal court seats with southerners. For example, among these was Seybourn H. Lynne, appointed to the U.S. District Court for the Northern District of Alabama. Lynne was educated in Alabama, got his law degree at the University of Alabama School of Law, practiced in Decatur, Alabama, and sat on the state supreme court before he joined the federal bench. "Old school" and courteous but rarely in sympathy with civil rights lawsuits, when civil rights lawyers practiced before him, they knew they would lose. After which, the Court of Appeals for the Fifth Circuit would overturn Judge Lynne. Lynne presided at the first attempt to force the trustees

---

1950, quoted in Goldman, *Picking Federal Judges*, 76; Abraham, *Justices, Presidents, and Senators*, 241; Lee Epstein and Jeffrey A. Segal, *Advice and Consent: The Politics of Judicial Appointments* (New York: Oxford University Press, 2005), 68; Mark Edward Lender, *"This Honorable Court": The United States District Court for the District of New Jersey, 1789–2000* (New Brunswick, NJ: Rutgers University Press, 2006), 160–61; Kermit L. Hall and Kevin T. McGuire, *Institutions of American Democracy: The Judicial Branch* (New York: Oxford University Press, 2005), 153; Sean J. Savage, "Truman in Historical, Popular and Political Memory," in *A Companion to Harry S. Truman*, ed. Daniel S. Margolies (Chichester, UK: Blackwell, 2012), 14.

    4. Goldman, *Picking Federal Judges*, 68; Michael R. Gardner, *Harry Truman and Civil Rights: Moral Courage and Political Risks* (Carbondale: Southern Illinois University Press, 2002), 152–53; Kermit Hall, "William Henry Hastie," in *Great American Lawyers: An Encyclopedia*, ed. John R. Vile (Santa Barbara, CA: ABC-CLIO, 2001), 343–49.

of the University of Alabama to allow admission of qualified blacks, with results described later in this book.[5]

✶

Before this array of judicial appointees, the LDF battled discrimination on many fronts, including transportation, employment, and, most importantly, education. It was the first "litigation campaign" for a public interest, for the LDF conceived of legal equality for blacks as a public good. The grueling pace would have worn down the strongest lawyer, but the leadership of the LDF were not ordinary men. For example, Thurgood Marshall grew up in Jim Crow Baltimore, to a father who worked as a dining car waiter and a mother who taught in the segregated elementary school. Marshall worked as a bellhop to put himself through college at Lincoln University in Pennsylvania and Howard University School of Law, both black schools, because Maryland denied blacks admission to its premier undergraduate and graduate institutions. Marshall's good humor and folksy public face concealed a burning desire for racial justice.[6]

Working at Marshall's side if often in his shadow, managing the New York office of the LDF, was Robert L. Carter. Unlike the often plainspoken Marshall, Carter was all business, a scholar and a man who understood the importance of detailed preparation of cases. He could be a little too bookish in the courtroom, but everyone who knew him respected his dedication.

Jack Greenberg remembered that the staff of the LDF was small when he joined it, and the board was not very prestigious in the elite legal community, but Marshall had friends everywhere among law professors and in government (in the North), and that network provided ideas and encouragement as well as small donations to the LDF. He and the other members of the staff would fly or ride out at a moment's notice to represent the local NAACP chapters in litigation of all sorts, not just constitutional cases. The latter actually represented a very small portion of the legal work the LDF did, but those cases became the landmarks by which the battle against state-mandated seg-

5. Patrick Dunn, "An Oral History of Alabama Civil Rights and the African-American Bar," May 6, 2015, http://blog.superlawyers.com/2015/05/an-oral-history-of-alabama-civil-rights-and -the-african-american-bar.shtml. Steven Knopper, "An Interview with U. W. Clemon," *Alabama Super Lawyers Magazine*, May 2015, https://www.superlawyers.com/alabama/article/an-interview -with-uw-clemon/d22c09ad-a222-4e38-88bf-deaf6ce81b97.html. Judicial biography from Federal Judicial Center, https://www.fjc.gov/history/judges/lynne-seybourn-harris.

6. Howard Ball, *A Defiant Life: Thurgood Marshall and the Persistence of Racism in America* (New York: Crown, 1999), 57–65, 115–40; Richard Kluger, *Simple Justice: The History of* Brown v. Board of Education *and Black America's Struggle for Equality* (New York: Knopf, 2011), 173–238.

regation progressed. Although his assistant attorneys did much of the grunt work, and Carter in the New York office and Spottswood Robinson from his office in Richmond did yeoman service for the LDF, at the center of everything stood the tall, energetic Marshall. After every victory, as they began to pile up, Marshall would hold a news conference, creating the impression that the LDF was a juggernaut that could not be stopped, an image increasingly frightening to southern legal and political officialdom.[7]

Like the board of the NAACP, the board of the new Legal Defense and Educational Fund was interracial and included major political, educational, and legal figures, including Herbert H. Lehman, the governor of New York. What may have been just as important, the board was drawn entirely from the Northeast. It had no southern members, despite the fact that there were NAACP local chapters all over the South. From these chapters came appeals for help. The NAACP lawyers were sometimes accused of looking down on the local lawyers, although their cooperation was essential to success in the courts and even more so with the black local community. In this sense, the LDF's fight was often, perhaps too often, a top-down one, a reprise of Reconstruction but without the aid of Republicans in the South, with local lawyers associated with NAACP chapters taking a secondary role to the LDF staff. The LDF sometimes had to fight for its independence from the NAACP, as Walter Francis White, president of the latter, did not always agree with the tactics of Marshall and Carter; but it was the lawyers of the LDF, not the membership of the NAACP at large, that utilized the legal tools against discrimination.[8]

Perhaps because of these regional and personnel constraints, but more likely because of its own drive to win every case, the LDF intentionally narrowed its focus from discrimination as a whole to racial discrimination under the law. Historians do not dwell on what might have been; however, some students of the past have engaged in hypotheticals—"what if" alternatives to actuality. By contrast, law professors rely on hypotheticals in their teaching, and one may ask if a road not taken by the LDF, bringing lawsuits to aid blacks in labor cases, would have borne fruit. For the field of civil rights litigation need not have been limited to undoing Jim Crow. There were opportunities for a wider campaign. True, cases like *Hodges v. United States* (1906) seemed to

7. Greenberg, *Crusaders*, 28–29, 34–35.

8. See, e.g., Tomiko Brown-Nagin, *Courage to Dissent: Atlanta and the Long History of the Civil Rights Movement* (New York: Oxford University Press, 2011), 402–3.While obviously bent in favor of the LDF and the lawyers' campaign against discrimination, Jack Greenberg's memoir, *Crusaders in the Courts*, is a wonderfully vivid account of these lawyers and their efforts that favors the top-down version of the story.

close the door to labor equality as firmly as *Plessy* had shut the door to equal-
ity in public accommodations, and *Cumming v. Richmond County Board of
Education* (1899) had locked the door to equality in education, but the New
Deal seemed to have opened the door to equality in federal labor contracts.
New Deal legislation protecting some rights of union members did not protect the black worker against discrimination within and by unions, however.
While the prospects for equal pay and equal treatment seemed to improve
as black labor became necessary to win World War II, again the legal rights
of blacks to work, much less to overcome discrimination in the workplace,
were not so bright. The most pressing evidence came from the rural South,
where Jim Crow's shadow in the form of anti-enticement, quasi-peonage, anti-
hitchhiking, vagrancy, and other laws limiting black laborers' ability to bargain
for their services fell on every black farm family. A challenge to the long tradition of extorting black labor and undervaluing black production found little
succor in the Department of Justice. These cases deeply moved the LDF, but
"once the [LDF] defined the problem as racial discrimination, rather than inequality or insecurity, it essentially defined the farm workers' problems out of
its litigation agenda." Although this decision sounds as though the LDF was
moved more by a tone-deaf formal legal reasoning blind to real human suf-
fering, one has to remember that the small staff were lawyers, and they had
to base cases on established legal doctrine. There were doctrinal grounds for
arguing against racial discrimination. There were no (and still are no) grounds
for arguing against a maldistribution of wealth.[9]

Whatever the legitimacy of the claims of black laborers, the NAACP made
the decision to target racial discrimination, first and foremost, in education.
Initially, the LDF focused its energies on insuring that allegedly separate but
equal facilities were actually equal. Facing the well-entrenched forces of Jim
Crow, the civil rights lawyers had to adopt what Greenberg called a "tacti-
cally cautious yet strategically bold technique." It might seem piecemeal, but
its real target was the entire Jim Crow system. The lawyers knew that a black
man or woman who sued Jim Crow was likely to face retaliation from white
neighbors. It was never easy to find willing and courageous plaintiffs—but the
LDF did.[10]

It was against this background—and with men like Marshall, Carter, Robinson, and Greenberg working together—that the LDF turned to graduate
and professional education lawsuits. As in the other areas of discrimination,
state trial and appeals courts found for the defendants, sustaining the denial

9. Goluboff, *Lost Promise*, 36–38, 51–52, 66–67, 186.
10. Greenberg, *Crusaders*, 107.

of equal access to public education. The first two cases came from Oklahoma. In *Sipuel v. Board of Regents of the University of Oklahoma* (1947), the Oklahoma Supreme Court held: "We conclude that petitioner is fully entitled to education in law with facilities equal to those for white students, but that the separate education policy of Oklahoma is lawful and is not intended to be discriminatory in fact, and is not discriminatory against plaintiff in law for the reasons above shown." Ada Sipuel could go out of state for her education with a tuition grant from the state not available to whites, so eager was Oklahoma not to provide equal opportunities for her in the state. "Or if she preferred, she might attend a separate law school for negroes in Oklahoma." There was no such school. Four days after the oral argument before the U.S. Supreme Court, it issued a per curiam opinion in *Sipuel v. Board of Regents of the University of Oklahoma* (1948) ordering the state to provide Sipuel with a legal education "in conformity with the equal protection clause of the Fourteenth Amendment and provide it as soon as it does for the applicants of any other group."[11]

Oklahoma sought to preserve segregation by hastily opening up a law school for "coloreds"—hiring three attorneys and setting aside three rooms in the state capitol and access to the capitol law library, hardly equal though obviously separate. Arguing against the state, Marshall did not challenge *Plessy* directly, but Justice Wiley Rutledge on the high court did: "The equality required was equality in fact, not in legal fiction." Oklahoma successfully evaded integration of its premier law school, but the maneuver only lasted one year. Although the Supreme Court had not ordered the state to admit her, in 1949 state authorities conceded, the makeshift law school closed, and Sipuel entered the real one. She graduated in 1951.[12]

In the meantime, the justices faced an even more egregious case of discrimination, again from Oklahoma. George McLaurin gained admission to the doctoral program in education under *Sipuel*, but the university, under a state law passed to deal with his admission, "required [him] to sit apart at a designated desk in an anteroom adjoining the classroom; to sit at a designated desk on the mezzanine floor of the library, but not to use the desks in the regular reading room; and to sit at a designated table and to eat at a different time from the other students in the school cafeteria." A unanimous U.S. Supreme Court ruled that these special arrangements failed constitutional tests. In *McLaurin v. Oklahoma State Regents* (1950), one can hear the same tone

11. Sipuel v. Board of Regents, 199 Okla. 36, 45 (1947) (Welch, J.); Sipuel v. Board of Regents of Univ. of Okla., 332 U.S. 631, 633 (1948) (per curiam).

12. Fisher v. Hurst, 333 U.S. 147, 152 (1948) (Rutledge, J.); Fowler V. Harper, *Justice Rutledge and the Bright Constellation* (Indianapolis: Bobbs-Merrill, 1965), 332; Klarman, *Jim Crow*, 205–6.

of sharp rebuke as in the Court's Alabama peonage case. "The Fourteenth Amendment precludes differences in treatment by the state based upon race." The Court limited its holding to the circumstances of the case, declining to deal with *Plessy*.[13]

Sweatt v. Painter (1950) then became the key case. Indeed, many of the arguments so often associated with *Brown v. Board of Education* were rehearsed in *Sweatt*. In *Sweatt* the LDF represented an applicant to the University of Texas School of Law denied admission explicitly because state law required segregation of the law school. Although the constitutional argument was familiar—separate but equal failed miserably in practice—the materials Marshall assembled represented a new kind of attack. The strategy was based on the old Brandeis brief, in which Louis Brandeis, acting as co-counsel for an Oregon hours limitation law (*Muller v. Oregon* [1908]), reached out to the social science community to prove that too many hours at work harmed women laundresses. Marshall later told an interviewer that the Brandeis brief idea was a key to his strategy. Marshall brought to court evidence that race had little to do with intellectual ability and that racial segregation produced palpable harm to black students. Did such social science information belong in law? The answer was yes, for testimony based on data collected in the real world that people of African ancestry were just as able to make use of higher education, and that racial stigma was a genuine psychological harm, would appear in every major LDF brief thereafter.[14]

Heman Marion Sweatt was born in 1912, and when he applied to the law school in Austin, he was a mailman. He was poorly prepared for it, according to recollections of one faculty member, but then the law school admitted all applicants, regardless of preparation. Plans were already afoot in the state legislature to expand separate but not quite equal (they would not have access to a special set aid fund from the legislature) schools for the professional education of black students. In 1946, however, the Special Joint Committee on Higher Education for Negroes in Texas had done little more than make recommendations to expand separate facilities for blacks in Houston. Meanwhile, public meetings in Austin, the state capital, inspired the local NAACP chapter to aid Sweatt's cause to enter the state law school. This brought Mar-

13. McLaurin v. Oklahoma State Regents, 339 U.S. 637 (1950).

14. Thurgood Marshall, "Reminiscences of Thurgood Marshall," in *Thurgood Marshall*, ed. Tushnet, 499. Targeting education: Tushnet, *The NAACP's Legal Strategy*, 25–27 (Margold report). On the so-called Brandeis Brief, see Nancy Woloch, *A Class by Herself: Protective Laws for Women Workers, 1890s–1990s* (Princeton, NJ: Princeton University Press, 2015), 65–67; and Melvin Urofsky, *Louis D. Brandeis: A Life* (New York: Schocken, 2009), 217–19.

shall, Carter, and the LDF to the capital city with plans to represent Sweatt,
joined by local attorney W. J. Durham. Support came from unexpected sources.
For example, the University of Texas student newspaper, the *Daily Texan*, ran
editorials in favor of desegregation of the law school. Thus from the outset of the litigation, there was white support for the integration of the law
program.[15]

There were two state trial court hearings of Sweatt's case after UT denied
his application for admission. The university cited the Texas law that forbade
racial mixing at the university. At the May 16, 1946, hearing in the circuit
court for Travis County, the response of the UT administration averred that
"the Constitution and laws of the State of Texas require equal protection of
the law and equal educational opportunities for all qualified persons but provide for separate educational institutions for White and Negro students. The
Respondents therefore deny that their refusal to admit Relator was arbitrarily
or illegal or in violation of the Constitutions of the United States and the State
of Texas, since equal opportunities were provided for Relator in another State
supported law school as hereinafter shown." Judge Roy C. Archer agreed that
the rejection of Sweatt was simply a matter of Texas law. "The Constitution
and laws of the State of Texas provide for the segregation of the white and
colored races in educational institutions maintained by the State of Texas; and
that such laws are valid and subsisting and must be sustained by this Court
unless they clearly and unmistakably deny to the relator his rights under the
Constitutions of the United States and of the State of Texas." He gave the state
six months to provide for a segregated alternative law school.

In the fall of 1946, with Marshall orchestrating publicity, the case was already a cause célèbre in the state. Six months after Judge Archer had ruled
on the original petition, Marshall and James Nabrit Jr. along with Durham,
returned to court to hear why the state had ignored Judge Archer's original
order. Marshall pointedly asked Judge Archer why little had been done to establish the promised black law school. Despite a plea by the dean of the law
school, Charles McCormick, that the state change its mind and admit Sweatt,
Attorney General Grover Sellers, counsel for the state, replied that everyone
had to obey Texas law, and the fault lay in the black colleges for not providing
a law school for their students.

15. Gary M. Lavergne, *Before* Brown: *Herman Marion Sweatt, Thurgood Marshall, and the
Long Road to Justice* (Austin: University of Texas Press, 2010), 125–28, 130, 132 (including W. Page
Keeton recollection); Thurgood Marshall, "Opening Remarks . . . Seventh Annual Institute of
Race Relations, Fisk University . . . June 26, 1950," in *Thurgood Marshall, Supreme Justice: Speeches
and Writings*, ed. J. Clay Smith Jr. (Philadelphia: University of Pennsylvania Press, 2001), 34.

Sellers had made up his mind about the case even before it was filed. A one-term attorney general, he would run for governor in 1946, lose, accept a post on the state bench, and return between sessions to his cattle ranch. He thought separation of the races was a "wise" policy. In short, the trial court once again wholly and without qualification adopted the position of the defendants. Archer repeated his earlier views on the case and extended the time for the establishment of the black law school. The tactic of ordering equalization then allowing delay was one that would soon find use in other venues. Needless to say, it was proof to Marshall that the delay showed bad faith, for stalling amounted to legally sanctioned inaction.[16]

Sweatt appealed but could not have hoped for victory. Southern state institutions of higher learning and professional training were not overawed by the LDF blitz. Instead, they marshalled their own battalion of lawyers. These included the states' attorneys general and their assistants, some specially hired, like Jack Greenberg was for the LDF, to battle in segregation cases. Although Texas attorney general Price Daniel signed the brief for the state in the state court of appeals, it was Assistant Attorney General Joseph Greenhill whom Daniel hired and assigned the drudge work of research and writing. A 1939 graduate of the University of Texas School of Law, Greenhill had been working as a researcher for the state supreme court when the post came along. It paid more and he was comfortable working with Daniel. Greenhill would later go on to a distinguished career on the state supreme court, an elective post. His boss, the attorney general, was a generation older (born in 1910) and had served in the Texas House of Representatives before his service in World War II. Elected to the attorney general post, he would later serve as a senator from Texas and the state's governor, also elective posts. The two men were thus what one could in justice regard as the best products of Texas legal training and political reputation. In addition to the tidelands oil case (involving federal versus state control of tax revenues from offshore oil), Daniel assigned

16. Response of the defendants and decision of the court, in Sweatt v. Painter, 126 Circuit Court, Travis County No. 74,945, May 1946, *Herman [i.e. Heman] Marion Sweatt, Petitioners vs. Theophilus Shickel Painter, et al.: [In the] Supreme Court of the United States* (Washington, DC: Judd & Detweiler, printers, 1948–49) 1:5–8; Lavergne, *Before* Brown, 135; "Judge Dodges Own Order in Sweatt Case," *Houston Informer*, December 14, 1946, 1; Rawn James Jr., *Root and Branch: Charles Hamilton Houston, Thurgood Marshall, and the Struggle to End Segregation* (New York: Bloomsbury Press, 2010), 206. Not every NAACP local leader was pleased. Some wanted Texas to fulfill its promise to separate but equal. But the voices for desegregation won the day. Meline Pitre, *In Struggle against Jim Crow: Lulu B. White and the NAACP, 1900–1957* (College Station: Texas A&M University Press, 1999), 91–94.

Sweatt to Greenhill, arguably one of the two most important cases the attorney general's office handled in the immediate postwar era.[17]

Of *Sweatt*, Greenhill recalled, "There was not any preconceived racism on my part. I had a job and I could do it or I could quit. My job was to represent the University of Texas, A&M [the other state university system] and school districts. At that time the Constitution of Texas required separation of the races and supposedly equal facilities." Greenhill had already met Marshall in court and bested him in "several cases," as he recalled, but the law school case was the only one that Marshall and his team appealed. Greenhill knew that there was no separate law school, much less an equal one. The legislature responded to the lawsuit; they wanted "an instant equal separate school." The idea originated after Sweatt applied and was turned down. So Marshall brought lawsuit in the trial court in Austin. Following the instructions of the legislature to create a law school for blacks in Austin, "we bought up all the law books you could buy . . . we bought all we could" and put them in a "three story building across the alley from the state capitol." Marshall watched every move Texas made. "One of the brightest things Thurgood Marshall did was establish that this old building that we were using . . . probably wasn't structurally sound enough to hold the weight of all those law books," Greenhill recalled, but it did not matter. "There wasn't any way we could [have] lost that case in Austin."

Eyewitness accounts of the trial recalled that Price Daniel led a vigorous cross-examination of Sweatt, introduced inflammatory racialist language, and generally acted as though the plaintiff and his counsel were cattle rustlers on trial for a crime rather than petitioners in a lawsuit for admission to a school. After losing in the trial court, Marshall brought the lawsuit to the Texas Court of Civil Appeals (the Texas Supreme Court declined to hear the appeal from the lower courts). In the interim, the legislature had provided a new law school in Houston. "They had fine facilities. Just beautiful," Greenhill thought. And approved by the ABA too. Greenhill knew that there were segregated (black) law schools in other southern states. "Some of them were ridiculous." Anyhow, Texas treated Marshall, as well as his comrades, "as an equal. I'm not sure that was completely true. But there were no racial overtones, no heated racial overtones in the trial of Sweatt." Greenhill added, almost as an afterthought, "He [Marshall] did have a problem in that then in Austin there wasn't any

17. Oral History interview with the Honorable Joe R. Greenhill, February 10, 1986, Rare Books and Special Collections, Tarlton Law Library, University of Texas at Austin; Oral History interview with Dean W. Page Keeton, July 28, 1986, Rare Books and Special Collections, Tarlton Law Library, the University of Texas at Austin.

place on Congress Avenue or for two blocks on either side where Marshall could get a room or buy a meal or go to the restroom." Some counsel were just more equal than others.[18]

The decision of the Court of Civil Appeals showed that Greenhill's work was persuasive and his prediction accurate. Delivering the opinion for a unanimous court was Chief Justice James Wooten McClendon. The chief justice was born in Georgia, in 1873, on the eve of the "Redemption" of the state by Democrats opposed to Reconstruction. He moved to Texas as a young man and earned his law degree at the then-still-new School of Law in Austin. After practicing law, he was named to the Texas Supreme Court in 1923, three years later moving his wife into a French medieval-style mansion in Austin, and serving as the court's chief justice at the time of his retirement in 1949. McClendon was a distinguished jurist, named to the American Law Institute and the National Conference of Judicial Councils among other prestigious offices. *Sweatt* was his last great case. He died in 1972.[19]

McClendon made clear from the outset that the crucial question of fact was stipulated by both sides—Sweatt was black. There was no question of him passing for white, like Homer Plessy. "On February 26, 1946, Heman Marion Sweatt, a Negro, applied for admission to the School of Law of the University of Texas, as a first year student. Admittedly, he possessed every essential qualification for admission, except that of race, upon which ground alone his application was denied, under Section 7 of Article 7 of the Texas Constitution . . . which reads: 'Separate schools shall be provided for the white and colored children, and impartial provision shall be made for both.'" Sweatt filed in the Texas courts against the president of the university, Theophilus Shickel Painter, and the members of the board of regents. The state had sovereign immunity, but the common way around this bar to lawsuit was to name individual officers of the state. The basis for the lawsuit was the Equal Protection Clause of the Fourteenth Amendment. Whatever the Texas Constitution might have said, the state was supposed to provide equal protection to all the citizens of the United States under this provision of the federal Constitution. The trial court denied the relief sought—an injunction compelling his admission, and he appealed.[20]

18. Greenhill Oral History interview, February 10, 1986; Kluger, *Simple Justice*, 262–63.

19. "McClendon, James Wooten," Texas State Historical Association, https://tshaonline.org/handbook/online/articles/fmc13; the McClendon Papers at the Tarleton Law Library, University of Texas School of Law, Austin, alas do not throw any light on his thinking in *Sweatt*. In all probability, it seemed to him like an open-and-shut case, governed by Texas law and federal constitutional precedent.

20. Sweatt v. Painter, 210 S.W. 2d. 242, 243 (Tex. Civ. App. 1948) (McClendon C.J.).

State courts are free to interpret federal law when that law is the basis of a lawsuit in the state court. McClendon rested the federal question on prior U.S. Supreme Court decisions. This is precedent, and in a common-law system, precedent is the most common way to rationalize a decision. "It should be borne in mind that the validity of state laws which require segregation of races in state supported schools as being, on the ground of segregation alone, a denial of due process, is not now an open question." A footnote—here a string citation of cases—listed these decisions. These referred to the Due Process Clause of the Fourteenth Amendment, the grounds on which prior petitioners sought to challenge state-mandated segregation. "The gist of these decisions is embodied in . . . *Plessy v. Ferguson*," from which McClendon quoted at length. In that case, Justice Harlan had dissented, but McClendon noted that Harlan had not dissented in a school segregation case coming from Georgia, three years later (*Cumming v. Richmond County* [1899]), and Chief Justice William Howard Taft, for the Court, upheld state segregation laws in *Gong Lum v. Rice* (1927).[21]

Marshall knew all about these cases and, facing them, then shifted to the Equal Protection Clause to show that "(1) There is no rational basis for racial classification for school purposes. (2) Public schools, 'separate but equal' in theory are in fact and in practical administration consistently unequal and discriminatory[.] [A]nd (3) [i]t is impossible to have the equality required by the Fourteenth Amendment in a public school system which relegates citizens of a disadvantaged racial minority group to separate schools." It was the third of these that made *Sweatt* the key case, for in this argument the LDF departed from the equalization claim and proposed that segregated schools could never satisfy the Equal Protection Clause. But even if this most thoroughgoing of claims failed, "The doctrine of racially 'separate but equal' public facilities is merely a constitutional hypothesis which has no application where racial segregation is shown to be inconsistent with equality."[22]

McClendon agreed with the petitioners that the case before him was a novel one because of the third claim, "Whether it is possible to have the equality required by the Fourteenth Amendment in a public school system which relegates citizens of a disadvantaged racial minority group to separate schools." Because of this claim, the case had far broader application than the admission of a student to Texas's law school. "Implicit in these quotations is the assertion that race segregation in public schools, at least in the higher and professional

21. 210 S.W. 2d at 244; Cumming v. Richmond County, 175 U.S. 528 (1899) (Harlan, J.); Gong Lum v. Rice, 275 U.S. 78 (1927).

22. 210 S.W. at 244; Marshall, "Reminiscences," 423 (*Sweatt* targeted segregation straight out).

fields, inherently is discriminatory within the meaning of the Fourteenth Amendment, and cannot be made otherwise." McClendon was not willing to take such a giant step, whatever his own views of segregation might be, because "this assertion in effect impeaches the soundness of the various decisions of the Federal Supreme Court which hold to the contrary. . . . To so hold would convict the great jurists who rendered those decisions of being so far removed from the actualities involved in the race problems of our American life as to render them incapable of evaluating the known facts of contemporaneous and precedent history as they relate to those problems." McClendon, a standard bearer of the Texas legal establishment, understood the scope of the case, and obviously sensed that a decision for the appellant would be a radical departure from established norms. But Marshall had not asked the court to overturn *Plessy* and its progeny much less to convict the 1896 Supreme Court of anything. He instead had asked McClendon's court to revisit "separate but equal" and ask whether it still made sense.[23]

McClendon then turned to the narrower claim that the provisions for black law students in the state were not equal to those provided for white students. "It is of course of the very essence of the validity of segregation laws that they provide for each segregated group or class facilities and opportunities the equivalent, or (as often stated) substantial equivalent of those provided for the other group or class. Our constitution (quoted above) so provides." The choice of the word "validity" was telling. Valid meant that reality must match the letter of the law. Against this staple of the pro-segregation legal doctrine, Marshall had replied that there could be no equality so long as the state forced separation by race. McClendon had a clever riposte: there was never perfect equality, not in the real world. If the races existed, as he presumed, and their qualities and capacities were not equal, as he assumed, then equal provisions for them must be predicated on these differences. Shades of Justice Brown in *Plessy*. "The framers of the Texas constitution of 1876 recognized the necessity (both inherent and under the 14th Amendment) of 'equal protection' in the must (shall) requirement (art. 7, Sec. 7) of 'impartial provision' for 'both' races. The question, and we think the controlling one, which this appeal presents is whether under the record showing in this case the State at the time of the trial had provided and made available to Relator a course of instruction in law as a first year student, the equivalent or substantial equivalent in its advantages to him of that which the State was then providing in the University of Texas Law School. We are not dealing here with abstractions but with realities."[24]

23. Id. at 245.
24. Id.

McClendon did not see those realities incorporating the supporting evidence that the LDF assembled, however. Playing something like a legal version of three-card monte, the court found that Marshall's evidence was "outside the judicial function." It was, in other words, not admissible, even though it dealt with the very realities that the court had cited for separation of the races. Thus, there were two sets of realities, one dictated by long custom and attitude, and the other by social science findings. Only the former were probative in McClendon's opinion. Indeed, the "factual bases" on which Texas based its "constitutional and legislative enactments" were so obvious to him that they were not fit "subjects of judicial review." The court incorporated the first set of realities—the realities of legislative racial prejudice—but not the realities of the impact of such prejudice on its victims. As a consequence of this artificially narrowed view of reality, the jerry-rigged arrangements that the legislature had made for a separate school in Houston—despite its paucity of students, library, and access to faculty—McClendon found substantially equivalent to the university's law school in Austin. Indeed, the court cited with approval the appropriation that the legislature made to acquire the property and other outward accoutrements of a law school. "The evidence shows, on the part of the State of Texas, an enormous outlay both in funds and in carefully and conscientiously planned and executed endeavor, in a sincere and earnest bona fide effort to afford every reasonable and adequate facility." The ruling of the trial court was affirmed.[25]

At the Civil Division hearings (the Texas Supreme Court declined to hear the appeal from the Court of Civil Appeals), Greenhill sat next to Daniel but did not speak for the state. Instead, he recalled, "my main job was to research the law." He unearthed *Plessy* and concluded that there was "no federal obligation to teach or to educate." States had to offer equal opportunities to all groups if they offered it to one. He studied the *Congressional Globe* and concluded that "the Fourteenth Amendment was not prosed or adopted to require integration of the races." In conclusion, "it was clear as it could be" that integration was not what the Congress wanted. Winning in Texas in 1948 and losing in the high court two years later, even in *Brown*, which Greenhill heard announced in the Supreme Court courtroom, "It wasn't any big deal to me. It was a lawsuit."[26]

Durham prepared a brief for the appellant for the U.S. Supreme Court, meant as a guide for oral argument. The argument began with the NAACP stance in *Sipuel*—the schools for blacks were funded at one-eighth the level

25. Id.
26. Greenhill Oral History interview, February 10, 1986.

of the schools for whites. It was a clear presentation of the evil of discrimination. Thus what had prior to *Sweatt* been proof that the standard of *Plessy* was not met here became evidence that the intent to discriminate was inherent in the Texas law. A state law based on *Plessy* was "illegal" because it barred Texas courts from considering any evidence of the disparate impact of discrimination. McClendon had said as much. He had added that the peace and welfare of the state required separation of the races. In Durham's thinking, however, segregation was the result of "brutal agitation by one race against another." Segregation endangered the peace and welfare of all Texans. The only reason for the mandate was racial stigma based on pure prejudice. Although Durham repeated the constitutional arguments that Marshall and the LDF had evolved, there was a personal tone in his brief—a tone of injury and long-suffered malice, that one did not see in the arguments the state made. Durham came from Sherman, Texas, the scene of a brutal race riot in 1930, during which his office was burned and his life endangered. He knew that the violence that state-imposed segregation bred fell heavily upon the very people that the law oppressed. But minority lawyers trained in the best schools could provide some relief from these wrongs, able to "match wits" with white lawyers trained by the same teachers in integrated schools.[27]

Durham was the local attorney who had served in the trenches, defending people of color in all manner of causes. Like so many of the local black attorneys, he was a bulwark of the NAACP. To him, Heman Sweatt had turned. He had presented the case to the local court, but as the stakes mounted and the LDF prepared the appeal for the U.S. Supreme Court, Durham stepped aside for the national office men. They were not from Texas. But they had paid their dues in the civil rights cause. If there was glory in the eventual victory, history will have to insure that William Durham gets his share.

Both sides' counsel presented their case in oral argument before the U.S. Supreme Court on April 3, 1950, Greenhill at the appellee's table with Price Daniel; Marshall across the aisle with Robert L. Carter, the cream of the LDF team. Durham did not participate in the oral argument. Nor was his draft the basis for the LDF presentation. Instead, oral argument followed the lines of the state case, with the clear exception that Marshall had now won the battle within the LDF and the NAACP to attack segregation directly. The absence of equality in the opportunities was no longer the gravamen. There could be

27. "Sweatt v. Painter, Brief of the Argument," 2, 4, 7, 9, 16. Texas Southern University Thurgood Marshall Law School Archives, Houston, Texas; John Browning, "Forged in Fire, the William J. Durham Story," *Rockwell County (TX) Herald Banner*, July 28, 2006.

no equality, hence the Equal Protection Clause could never be satisfied, so long as a state mandated separate schools. Separate but equal was impossible, and that was that. But that was not where Marshall stopped. Sweatt's right was a constitutional one, not merely a matter of bricks and mortar, books, and desks.[28]

Daniel's oral response was that racial separation was reasonable so long as the state provided substantially equal facilities. Daniel was arguing, in effect, that the state law should be viewed not under the "strict scrutiny" standard, wherein the state had to prove a compelling rationale for the law and that its strictures were closely tailored to that compelling need, but under a rational relation standard, in which the state had only to show that its law was a reasonable application of its concern for the welfare of all its citizens. The distinction went back to the beginning of the twentieth century and was generally applied to state health and police powers under the Due Process Clause of the Fourteenth Amendment. The application of the rational relation doctrine to Equal Protection cases was a stretch. In keeping the races separate, the state of Texas was merely trying to avoid unpleasantness for its black citizens and keep good order among its whites. Greenhill, given the chance to add to his boss's comments, reminded the justices that education was a subject long left to the states.[29]

To pass over Greenhill's arguments was a bridge too far for some members of the Court, however. They had come to maturity in politics and law in a world where segregation was the norm. They thus faced, in microcosm, the same difficulty that the LDF and the NAACP faced—should they decide to reverse the Texas ruling in *Sweatt*, must they reverse *Plessy* as well? Biography—personality and personal experience—may not dictate judicial views, but it certainly has an influence on them. The judges who faced Marshall and Daniel from the high bench were all white men, and only a few could be assumed to be opponents of Jim Crow. Despite the weak record of the New Deal Department of Justice on racial equality, four of the holdovers from the New Deal Court—Justices Hugo Black, Felix Frankfurter, William O. Douglas, and Robert H. Jackson—had already given hints that they

28. Oral Argument in Sweatt v. Painter, April 3, 1950, in Lavergne, *Before* Brown, 245–47. (No stenographic record of the oral argument exists.)

29. Oral Argument in Sweatt v. Painter, April 3, 1950, in Lavergne, *Before* Brown, 246–47. Lavergne regarded Daniel's conduct between January and April 1950 as little more than cheap political posturing, an attempt to wring higher office in the state out of the case. By contrast, Greenhill was a serious student of law rather than a pol and his presentation was more workmanlike.

were favorable to the end of segregation in higher education. But Justice Stanley Forman Reed and the newer members of the Court, all Harry S. Truman appointees, could not be counted on, and a unanimous opinion was vital to the desegregation cause.

The briefs and oral arguments submitted, on April 8, 1950, the conference of the Court convened. The justices offered their views on *Sweatt* in order of seniority. Chief Justice Fred Vinson offered a short course in the constitutional precedents, conceding that there was no equality in the school that Texas was setting up for black students, the rule in older precedents, but "it may be that now we should expand the constitution." Then again, "the problem is so sensitive." So long as the decision was limited to the professional schools, however, "no great harm would result from the mingling of the races in professional schools." On the other hand, he did not see how the Court could draw a line between the rights of applicants to professional schools and the rights of children in elementary schools, and this greatly troubled him. He would affirm the Texas courts' rulings.[30]

Vinson was in many ways the least likely member of the Court to support the LDF program. When he was named to the center seat in 1946, he was serving as Truman's secretary of the treasury. He did not have a distinguished legal career, nor was he a much-respected jurist. He did have a career very similar to Truman's. Born in 1890 in the small town of Louisa, Kentucky, Vinson overcame many obstacles to reach the pinnacle of American judicial office. Like Truman, he served in the armed forces during World War I. Thereafter, Vinson was a quintessential local politician, easy to know and work with, earning election as commonwealth attorney in 1921 and successive terms in Congress from 1924 to 1938, with the exception of one election in 1928 when the national Democratic Party's stand on Prohibition briefly cost him his seat. Roosevelt appointed him to the D.C. Circuit Court of Appeals. On the court of appeals, he sided with the government and deferred to the legislative branch. After his service as an administrator during the war, President Truman appointed him secretary of the treasury, and on June 6, 1946, tabbed him for the chief justiceship. Confirmation followed easily. But Vinson would prove unable to apply his administrative experience to managing what had become a bitterly divided bench. Vinson seemed to favor civil rights when it did not threaten to upset white majorities.[31]

30. Chief Justice Vinson, April 8, 1950, Conference, in Del Dickson, ed., *The Supreme Court in Conference, 1940–1985* (New York: Oxford University Press, 2001), 641–42.

31. Truman and Vinson: James E. St. Clair and Linda C. Gugin, *Chief Justice Fred M. Vinson of Kentucky: A Political Biography* (Lexington: University of Kentucky Press, 2002), 154, 176–78,

Hugo Black, the justice with the greatest seniority hence the next to speak, voted to reverse the Texas court. The Supreme Court had already spoken on *McLaurin*. The two cases seemed aligned to him. Black, an Alabama senator and staunch friend of the New Deal, sometimes embarrassed the New York plutocrat in the White House with his attacks on privilege, corporate arrogance, and special deals. In this sense, Black was a Populist. He even supported the unions, a dangerous position to take in the Deep South, particularly when his wealthy Birmingham friends were fighting so hard to prevent unionization of the mines and mills. After his confirmation, it was discovered that he had briefly belonged to the Klan, but he had long since renounced its racism and his views of school desegregation made him, perhaps, a reliable ally on the Court of the LDF campaign.[32]

Justice Reed voted to affirm. For all intents and purposes, the facilities would meet the separate but equal standard. Reed—a Kentucky Democratic corporate attorney, state legislator, and federal bureaucrat—was Roosevelt's choice for solicitor general of the United States in 1935, and he won many key New Deal cases in the Supreme Court as counsel for the federal government. His views on segregation were troubled, for he was hesitant to overrule so many precedents that undergirded Jim Crow. On the other hand, he thought, perhaps law schools were a special case, in which the "intangibles" of the quality of faculty and the connections that prestigious institutions offered to their students outweighed other factors like expenditures per student. He would have to be persuaded, however, that the courts were the right place to strike down segregation.[33]

Justice Frankfurter voted to reverse. In January 1939, Frankfurter had joined the Court. Frankfurter was an immigrant, his family fleeing to the Lower East Side of New York in 1894 to escape anti-Semitism in Eastern Europe. Frankfurter starred as a student at Harvard Law School, returning in 1914 to the school from a brief stint in private practice and government service. As a professor, he introduced a seminar in administrative law. In it he mentored

190; Justice Douglas, quoted in William Domnarski, *The Great Justices, 1941–54: Black, Douglas, Frankfurter, and Jackson in Chambers* (Ann Arbor: University of Michigan Press, 2006), 46–47; Noah Feldman, *Scorpions: The Battles and Triumphs of FDR's Great Supreme Court Justices* (New York: Hachette, 2010), 298ff.; Kluger, *Simple Justice*, 244, 589; Michal Belknap, *The Vinson Court: Justices, Rulings, and Legacy* (Santa Barbara, CA: ABC-CLIO, 2004), 35–41; Clare Cushman, *Courtwatchers: Eyewitness Accounts in Supreme Court History* (Lanham, MD: Rowman and Littlefield, 2011), 175.

32. Roger K. Newman, *Hugo Black: A Biography* (New York: Fordham University Press, 1997), 13; Kluger, *Simple Justice*, 591–93.

33. Klarman, *Jim Crow*, 208, 211; Kluger, *Simple Justice*, 596.

able and eager young men ready to enter and reform government. He was greatly loyal to Roosevelt and patriotic to a fault, lest anyone hold his Jewish background or his foreign birth against him.[34]

In oral argument, Frankfurter reverted to his professorial manner, posing sharp questions to counsel. In conference, however, he could go on speaking far too long, treating the other justices as though they were his students. His opinions and comments on other justices' drafts were miniature law school lectures. In his own opinions, many of them concurrences, Frankfurter advocated judicial restraint, husbanding the political capital of the Court by deferring to the other branches of the federal government. He looked for ways to avoid deciding questions on constitutional grounds, including denying that a plaintiff had standing to sue, or finding that lawsuits were moot or unripe for decision. He was worried about the ability of the Court to enforce unpopular decisions, but he was clearly opposed to Jim Crow.[35]

Frankfurter had a personal stake in the case. He had served as a consultant to the NAACP for years before he was elevated to the Court and had been a law professor for over two decades. He understood the claim that the strength of a law school was the quality of its student body, and nothing that Texas could provide for minority students would match what the flagship university provided to its law students. Still, he claimed, "we need not go beyond the needs of graduate education," not yet at least. In this, Frankfurter was thinking about the same thing as Vinson—the Court would be hard-pressed to draw a line between Equal Protection in graduate education and the same Fourteenth Amendment doctrine in elementary education. Cautious to a fault, he would prefer not to have the Court step out in front of that issue. "We should not go beyond what is necessary here." Justices William O. Douglas, Robert H. Jackson, Harold H. Burton, Tom C. Clark, and Sherman Minton all voted to reverse, Clark making clear his view that desegregation orders should only apply to graduate schools.[36]

Douglas was a New Dealer and like Frankfurter a former law professor. Growing up in Yakima, Washington, after the death of his father, Douglas endured family poverty and polio. He countered the former by hard work and the latter by a vigorous outdoor life. He went on to a storied career as a law

34. Feldman, *Scorpions*, 38–39; Jeff Shesol, *Supreme Power: Franklin Roosevelt vs. the Supreme Court* (New York: Norton, 2011), 51–53; Melvin I. Urofsky, *Felix Frankfurter: Judicial Restraint and Individual Liberties* (Boston: Twayne, 1991), 32ff.; H. N. Hirsch, *The Enigma of Felix Frankfurter* (New York: Basic, 1981), 106, 144 (flattery).

35. Kluger, *Simple Justice*, 599.

36. Justices Black, Reed, Frankfurter, Jackson, Burton, Clark, and Minton, April 8, 1950, Conference, in Dickson, ed., *Supreme Court in Conference*, 642–44.

professor at Yale and Columbia and then to head the Securities Exchange Commission. He was elevated to the Court in 1939.[37]

Douglas was ambitious for the highest elective political office, and that meant that he could not afford to offend southern voters, but he was a staunch liberal nonetheless. At the same time, he was a brilliant writer, giving speeches and publishing essays, in addition to dashing off stunning opinions "of creativity, novelty, and importance." From the first, he was outspoken in his enmity for Jim Crow.[38]

The last of the New Dealers on the Court was former attorney general Robert H. Jackson. Jackson grew up on a farm in upstate New York. After completing high school, he took classes at Albany Law School and observed New York Court of Appeals arguments. In 1913, at the age of twenty-one, he gained admission to the bar. He was immensely successful in private practice, but took time to represent the poor and downtrodden as well as the well-to-do.[39]

Jackson's reputation as a lawyer and his steadfast Democrat politics brought him to FDR's attention as a friend and advisor, and then in 1938 as solicitor general and in 1940 as attorney general. A year later, Jackson joined the Court. Reliably deferential to government, he explained in *The Struggle for Judicial Supremacy: A Study of a Crisis in American Power Politics* (1941) how a pre-1937 activist court was "substituting its judgment for that of Congress and the way in which judicial review governed our society." On the bench he believed that liberty must make some concessions to order, and the rights that every citizen had did not include the right to undermine elected officials or the Constitution itself. The Bill of Rights was not "a suicide pact." It was not clear where he would stand on the issue of segregation, but he was closely aligned with Frankfurter on the Court and Truman's support for desegregation led him into the desegregation camp.[40]

37. Douglas told his own story in *Go East, Young Man: The Early Years: The Autobiography of William O. Douglas* (New York: Random House, 1974), and *The Court Years, 1939–1975* (New York: Random House, 1980).

38. Stephen B. Duke, "Justice Douglas and the Criminal Law," in *"He Shall Not Pass This Way Again": The Legacy of Justice William O. Douglas*, ed. Stephen L. Wasby (Pittsburgh: University of Pittsburgh Press, 1990), 133–34; James F. Simon, *Independent Journey: The Life of William O. Douglas* (New York: Harper and Row, 1980), 354; Douglas, memo to Frankfurter, May 29, 1954, in *The Douglas Letters: Selections from the Private Correspondence of William O. Douglas*, ed. Melvin I. Urofsky (Bethesda, MD: Adler and Adler, 1987), 85.

39. Gregory Caldieera, "Robert Houghwout Jackson," in *Oxford Companion to the Supreme Court of the United States*, ed. Kermit Hall et al. (New York: Oxford University Press, 1992), 443–45.

40. Robert H. Jackson, *The Struggle for Judicial Supremacy: A Study of a Crisis in American Power Politics* (New York: Knopf, 1941), 109. "The Constitution is not a suicide pact": Terminiello v.

President Harry S. Truman looked to his former Senate comrades to fill vacancies on the Supreme Court. The first was Harold Burton, in 1945, then serving as Republican senator from Ohio, and his last was former Democratic senator Sherman Minton, from Indiana, in 1949. Minton, unlike Burton, had judicial experience, confirmed to a seat on the Seventh Circuit Court of Appeals in 1941 after losing his seat in the Senate. Truman knew, liked, and had worked with both men when Truman represented Missouri in the Senate.[41]

Another of these government men whose service recommended them for the bench was Truman's attorney general, Tom C. Clark. Born in Dallas, Texas, in 1899, Clark attended the Virginia Military Institute until financial reasons forced him home. Like Vinson, he volunteered for service in World War I but did not see combat. He earned his bachelor's and LLB from the University of Texas and joined his father and brother in the family law firm before becoming a successful assistant district attorney. Local politics led to federal office. In 1937, after another stint in private practice, he went to Washington to serve in the Department of War, and after the United States entered World War II, he was the special assistant in the War Risk Insurance Office, the first of a series of offices including civilian coordinator for Japanese internment. Much later in life, he admitted that the latter was "the biggest mistake of my life." Truman made Clark attorney general, where he continued his antitrust work and, unlike Vinson, vigorously aided the civil rights movement, filing friends of the court briefs in NAACP law lawsuits, urging the FBI to investigate racial violence, and supporting an anti-lynching bill in Congress. Clark also undertook a thorough campaign against communism through Smith Act prosecutions of American Communist Party leaders. But by 1948, he soured on red-baiting, now a cause championed by Republican-dominated organs like the House Un-American Activities Committee. From this platform of friendship and service to Truman, Clark ascended to the Court.[42]

A few months after the Clark appointment, Truman put another friend, Sherman "Shay" Minton, forward. Liberal groups favored the former senator from Indiana whose 1934 Senate campaign featured the slogan "You can't

City of Chicago, 337 U.S. 1, 36 (1949) (Jackson, J.); Brown v. Allen, 344 U.S. 443, 540 (1953) (Jackson, J.); Kluger, *Simple Justice*, 583–86, 609–10; Klarman, *Jim Crow*, 210.

41. Eric A. Chiappinelli, "Harold Hitz Burton," in Oxford Companion, ed. Hall et al., 106–7; "Sherman Minton," in ibid., 551–52.

42. Alexander Wohl, *Father, Son, and Constitution: How Justice Tom Clark and Attorney General Ramsey Clark Shaped American Democracy* (Lawrence: University Press of Kansas, 2013), 88–93 (civil rights work), 82–154 (Vinson Court).

eat the Constitution." A stint on the Seventh Circuit Court of Appeals, from 1941, had shown Minton as an advocate of restraint, deference, and practicality. The committee and the full Senate approved his appointment in October 1949. Minton remained committed to judicial restraint on the Supreme Court bench, consistently voting to uphold government actions. He was not a supporter of Jim Crow, however, nor antipathetic to civil rights.[43]

Originally in the minority (Justice Black, as the senior man in the majority, was preparing the opinion for reversal), the chief justice changed his mind after seeing that he and Reed might be the lone holdouts and assigned himself the opinion. Reed joined him and, after some negotiation with Black on the wording of the opinion, Vinson delivered the opinion of the unanimous Court on June 5, 1950. "This case . . . present[s] . . . aspects of this general question: to what extent does the Equal Protection Clause of the Fourteenth Amendment limit the power of a state to distinguish between students of different races in professional and graduate education in a state university?" Relying on the plain text of the Equal Protection Clause was the wrinkle in the *Sweatt* strategy. Leave out *Plessy* and the flotilla of precedent that sailed with it, and go back to the text. But the Court would not accept the invitation to revisit *Plessy*. "Broader issues have been urged for our consideration, but we adhere to the principle of deciding constitutional questions only in the context of the particular case before the Court."[44]

Frankfurter's influence was clear in the next passage. "We have frequently reiterated that this Court will decide constitutional questions only when necessary to the disposition of the case at hand, and that such decisions will be drawn as narrowly as possible." That meant disposing of "much of the excellent research and detailed argument presented in these cases." A review of the Texas courts' findings followed, for these were judicially cognizable facts, as opposed to facts about the effects of segregation. The Court's reading of the state proceedings was able and concise, but the way it was phrased gave a clue to the justices' reading of the law. "The state trial court recognized that the action of the State in denying petitioner the opportunity to gain a legal education while granting it to others deprived him of the equal protection of the laws guaranteed by the Fourteenth Amendment. The court did not grant

43. Linda C. Gugin and James E. St. Clair, *Sherman Minton: New Deal Senator, Cold War Justice* (Indianapolis: Indian Historical Society, 1997), 179, 180, 204, 210, 215, 217; N. E. H. Hull, "Sherman Minton," in *Oxford Companion*, ed. Hall et al. On changing titles of appeals courts: Judicial Code of 1948, Act of June 25, 1948, 62 Stat. 869, 985.

44. Sweatt v. Painter, 339 U.S. 629, 631 (1950) (Vinson, C.J.); St. Clair and Gugin, *Vinson*, 312–13.

the relief requested, however, but continued the case for six months to allow
the State to supply substantially equal facilities."[45]

Texas then scrambled to provide facilities, but in the view of the justices,
those facilities were not, and could not, equal those denied to Sweatt at the
University of Texas's law school. Now the Court looked at a mixture of facts
about the UT School of Law and comparisons of it with the proposed school
for blacks. "The University of Texas Law School, from which petitioner was
excluded, was staffed by a faculty of sixteen full-time and three part-time
professors, some of whom are nationally recognized authorities in their field.
Its student body numbered 850. The library contained over 65,000 volumes.
Among the other facilities available to the students were a law review, moot
court facilities, scholarship funds, and Order of the Coif affiliation. The
school's alumni occupy the most distinguished positions in the private practice of the law and in the public life of the State. It may properly be considered
one of the nation's ranking law schools." This characterization of the white
law school's qualities was not a legal judgment. That is, it did not report or
rely on either Texas's own law or federal law. By including it, the Court had
taken the step that the first passages of the opinion had refused to take—a
step into the real world where racial discrimination in professional education
had its impact. "The law school for Negroes which was to have opened in
February, 1947, would have had no independent faculty or library. The teaching was to be carried on by four members of the University of Texas Law
School faculty, who were to maintain their offices at the University of Texas
while teaching at both institutions. Few of the 10,000 volumes ordered for the
library had arrived, nor was there any full-time librarian. The school lacked
accreditation." A second attempt by Texas to ameliorate had led to a slightly
better school, on the "road to full accreditation."[46]

The court said that it did not matter "whether the University of Texas Law
School is compared with the original or the new law school for Negroes, we
cannot find substantial equality in the educational opportunities offered white
and Negro law students by the State." Apart from the differences in "number
of the faculty, variety of courses and opportunity for specialization, size of the
student body, scope of the library, availability of law review and similar activities," the subjective inferiority of the black school could not be overcome
by further recruitment of faculty or expenditure on facilities. "What is more
important, the University of Texas Law School possesses to a far greater de-

45. 339 U.S. at 632.
46. 339 U.S. at 633.

gree those qualities which are incapable of objective measurement but which make for greatness in a law school." The Court supplied its own judgment of these qualities and, in so doing, accepted a kind of pedagogical jurisprudence parallel to the sociological jurisprudence that Marshall had offered the Texas courts. Qualities external to the law but not external to the real world of legal practice mattered under Equal Protection. "The law school, the proving ground for legal learning and practice, cannot be effective in isolation from the individuals and institutions with which the law interacts. Few students and no one who has practiced law would choose to study in an academic vacuum, removed from the interplay of ideas and the exchange of views with which the law is concerned." Moreover, the composition of the state's population mattered. "The law school to which Texas is willing to admit petitioner excludes from its student body members of the racial groups which number 85% of the population of the State and include most of the lawyers, witnesses, jurors, judges and other officials with whom petitioner will inevitably be dealing when he becomes a member of the Texas Bar."[47]

The Court was aware of Justice Brown's argument in *Plessy*, revived by Daniel and Greenhill in defending segregation. "It may be argued that excluding petitioner from that school is no different from excluding white students from the new law school. This contention overlooks realities." It overlooked the realities that the Court thought relevant—facts about the impact of discrimination. The opinion thus edged toward the sociological and psychological facts that the LDF wanted included. "It is fundamental that these cases concern rights which are personal and present. This Court has stated unanimously that the State must provide [legal education] for [petitioner] in conformity with the equal protection clause of the Fourteenth Amendment and provide it as soon as it does for applicants of any other group."[48]

This was as far as the Court was willing to go. Its unanimity on the questions the case raised had always been fragile, and Vinson did not have the charisma (or the desire) to ask it to go further. "Petitioner may claim his full constitutional right: legal education equivalent to that offered by the State to students of other races." Although both sides wanted the Court to address the *Plessy* precedent, appellant to overrule it, appellee to sustain it, the Court explicitly refused to do either. The fact that it made its refusal explicit was itself evidence that *Plessy* was now vulnerable.[49]

47. 339 U.S. at 634.
48. 339 U.S. at 634–635.
49. 339 U.S. at 635–636.

Daniel heard the Court's decision over the phone, in his Austin office. Though before the final decision Daniel had characterized himself as a hard-line, fighting attorney general, he ordered Heman Sweatt admitted. Letters on the case had poured into his office before the high court rendered its judgment. They urged him to hold firm to the state's segregated regime. After the Court's ruling, the tenor of the letters began to shift. When it became clear that he intended to order the end of segregation at all of the state's universities, he faced a very different public reaction. He "backtracked," correctly noting, in public at least, that the court had not found segregation per se unconstitutional. Privately, he conceded that the end of segregation was near. Fortunately for what would become a notably successful career at the national level, his reputation for probity and his service to the state kept the diehards from ousting him from office.[50]

Sweatt was admitted along with five other black students. According to Page Keeton, then dean of the University of Texas School of Law, some white students did not accept the desegregation of the school. "There were a group of students who came to me and said, 'We don't want to go to the same rest-room . . . as these blacks are going to.'" They wanted segregation within the law school. Keeton, who supported Ada Sipuel's admission to Oklahoma's law school while he was dean there, would have none of this at his new post in Texas. "That might have been lawful at that time, I don't know, but I wasn't about to do it." He convinced the black students to use one restroom for men voluntarily and put off the "rednecks" by telling them they could use the other. Presumably the two accommodations were equal. But the result was not a flood of black applicants. "And there's no question but what the blacks felt that they would not be treated fairly, and so the University of Texas was not a popular place." The students' conduct was modest compared with the thugs who burned a cross on the lawn of the school one night, as Sweatt left classes.[51]

Many white students and faculty members at the law school had a some-what different view of the matter. Students signed petitions in favor of admitting Sweatt, and the faculty generally sided with the applicant. There was a rally on the grounds. Opinion polls at the time showed that a majority of the

50. Lavergne, *Before* Brown, 133, 259; Amilcar Shabazz, *Advancing Democracy: African Americans and the Struggle for Access and Equity in Higher Education in Texas* (Chapel Hill: University of North Carolina Press, 2004), 107–8.

51. Oral History interview with Dean W. Page Keeton, July 28, 1986, Rare Books and Special Collections, Tarlton Law Library, the University of Texas at Austin; Shabazz, *Advancing Democracy*, 116.

law school students thought that the time had come for the end of segregation at the law school. One of the justices who heard the case at the U.S. Supreme Court agreed. Tom Clark, who obtained his law degree there many years earlier, believed that fears of student resistance were groundless.[52]

But resistance to a broader intervention of federal courts into the regime of Jim Crow would be another matter entirely, and that broader intrusion was exactly what the LDF had in mind. For the next step was the desegregation of the public schools. Cases of this type were already making their way up the ladder of the state and federal courts.

52. Clark, quoted in Klarman, *Jim Crow*, 210.

Brown v. Board of Education

President Truman declined to run for reelection in 1952 and newly installed President Dwight D. Eisenhower, a World War II military leader, had limited interest in the civil rights initiatives that Truman inaugurated. Eisenhower had grown to manhood in an army that was as segregated as any Jim Crow state, but as president, he believed that inequalities based on race "in areas of federal responsibility," for example, federal contracts on military bases in the South, must yield. As he wrote to Governor James F. Byrnes, of South Carolina, where such executive action might "run counter to customs in some states," the federal government's writ must nevertheless run unobstructed. Nothing in this program intruded into those areas of policy—for example, education—traditionally assigned to the states, however, although Eisenhower had opened the communication with mention of the first round of argument over desegregation in the schools. Byrnes's reply, unanswered, was that "the Court has no right to legislate." Byrnes insisted that the "right of the state to exercise its police powers to make distinctions among people" was well established, and that Eisenhower himself had agreed that such matters were "local," not federal. When pressed to support an anti-lynching bill in Congress, Eisenhower declined.[1]

Thus, although Eisenhower presided over the next stage of civil rights litigation, he took little part in it. As he said in his first State of the Union ad-

1. Klarman, *Jim Crow*, 325 ("Not until 1959 did he declare that 'segregation is morally wrong'"); Dwight Eisenhower to James Byrnes, August 14, 1953, Eisenhower Presidential Library, Abilene, Kansas; James Byrnes to Dwight Eisenhower, November 20, 1953, Eisenhower Presidential Library; Michal Belknap, *Federal Law, Southern Order: Racial Violence and Constitutional Conflict in the Post-Brown South* (Athens: University of Georgia Press, 1995), 62–63.

dress, "We know that discrimination against minorities persists despite our allegiance to this ideal. Such discrimination—confined to no one section of the Nation—is but the outward testimony to the persistence of distrust and of fear in the hearts of men. . . . This fact makes all the more vital the fighting of these wrongs by each individual, in every station of life, in his every deed. . . . Much of the answer lies in the power of fact, fully publicized; of persuasion, honestly pressed; and of conscience, justly aroused. These are methods familiar to our way of life, tested and proven wise." Missing from that invocation of the value of individual tolerance was a commitment to any executive or legislative civil rights program (other than in the military and the District of Columbia). Eisenhower did understand, however, that foreign eyes were closely watching how Jim Crow divided the nation in two. The leaders of the Communist bloc recognized that Jim Crow was a powerful tool in their contest for the minds and hearts of people of color in the Third World. In appealing to African and Asian peoples, Soviet propagandists could point to state-mandated segregation of the races in a large portion of the United States.[2]

No surprise then that Eisenhower appointees to southern seats were southerners. But they were not all antipathetic to civil rights. For example, to the Northern District of Alabama District Court Eisenhower named Harlan H. Grooms. Grooms, a Kentucky native, practiced law in Birmingham, but in 1955 barred the University of Alabama from denying admission to students based solely on their race, and in 1962 ordered the University of Alabama to admit Vivian Malone and two other black students to the school. Then-governor George Wallace resisted, briefly standing in the way, but he finally relented. Eisenhower also appointed Frank Johnson, of whom more anon.[3]

It was in this context of limited expectations of support from the state and federal judiciary in the South that the LDF nevertheless moved its focus from the area of graduate and professional education to the instruction of the young and impressionable. Jack Greenberg recalled that the LDF called these the "school cases" and Thurgood Marshall was somewhat hesitant to bring them. He wanted to win, and the odds looked long. "The old dilemma reappeared: to fight for equalization or for an end to segregation." As in the Texas NAACP on the eve of *Sweatt*, members of the black communities were

2. Dwight D. Eisenhower, Address to Congress, February 2, 1953, http://www.eisenhower.archives.gov/all_about_ike/speeches/1953_state_of_the_union.pdf; Mary Dudziak, *Cold War Civil Rights: Race and the Image of American Democracy* (Princeton, NJ: Princeton University Press, 2011), 27ff.

3. Lucy v. Adams, 134 F. Supp. 235 (1955); E. Culpepper Clark, *The Schoolhouse Door: Segregation's Last Stand at the University of Alabama* (New York: Oxford University Press, 1995), 39–44; "Harlan H. Grooms, 90, Judge in Rights Case," *New York Times*, August 26, 1991.

divided, reckoning that white resistance to desegregation would be immediate and violent, or that true equalization was better for minority interests than desegregation. Local black lawyers were similarly of two minds. Some lagged behind the LDF decision, but Marshall convinced them to join the battle for desegregation. It was important to lead, but not to go "so far ahead" that the local lawyers would not follow.[4]

The school cases went not to state courts, but directly to federal district courts in which the LDF directly attacked "separate but equal." This was a shift in tactics. State courts were very unlikely to overturn state constitutions or state statutes on federal constitutional grounds, although they could apply federal law if they wished. Federal courts were only slightly more amenable to voiding state law on federal grounds, but because the LDF sought injunctive relief against the state, federal civil procedure required the empaneling of a three-judge court. One of or more of those judges might be willing to rule in favor of the plaintiffs. Even if the panel upheld the state law, appeal from the three-judge panel went directly to the U.S. Supreme Court, and given the result in *Sweatt*, that is exactly where Marshall wanted to go.[5]

In the school cases, lower federal courts in South Carolina, Virginia, and Kansas upheld state-mandated separation of the races. All but one of the judges in these courts averred that they were bound by earlier Supreme Court decisions. They had no discretion to rule otherwise. Only the Supreme Court could overrule its own precedents. In fact, a trial court may interpret the application of a Supreme Court according to the judge's own reading of the decision—as happened when some judges resisted full implementation of *Brown* II. Also, a trial court judge is sometimes free to choose among diverse competing precedents.[6]

In the Kansas case, *Brown v. Board of Education*, the state permitted school districts to segregate or integrate. Topeka chose to segregate its elementary schools. The three-judge federal court assembled under the Three-Judge Court Act that heard *Brown* would not override the state law and would not order white schools to admit black students. As Tenth Circuit judge Walter Huxman, a former Democratic governor of the state, wrote for his brethren on the

4. Greenberg, *Crusaders*, 118–19.

5. The requirement that only a three-judge panel could enjoin a state from obeying its own laws originated in the Progressive Era, part of the complex effort to regulate railroad freight rates. When states passed various acts creating commissions to do this, railroad companies sought injunctive relief in federal courts against the imposition of the state laws. The Mann-Elkins Act (Three Judge Panel Act of 1910), 36 Stat. 557, was a response. Later cases limited its application in criminal matters, deferring to state court interpretations of state law.

6. On the choice of precedents, see Richard A. Posner, *How Judges Think* (Cambridge, MA: Harvard University Press, 2008), 45.

Brown district panel, "As a subordinate court in the federal judicial system, we seek the answer to this constitutional question in the decision of the Supreme Court when it has spoken on the subject and do not substitute our own views for the declared law by the Supreme Court." In a later interview, Judge Huxman revealed that "there was no way around" *Plessy*, but he hoped that the Supreme Court would find a way. Petitioners appealed his decision to the Supreme Court. *Brown* was the lead case, joined by the Court with three other cases, from South Carolina, Virginia, Delaware, and another from the District of Columbia decided at the same time.[7]

The three-judge district court that heard and decided *Briggs v. Elliott*, with an opinion by circuit judge John J. Parker, found that the facilities for black students in South Carolina's rural Clarendon County schools were not equal, but the reason was not discrimination so much as the economic deficiencies of the Clarendon County region. Marshall—along with Robert Carter, Spottswood Robinson, and local attorney Harold R. Boulware of Columbia, South Carolina—led the plaintiff's case, relying on the expert witness testimony that Marshall had helped pioneer in the graduate school cases. Kenneth Clark, for example, repeated his black dolls/white dolls test with children from the Clarendon district and found that the black children once again thought the white dolls were good and the black dolls were bad.

On the other side of the aisle, Robert McC. Figg—a longtime Charleston, South Carolina, politician, representing the state alongside its attorney general, T. C. Callison—insisted that the outside academic experts were not qualified to speak to the conditions or the attitudes of a rural South Carolina county. Instead, the court should listen to the county's former school superintendent, E. R. Crow, currently the director of the South Carolina Educational Finance Commission. Marshall cross-examined, seeking to know whether the state would actually close its public schools rather than desegregate them. Would the government refuse to obey an order to desegregate, if such were issued? No answer. Marshall won the day, but not the case.[8]

Judge Parker, joined by district judge George Bell Timmerman, was not persuaded to order desegregation. Parker was a distinguished jurist, had served on the Fourth Circuit Court of Appeals from 1925 to 1958, the last ten years of

7. Brown v. Board of Education, 98 F. Supp. 797, 798 (D.C. D. Kans. 1951) (Huxman, J.); Kluger, *Simple Justice*, 424; Note, "The Three-Judge Court Act of 1910 Purpose, Procedure and Alternatives," *Journal of Criminal Law, Criminology, and Police Science* 62 (1971): 205–19.

8. Tinsley E. Yarbrough, *A Passion for Justice: J. Waties Waring and Civil Rights* (New York: Oxford University Press, 1987), 184. Material here and after adapted from Peter Charles Hoffer, Williamjames Hull Hoffer, and N. E. H. Hull, *The Federal Courts: An Essential History* (New York: Oxford University Press, 2016), 352–64.

which he was its chief judge, and had been nominated for a seat on the Supreme Court in 1930. There is some evidence that President Eisenhower had
considered Parker for the center seat of the high court when Chief Justice Vinson died. A born and bred North Carolinian, he did not hide his sympathy for
the defeated South, telling one gathering of Georgia lawyers, "When I think
of the lawyers of Georgia . . . whom I know and love and respect, . . . I think
also of the great figures who have added glory to this bar in the past . . . Judge
[T. R. R.] Cobb . . . and Alexander H. Stephens. . . . I feel that their spirits still
linger here and that their presence add to the dignity of all your deliberations."
Parker knew that Cobb was a staunch defender of slavery who wrote the Confederate Constitution and died in its army. Stephens was vice president of the
Confederate States of America and spent a brief time in a federal prison. If
their spirits still lingered nearby, they probably still harbored thoughts of the
"lost cause" of the Confederacy. Parker had also given a speech in which he
defended the "Grandfather Clauses," exemptions from literacy tests for voting if
an individual's ancestor had voted, effectually subjecting would-be black voters
(whose ancestors were slaves) to franchise restrictions that white voters did not
face. In an echo of Chief Justice Taney in *Dred Scott*, he added that he thought
it unlikely that the mass of African American voters could ever fulfill the obligations of republican citizenship.[9]

Parker's opinion rested upon local knowledge, a set of supposed facts that
he shared with judges like McClendon and Timmerman. "The defendants
contend, however, that the district is one of the rural school districts which
has not kept pace with urban districts in providing educational facilities for
the children of either race, and that the inequalities have resulted from limited
resources." Governor James F. Byrnes and the state legislature had promised
in the future to make up the difference, although no positive steps had been
taken. Nevertheless, as equity presumed good faith on the part of the defendant state (petitioners sought injunctive relief), Parker continued, "How this
shall be done is a matter for the school authorities and not for the court, so
long as it is done in good faith and equality of facilities is afforded." Petitioners had asked the federal courts to provide appropriate relief. Parker replied,
"One of the great virtues of our constitutional system is that, while the fed-

9. Robert Mickey, *Paths Out of Dixie: The Democratization of Authoritarian Enclaves in
America's Deep South, 1944–1972* (Princeton, NJ: Princeton University Press, 2015), 472n4;
Kluger, *Simple Justice*, 141–44; John J. Parker, "The Federal Jurisdiction and Recent Attacks upon
It," address to the Georgia Bar Association, June 8, 1932, *American Bar Association Journal* 18
(1932): 433. The U.S. Supreme Court found that the grandfather clauses violated the Fifteenth
Amendment in Guinn v. U.S., 238 U.S. 347 (1915). The failed nomination of Parker is discussed in
Stephen W. Stathis, *Landmark Debates in Congress* (Washington, DC: CQ Press, 2008), 303–10.

eral government protects the fundamental rights of the individual, it leaves to the several states the solution of local problems. . . . [L]ocal self government in local matters is essential to the peace and happiness of the people in the several communities." The "peace and happiness" Parker cited referred to the potential for white violence against blacks if the court should order the end of segregation, an argument that would be repeated by southern officials for the next twenty years. He did, however, order the state to equalize facilities in Clarendon County. A few years earlier, the LDF might have counted this as a victory. When, six months later, the state reported tentative financial steps toward compliance, Judge Parker was content that the state had fulfilled its constitutional obligations: "There can be no doubt that as a result of the program in which defendants are engaged the educational facilities and opportunities afforded Negroes within the district will, by the beginning of the next school year in September 1952, be made equal to those afforded white persons."[10]

Parker's opinion in *Briggs* was lauded by the state's white leaders. Judge Timmerman signed on, as one would expect. Timmerman (Sr.) (his son was governor for a time during the adjudication) was a longtime Democratic power in central South Carolina, serving in the state House of Representatives as well as in appointive positions. A much-respected lawyer and judge and a deeply religious man, Timmerman believed that the Bible provided sufficient authority for segregation of the races. Governor Byrnes called the opinion unanswerable, but that was not surprising, as he had warned that he would close the state's public schools if the court ordered them desegregated.[11]

None of this persuaded the dissenter on the panel, District Judge J. Waties Waring. He was educated in Charleston, the descendant of Confederate

10. Briggs v. Elliott, 98 F. Supp. 529, 531, 532 (E.D. S.C. 1951) (Parker, J.); Briggs v. Elliott, 103 F. Supp. 920, 922 (E.D. S.C. 1952) (Parker, J.). On Parker's "venerable dictum of restraint" after *Brown* that the decision merely barred state-mandated segregation rather than contemplating unitary school systems, see J. Harvie Wilkinson, *From* Brown *to* Bakke: *The Supreme Court and School Integration, 1954–1978* (New York: Oxford University Press, 1981), 113, 81–82. Note that deference to states when it came to their peacekeeping role (and claims of its importance by judges) was not confined to segregation cases. As Justice Reed wrote in Brown v. Allen, 344 U.S. 443, 487 (1953) (Reed, J.), denying relief to a black convict in North Carolina whose confession was coerced and from whose jury persons of color were systematically excluded, "the states are the real guardians of peace and order within their boundaries," and state supreme court findings must be given deference by the federal courts.

11. Mark Newman, *Getting Right with God: Southern Baptists and Desegregation, 1945–1995* (Tuscaloosa: University of Alabama Press, 2001), 43, 54–55; Vernon Burton and Lewie Reece, "The Palmetto Revolution: School Desegregation in South Carolina," in *With All Deliberate Speed: Implementing* Brown v. Board of Education, ed. Brian J. Dougherty and Charles C. Bolton (Fayetteville: University of Arkansas Press, 2011), 66, 69, 70, 73.

leaders, a son of the South deeply wedded to its traditions. He practiced law in Charleston for nearly forty years before Franklin D. Roosevelt named him to the Eastern District Court in 1942. By the time the case came to the district court, he had become frustrated by the injustice of separate and invariably unequal laws. After listening to Thurgood Marshall argue the case for the petitioners, Waring grew impatient with Judge Parker's temporizing, and his dissent hinted what everyone in the courtroom and on the bench knew or should have known—South Carolina had no more intention of equalizing its educational facilities for the two races than it did of abolishing segregation itself. "If this method of judicial evasion be adopted, these very infant plaintiffs now pupils in Clarendon County will probably be bringing lawsuits for their children and grandchildren decades or rather generations hence in an effort to get for their descendants what are today denied to them." In effect, he was accusing his brethren of conspiring with the state government to deny the petitioners their long overdue rights. Waring did not agree with Parker when the state reported its plan for equalization, writing to Parker that he would not sign off on anything short of the end of segregated schools. For his courage, Waring was ostracized by polite society and threatened by racist terrorists, ultimately leaving the court and the city for northern climes. In the meantime, plaintiffs appealed to the Supreme Court.[12]

Prince Edward County in Virginia exhibited much the same socioeconomic and demographic characteristics as Clarendon County, South Carolina. Fifty miles west of Richmond, today the county is still largely rural and poor. Race relations there were not as hostile as in Clarendon, but in 1951 black students refused to attend schools admittedly inferior in physical plant, curricula, and transportation to local white schools. In *Dorothy E. Davis, et al. v. County School Board of Prince Edward County* (1952), the district court ordered the defendants forthwith to provide substantially equal curricula and transportation, but would not order the end of the discriminatory system itself. The petitioner's attorney, Spottswood Robinson III (later a judge in the District Court and then the Court of Appeals for the District of Columbia), argued that "Virginia's separation of the Negro youth from his white contemporary stigmatizes the former as an unwanted, that the impress is alike on the minds of the colored and the white, the parents as well as the children, and

---

12. Christopher W. Schmidt, "J. Waties Waring," in *The Yale Biographical Dictionary of American Law*, ed. Roger K. Newman (New Haven, CT: Yale University Press, 2009), 570–71; Yarbrough, *Waring*, 195–97, 208; 98 F. Supp., at 540 (Waring, J.). Waring had committed the unpardonable sin, according to his neighbors, of marrying a northern liberal and adopting her views of Jim Crow.

indeed of the public generally, and that the stamp is deeper and the more indelible because imposed by law." Robert L. Carter led the examination of expert witnesses, including Kenneth Clark, that segregation stigmatized black children. Arguing for the state, Attorney General J. Lindsay Almond disparaged such witness testimony. He had attended the *Briggs* hearing and seen how South Carolina had failed to undermine the LDF experts' credentials. He did not make the same mistake. He "led the fight" for segregation, he later recalled, but "mine was not a spirit of defiance." After all, he was a lawyer and, as such, tried to "find some legal avenue of accommodation." In his three-page opinion for the defendants, Judge Albert Bryan did not find that Robinson's argument or Carter's witnesses testimony compelled a desegregation order. To his thinking, and that of the other members of the three-judge court, Armistead Dobie and C. Sterling Hutcheson, there was sufficient evidence from "distinguished and qualified educationists and leaders in the other fields" that separate and truly equal would not stigmatize black students. Custom trumped any disparity in expert evidence. "Separation of white and colored 'children' in the public schools of Virginia has for generations been a part of the mores of her people. To have separate schools has been their use and wont." Bryan, a Truman nominee in 1947, knew whereof he spoke. He was born, bred, and educated in eastern Virginia. President Kennedy would name him in 1961 for the Fourth Circuit, where he sat until his death in 1984.[13]

Among the cases joined in *Brown*, there was one ray of light for the LDF. In Delaware, Chancellor Collins Seitz (confirmed to the Court of Appeals for the Third Circuit in 1966), whose powers included the provision of equitable remedies, took a step that the federal judges in South Carolina and Virginia refused to take. In *Gebhart v. Belton*, parents of black students living in New Castle County brought a lawsuit in the Delaware Court of Chancery. They sought to enjoin enforcement of provisions in the state constitution and statutory code that required racial segregation in public schools. Jack Greenberg and Louis Redding, a Wilmington lawyer, argued for the petitioners. Greenberg and Redding worked well together. Redding was often described as cold and taciturn, which may have been true, but he was a Brown University– and Harvard Law School–educated lawyer and was the first black attorney admitted to the Delaware bar. He commanded respect and got it. Two years before the *Gebhart* case, Redding had represented black students seeking to enter

13. Davis v. County Sch. Bd., 103 F. Supp. 337, 338, 339 (D.C. E.D. Va. 1952) (Bryan, J.); Peter Irons, *Jim Crow's Children: The Broken Promise of the* Brown *Decision* (New York: Viking, 2002), 88, 90, 93; J. Lindsay Almond, "Oral History," February 7, 1968, John F. Kennedy Library, Boston, Massachusetts, p. 4.

the University of Delaware. He won that case before Vice Chancellor Seitz. In *Gebhart*, Seitz gave judgment for the plaintiffs and ordered their immediate admission to schools previously attended only by white children. The Delaware Supreme Court affirmed his decision. The defendants, the school board, appealed to the Supreme Court to prevent desegregation. Seitz was a scion of Wilmington, Delaware, went to school at the University of Virginia School of Law, then returned to his home state to practice. He was appointed chancellor in 1951, after five years on the court of chancery. The Delaware Court of Chancery was a busy one, as many businesses incorporated in Delaware to take advantage of its friendly tax laws. A much-respected jurist, Seitz was also sensitive to the evils of racism.[14]

Oral argument for segregation in the school cases followed the tropes and themes of the oral argument in *Sweatt* and the briefs and argument in the district court cases. In many ways, *Briggs* was the most important of the five cases, in part because it was the first of the school cases heard by the Supreme Court; in part because the state of South Carolina was the most adamant of all the appellees; and in part because it was argued before the high court by John W. Davis, one of the foremost lawyers in the land. When it was initially appealed, the judgment of the district court was vacated, the case was returned to the lower court for a second hearing. Waring had retired and left the state, replaced on the three-judge panel by circuit judge Armistead Mason Dobie, a Roosevelt appointee.

One might have expected Dobie to reproduce something like Waring's dissent. Dobie had a distinguished career in Virginia law, including a stint as dean of the University of Virginia School of Law. There he was a progressive educator and highly regarded lecturer. While a law dean, Dobie would serve on the panel that wrote the Federal Rules of Civil Procedure. He was hardly a hard-line defender of Jim Crow. In *Corbin v. County School Board of Pulaski County* (1949), for example, Dobie wrote for the Court of Appeals for the Fourth Circuit that the school board of Pulaski County denied to black children equal protection of the laws. Joined by Parker, with whom he had long enjoyed a friendship, Dobie declined to discuss the question of segregation itself, however. He deferred to the state law. Under Virginia law, "the segregation of the white and colored races is required in the public schools. While plaintiffs do not concede the validity of such segregation, they do not seem here to contest its validity, provided substantially equal educational facilities

---

14. Kluger, *Simple Justice*, 423ff.; Annette Wolard-Provine, *Integrating Delaware: The Reddings of Wilmington* (Newark: University of Delaware Press, 2003), 105, 121; Gebhart v. Belton, 33 Del. Ch. 144 (1952) (Seitz, Ch.); affirmed 91 A.2d 137 (Del. 1952).

are afforded to members of both races. In any event, we think this question would be foreclosed against plaintiffs by decisions of the United States Supreme Court [i.e., *Plessy* and its progeny] and no useful purpose could be served by our adding to the able discussion of this problem in the opinion below." But Dobie would not accept separate but unequal. "When the picture before us is viewed as a whole, and we must so view it, we are led to the conclusion that the record in the case before us discloses rather glaring inequality when the facilities for public high school instruction in Pulaski afforded to white students are compared to those furnished to Negroes. And it can hardly be denied that this discrimination is due to race and color. Where, as here, a right guaranteed by the Fourteenth Amendment has been breached, we cannot concern ourselves with questions of either more expediency or the difficulties which school authorities may have in securing that constitutional right. Whenever the forbidden racial discrimination rears its head, a solemn duty to strike it down is clearly imposed upon the courts."[15]

When the *Briggs* case came back to the three-judge panel in the winter of 1952, Dobie joined in Parker's opinion for the court. "For the reasons set forth in our former opinion, we think that plaintiffs are not entitled to a decree enjoining segregation in the schools but that they are entitled to a decree directing defendants promptly to furnish to Negroes within the consolidated district educational facilities and opportunities equal to those furnished white persons." The good-faith presumption of the court was that the state legislature would provide and the governor would approve funding to equalize facilities and salaries for the two school systems. It was promised in 1950, when the lawsuit was filed with the district court, again when the district court authored its first opinion, and again in the six months between the first and second opinions. The promise was an empty one, indeed a cynical one, from a racially gerrymandered legislature and a Jim Crow governor. Surely Parker knew all this, but he refused to look behind the veil of the defendant state's promise.[16]

When *Briggs* was joined with *Brown*, Marshall argued for the appellant in the two rounds of oral argument at the U.S. Supreme Court, first before the Vinson Court, on December 9, 1952, and then before newly installed Chief Justice Earl Warren's Court, on December 7, 1953. His line of attack was twofold. First,

15. F. D. G. Ribble, "Armistead Mason Dobie: A Reminiscence," *Virginia Law Review* 49 (1963): 1079–81; Armistead Mason Dobie, "The Federal Rules of Civil Procedure," *Virginia Law Review* 25 (1939): 261 (thanking Judge Parker for his support for the new rules); Corbin v. County School Board, 177 F.2d 924, 925, 928 (4th Cir. 1949) (Dobie, J.).

16. Briggs v. Elliott 103 F. Supp. 920, 923 (1952) (Parker, J.); Wolfgang Saxon, "George B. Timmerman Jr., Segregationist Leaders in the 50's," *New York Times*, December 3, 1994.

he had to explain why the LDF had no interest in equalizing facilities. Second, he had to convince the Court that its task was to redefine the Equal Protection Clause to omit "separate but equal," without requiring the Court to overrule *Plessy*. To accomplish both objectives, he focused on the errors of the district court. First, he argued that they had misunderstood his case, thinking it was still about equalizing expenditures for separate schools. He wanted the district court to listen to what his expert witnesses were saying—that state-mandated segregation held back black schoolchildren, stigmatizing them emotionally and damaging them intellectually. The district court had disregarded the testimony of these witnesses, who were the national expects in the field of primary education. Instead, the lower court believed the witnesses for the state, local school administrators, who insisted that whites and blacks both wanted segregated schools. In effect, Marshall implied that the lower court could not tell the difference between real experts, with national reputations in educational psychology, and local school administrators with a personal stake in the outcome of the case. One might regard this as his own disregard for local knowledge, but there was no question that the LDF had assembled a team of experts whose qualifications and reputation far exceeded that of the state's witnesses. At the very least, the state could not produce expert witnesses whose academic credentials came close to Marshall's team. In sum, the battle of expert witnesses was one between national and local authorities, a mirror of the divide between national thinking on desegregation and local attachment to it.[17]

Marshall opened the oral argument at the Supreme Court by asserting that the South Carolina statutes were extreme versions of Jim Crow education in that "no child of either race shall ever be permitted to attend a school provided for children of the other race." This was the third of three provisions in the state code requiring separation of the races, each time with greater vehemence. The adverb—"ever"—was unnecessary except in the way that it expressed South Carolina's version of the Lost Cause, an emotional response to the failure of secession and the end of slavery. South Carolina had argued in the lower court that substantial steps toward equal facilities were under way, although there was no evidence that such steps had resulted in any improvement of the black schools. Marshall was not interested in such promises. They were empty, as his expert witnesses testified in the district court hearing.[18]

17. Greenberg, *Crusaders*, 121–26; Marshall, oral argument in Briggs v. Elliott, Supreme Court of the United States, December 9, in *Landmark Briefs and Arguments of the Supreme Court of the United States*, ed. Philip B. Kurland and Gerhard Casper (Washington, DC: University Publications of America, 1977), 49: 308–9.

18. Marshall, oral argument, December 9, in *Landmark Briefs*, ed. Kurland and Casper, 49: 309.

Marshall's remarks were not just well-rehearsed legalisms. There was a personal tone, a moral outrage that had fueled his leadership of the entire school case campaign like Durham's in *Sweatt*. How to fit that outrage into legally cognizable categories was his problem, but letting the Court know that his argument was as much personal as professional gave him no pause. During the 1952 oral argument, he reproduced a portion of his exchange with Judge Parker, not quite sneering at the judge, but very close to showing open disrespect for the senior jurist. Parker had not wanted to hear argument that went beyond the equalization question, and Marshall did not want to argue the equalization question. So the two sparred. The exchanges, which Marshall read to the Vinson Court, were civil but edgy, and Vinson had intervened to prevent Marshall from going too far, if Marshall had any such intention, which he did not. But Marshall insisted that "for all intents and purposes the district court ruled out the question of all of this argument that segregation had the effect on these children to deny the children their rights under the Constitution," instead limiting the question to facilities, and then accepting the state's promise that the facilities would, in some distant time, be equalized. The court, in effect, had tilted the playing field.[19]

As much as Marshall insisted that the rule in *Sweatt* should be applied in *Briggs*, *Plessy* would not go away. Neither case was exactly on point, but *Gong Lum* was, and Vinson raised it. Vinson wanted to know why Harlan's dissent in *Plessy* did not mention education. Marshall did not know. Justice Frankfurter joined the colloquy with a reference to *Roberts v. City of Boston* (1849), in which the Massachusetts Supreme Judicial Court upheld a school board decision to segregate schools in that city. Did that have any application? Marshall opined that the times were different then. Frankfurter next offered a quotation from Justice Oliver Wendell Holmes Jr. about the Fourteenth Amendment that must have puzzled everyone in the room—it did not "destroy history for the state and substitute mechanical departments of law." Marshall simply agreed, not daring to contest a reference so oblique that no one but Frankfurter could have understood it. Frankfurter then made the point less obscurely: "that behind this are certain facts of life, and the question is whether a legislature can address itself to those facts of life in spite of or within the Fourteenth Amendment." These were sociological facts too. Was Frankfurter agreeing with South Carolina that "where there is a vast congregation of Negro population," a state might decide it was better, as a matter of fact, to segregate the races? Frankfurter did not see segregation as a natural rights question, whose resolution could be affected separate from times,

19. Id. at 314.

place, and fact. In reply, Marshall was adamant: The rights of the black children of Clarendon County were "personal and present" and did not depend on how many blacks and how many whites lived in the county or the state.[20]

Frankfurter was carrying on in his wonted fashion, a law professor engaging in Socratic dialogue with a student. Marshall was carrying on in his wonted fashion, the advocate for a wronged people. Questions and answers thus did not entirely match each other. It was not that Frankfurter and Marshall did not get what the other was saying or doing, but that they had different purposes in their remarks. Marshall wanted the state to produce evidence, including experts, to defend their statute. It was their burden, not his. Frankfurter, whose career as a progressive jurisprudent relied on the production of relevant facts, agreed with Marshall: "I follow you when you talk that way," but when Marshall simply asserted that "you cannot have segregation," Frankfurter worried that Marshall simply begged the question.[21]

Frankfurter was worried from the start of the litigation about the enforceability of a decision that would bar segregation, a set of traditions and social arrangements that were "so imbedded in the conflict of the history" of the South. Marshall conceded that "we have to deal with realities," but the realities that he wanted the Court to consider were the realities of the effect of discrimination on black people. The realities that Frankfurter wanted to consider were those that he feared would arise when southern localities and states simply refused to obey the Supreme Court. These did not arise in the graduate school cases. He assumed they would arise when school-age children were involved. Hence both men agreed, in Marshall's words, "it is not only complicated. I agree that it is a tough problem. But I think that it is a problem that has to be faced." Frankfurter then conceded, "That is why we are here." As counsel for the black families and their children, Marshall could not accede to further delay. "Granting that there is a feeling of race hostility in South Carolina, . . . granting that there is that problem, we cannot have the individual rights subjected to this consideration of what groups might do."[22]

Frankfurter then asked for specifics of enforcement—could Marshall "spell out in concrete what would happen" if the Supreme Court reversed the district court. Marshall suggested that the school board could redraw the school district lines so that children went to the nearest school. The Court would issue a decree barring the school board from segregating students in

20. Id. at 315–17.

21. Id. at 318.

22. Id. at 318–19. Frankfurter's concerns about implementation were well documented. See, e.g., Klarman, *Jim Crow*, 315.

schools on the basis of color. If the school board violated the injunction, it would be in contempt of the Court. But both men understood that pupil placement would depend on residence, and residence was as de facto segregated as schools were segregated de jure. Poor black families lived amid other poor black families. What was more, if pupil placement was permissive, then white students' parents were more likely to seek to place their children in whites-only schools than black parents would want to place their children in whites-only schools. If the LDF wanted integrated schools rather than the end of state-mandated segregation, the Court's decree would not accomplish that goal. Of course, parents could "move over into that district" to integrate a school. Neither man seemed to anticipate that parents would move away from a desegregated school, the pattern of "white flight" that actually followed desegregation of the public schools in many districts.[23]

Courts in the American government system are not miniature legislatures. Courts, in theory at least, deal with past wrongs rather than try to anticipate future conditions. When federal courts departed from this (admittedly self-enforced) role, they sometimes found their decisions controversial or even disregarded. Such was the case with *Dred Scott v. Sandford* (1857). Thus it is somewhat unfair of those scholars gifted with hindsight to remark that neither Marshall nor Frankfurter tried to see the future consequences of desegregation, or to project the path of integration. Frankfurter's concern was southern reaction to such a sweeping decree by the high court; Marshall's concern, under Frankfurter's prompting, was to gain immediate relief for his clients rather than to change the entire landscape of Jim Crow.

There was some heat in the colloquy between Marshall and Frankfurter, not between the two men, who clearly agreed that segregation must end, but heat in their sense of the stakes of the case. By contrast, John W. Davis was almost unemotional and so were the very brief interrogatories the justices posed to him, save by Frankfurter at the close of Davis's testimony. It may be that the justices respected Davis's age and reputation, or simply understood his position so clearly that they needed no clarification. Without question he believed in his cause, that is, in the need for and legal propriety of state-mandated segregation, just as strongly as Marshall opposed it, but he avoided any hint of personal involvement in the maintenance of Jim Crow. Ironically, both men had come from lower-class families in border states, but Davis's

---

23. Kurland and Casper, eds., *Landmark Briefs*, 49: 319–21; on white flight, see Charles T. Clotfelter, *After* Brown: *The Rise and Retreat of School Desegregation* (Princeton, NJ: Princeton University Press, 2004), 75–96; Reica Frankenberg and Gary Orfield, eds., *The Resegregation of Suburban Schools* (Cambridge, MA: Harvard Educational Press, 2012), 39–40.

father had all the opportunities that able white men enjoyed, and Marshall's father faced all the debilities that the law imposed on the ablest of black men. From these origins came their divergent approach to South Carolina's version of apartheid.

The brief and the oral argument that Davis prepared for the state was in many ways the best example of southern anti–civil rights lawyering, perhaps because he was rightly reputed to be one of the finest appellate advocates in the nation. Governor Byrnes, a former justice of the Supreme Court himself, could not have chosen a more distinguished counsel for the state in *Briggs v. Elliott*. Davis, born and educated in West Virginia, was remarkable in his scholarship even as a teenager. His family was not wealthy and he had to work his way through college and later law school as a teacher. He began practice in his native state and, following in his father's footsteps, entered state politics and then the U.S. House of Representatives. He remained a Democrat throughout his life, but rejected the progressivism of other southern Democrats like Woodrow Wilson, sharing only Wilson's views on segregation. In 1924, Davis ran for the presidency and lost, but won a seat on the most prestigious New York City law firm and for it spoke against the New Deal and for many corporate clients, including the J. P. Morgan bank and U.S. Steel. During this period, he served as the president of the American Bar Association. He was, in short, a conservative southern lawyer who represented the very highest traditions of his craft.[24]

Davis's presentation went largely uninterrupted by the justices. He said that the mandate to provide black students with equal facilities "has been fully complied with." He meant that the district court had so ordered, not that in fact, on the ground, the facilities were any more equal than they had been before the district court heard the case. He continued, inequality was "no longer the case." That is, the district court had ordered the state to report its progress within six months. Of course, no man would expect equalization in buildings and such to come immediately by "rubbing an Aladdin's lamp." Between the time of the district court decree and the present, the court reported, based on the state's self-report, that South Carolina "had made every possible effort to comply with the decree of the [district] court, that they had done all that was humanely possible." A state commission went to Clarendon County and found that local arrangements, that is, arrangements by the all-white school boards, were so chaotic, that steps to accelerate equalization would require new schools for the blacks. Land had to be purchased and additional funds

24. William Henry Harbaugh, *Lawyer's Lawyer: John W. Davis* (New York: Oxford University Press, 1973), 221–68, 399–420.

appropriated. One could, of course, have achieved equalization by allowing black students to share facilities formerly reserved for white students, but Davis did not contemplate this possibility. Nor could Davis "with equanimity" imagine allowing the minority of white students in black-majority school districts to attend black schools. In any event, state law made such provisions illegal, and the district court had not overturned the state segregation law.[25]

In addition, Davis offered that the state law mandating separation of the races did not "offend the Fourteenth Amendment." The state's "right" to classify students based on sex, age, and mental capacity, like that based on race (or color), "is not impaired or affected by that Amendment." This was the "crux" of the state's case. On this, the "opinion of Judge Parker . . . is so cogent and complete that it seems impossible to add anything to its reasoning." Davis then instructed the Court that amendments to the Constitution should be read in light of the understanding of those who wrote and ratified the amendment. As far as he was concerned, segregation in the District of Columbia proved that the framers of the amendment did not intend it to apply to desegregation of the public schools. Justice Burton wondered if what might have been constitutional then would be unconstitutional in 1952. After all, "the Constitution is a living document that must be interpreted in relation to the facts of the time in which it is interpreted." The Child Labor Cases, in which federal law was struck down in 1918 and then was upheld in 1937, were an example. Davis disagreed. "Circumstances may bring new facts within the purview of the constitutional provision, but they do not alter, expand or change the language that the framers of the Constitution have employed."[26]

This comment brought Frankfurter into the conversation. He had taken part in the effort to reform child labor conditions in the 1910s. Now he wondered whether the word "equal" in the amendment did not mean equal. Davis was adamant. "I am saying that equal protection in the minds of the Congress of the United States did not [then] contemplate mixed schools as a necessity." In case after case, the Supreme Court had upheld that view and, Davis continued, citing *Plessy* and its progeny, "this Court has spoken in the most clear and unmistakable terms to the effect that this segregation is not unlawful."[27]

Davis rejected the LDF's outside experts. They were all "professors and associate professors," and he said, "I am not sure exactly what that means . . . but there are two things notable about them . . . not a one of them has had to

25. Davis, oral argument, December 9, 1952, in *Landmark Briefs*, ed. Kurland and Casper, 49: 320–21; Davis, oral argument, December 10, 1952, in ibid., 329.

26. Id. at 333.

27. Id. at 334.

consider the welfare of the people from whom they are legislating." In other words, none of them sat in the South Carolina legislature or were elected officials, and only one of them had "the slightest knowledge of conditions in the states where separate schools are now being maintained." Thus nothing of the expert evidence the LDF had offered in the lower court was fit for the consideration of the courts. If having any worth at all, their views were matters of policy, not legality.[28]

Davis could not dismiss the LDF expert witnesses' testimony on its face, because the district court had admitted the testimony, but he could diminish its probative value. He did this not by challenging the credentials of the witnesses, although the aside about their academic rank implied something of this, but by arguing that local knowledge and legislative position—that is, being an elected official—trumped academic or social science knowledge. The experts were outsiders. Davis did not add the word "agitator" to outsider, although that phrase would reappear when northerners began to come south to aid in civil rights demonstrations. It was nevertheless hiding in the penumbras of his argument. South Carolina's white governors, however, had a wealth of experience, including, for a time during Reconstruction, mixed schools, which had proven a failure. He found a quotation from W. E. B. Du-Bois that such forced mixing of the races was, for both, a living hell.[29]

Marshall directed his rebuttal time to the local knowledge question: "In the year 1952, when a statute is tested, it is not tested as to what is reasonable insofar as South Carolina is concerned; it must be tested as to what is reasonable to this Court." The Fourteenth Amendment must be read in light of national law, not the law of an independent South Carolina. The science of the expert witnesses was national, as was their reputation, and it overcame any local prejudices that South Carolina officials might share, and although Marshall did not use the word "prejudice," it was clearly implied. In these national terms, black people were no different from others; in particular they were not, as Davis implied, inferiors needing special treatment.

Frankfurter interrupted Marshall. What was the constitutional basis for excluding racial segregation. Was it a sociological one—that racial classification was harmful? Marshall found himself defending the proposition that constitutional rights could be based on scientific findings of harm. Here the term "protection" was more important than "equal," that is, a reading of the amendment that implied a positive duty of the state to insure the welfare of all citizens of the United States, although neither Frankfurter nor Marshall

28. Id. at 335.
29. Id. at 337–38.

grasped the distinction at the time. In part this was because both were responding, in different ways, to Davis's attack on the value of the experts.[30]

A final passage of arms at the end of the oral arguments in this term of
the Court involved Justice Reed and Marshall. Reed wanted to know whether
the South Carolina segregation laws were "passed for the purpose of avoiding racial friction." Marshall had a somewhat different view of the relations
between the races in the Redemption Era after Reconstruction. It was not
friction, but violent suppression of blacks' attempts to retain the gains of
Reconstruction, that motivated the restored lily-white legislature. "I hate to
mention it—but that was right in the middle of the Klan period. . . . There
were racial statements made in the debates, some of which could be interpreted as just plain race prejudice." At last Marshall introduced the P-word
into the oral argument. Look around the country, he told Justice Reed, and
you would see white people and black people working and living side by side.
They went to war together and together fought for their country. Why should
they not go to school together? Reed remained unconvinced. And with that,
the oral argument ended.[31]

Justice Frankfurter could count votes for the appellants, and he could not
arrive at nine. At the conference of the justices after the case was submitted,
there were considerable differences of opinion on how to rule. Frankfurter
maneuvered Vinson into agreeing to a delay. He asked one of his judicial
clerks, Alexander Bickel, to conduct a thorough search of the historical record to see if there was conclusive evidence that the framers of the Fourteenth
Amendment were comfortable with segregated schools. The case was restored
to the docket in June and reargument was scheduled for the next term, beginning in October 1953, with the parties asked to respond to five questions. In
brief, these were (1) What historical evidence was there on the attitudes of
the framers of the amendment toward segregated schools? (2) Did the framers contemplate the possibility that future Congresses might use the fifth
clause of the Fourteenth Amendment (giving Congress the power to enforce
it by legislation) to impose desegregation on the states? (3) Was it within the
judicial power to abolish segregation based on the amendment? (4) Should
the Court issue a decree ordering desegregation "forthwith" or provide for a
"gradual adjustment" for desegregation in the schools? (5) If the Court ordered a gradual adjustment, which courts should oversee state compliance?
The Court also invited newly elected President Dwight Eisenhower's attorney

30. Marshall, oral argument, December 10, 1952, in *Landmark Briefs*, ed. Kurland and Casper, 49: 342–43.

31. Id. at 334–36.

general to take part in the oral argument, given that Truman's attorney general had submitted a friend of the court brief in support of desegregation.[32]

Davis's arguments did persuade one bystander, Justice Jackson's judicial clerk William Rehnquist. Rehnquist was a brilliant young lawyer, first in his class at Stanford Law School, and something of a rival of Bickel among the justices' clerks. Donald Cronson, Rehnquist's fellow Jackson clerk in the 1952–53 term, later recalled that he had prepared a short memo for the justice saying that *Plessy* was wrongly decided. The Court should take this opportunity to overturn *Plessy* but should leave to Congress the task of undoing its effects. Jackson was amenable but told Cronson that the other members of the Court would not join that opinion. Cronson next recalled that Justice Jackson asked Rehnquist to prepare a memo to the opposite effect, to wit, that *Plessy* was still good law and should not be toppled.[33]

Rehnquist complied with Justice Jackson's request. It was not a memo, but a miniature judicial opinion entitled "A Random Thought on the Segregation Cases." Taken as a whole, it was coherent, well argued, and persuasive, if one needed some persuading to support the appellees' view of the matter. It was very close to what Chief Justice Vinson and Justice Stanley Reed initially thought, and with Jackson presumably on the fence, Rehnquist's writing might have become the basis for a strong dissent. The memo opened as an answer to Bickel's historical researches, taking up where Bickel had left off. "One-hundred fifty years ago this Court held that it was the ultimate judge of the restrictions which the Constitution imposed on the various branches of the national and state government. . . . This was presumably on the basis that there are standards to be applied other than the personal predilections of the Justices." Here was the first hint that the Court was either bowing to political pressure or imposing its own politics on the issue of desegregation. To accuse the justices of this kind of judging was as close to lèse-majesté as a clerk could come, and Rehnquist, having hinted at it, stepped back into the safer waters of checks-and-balances theory. "As applied to questions of inter-state or state-federal relations, as well as to inter-departmental disputes within the federal government, this doctrine of judicial review has worked well. . . . As applied to relations between the individual and the state, the system has worked much less well."

Rehnquist then donned the robes of a justice of the Court, presciently as time would prove, to weigh precedent. "As I read the history of this Court, it

32. Kluger, *Simple Justice*, 615–16.

33. Donald Cronson to William H. Rehnquist, December 9, 1975, in *In Chambers: Stories of Supreme Court Clerks and Their Justices*, ed. Todd C. Peppers and Artemus Ward (Charlottesville: University of Virginia Press, 2012): 353–54.

has seldom been out of hot water when attempting to interpret these individual rights. . . . [*Dred*] *Scott v. Sandford* was the result of Taney's effort to protect slaveholders from legislative interference. . . . [E]ventually the Court called a halt to this reading of its own economic views into the Constitution [in cases like *Lochner v. New York* (1904)]." Precedent warned against the Court once again reaching for some version of substantive due process, the constitutional doctrine that misled early twentieth-century Courts to overturn state legislation. "Apparently it recognized that where a legislature was dealing with its own citizens, it was not part of the judicial function to thwart public opinion except in extreme cases." That wholesome prudence was once again in danger, however. "In these cases now before the Court, the Court is, as Davis suggested, being asked to read its own sociological views into the Constitution. Urging a view palpably at variance with precedent and probably with legislative history, appellants seek to convince the Court of the moral wrongness of the treatment they are receiving." The moral sensibilities of the justices notwithstanding, Rehnquist wrote, "I would suggest that this is a question the Court need never reach; for regardless of the Justice's individual views on the merits of segregation, it quite clearly is not one of those extreme cases which commands intervention from one of any conviction." Rehnquist, whose own politics were conservative, feared that the Court would be swayed by the petitioners "because its members individually are 'liberal' and dislike segregation." But politics should not entire into the justices' decision at all. "To the argument made by Thurgood Marshall that a majority may not deprive a minority of its constitutional right, the answer must be made that while this is sound in theory, in the long run it is the majority who will determine what the constitutional rights of the minority are." He closed the memo: "I think *Plessy v. Ferguson* was right and should be re-affirmed."[34]

Davis could not have put the matter more succinctly, either as to precedent or to prophecy, but his efforts had failed by the time that Rehnquist had departed his clerkship and the unanimous opinion came down. Were these ideas Rehnquist's? Was he trying to help his justice express his own views? In 1955 Rehnquist, then in private practice in Arizona, wrote a letter to Justice Frankfurter about Justice Jackson after the justice had died. Its text, now lost, threw some light on the memo, assuming that Frankfurter was likely to know what was in the memo, as he and Jackson were close friends and allies on the Court. Surely Jackson showed Frankfurter the memo, and

34. Texts of William Rehnquist Memo to Justice Robert H. Jackson, 1952, on Rights Cases, *New York Times*, December 9, 1971, 26 (original, signed WHR, in Robert H. Jackson papers, Library of Congress).

Frankfurter helped Jackson to reject Rehnquist's argument? As it happened, Frankfurter and Rehnquist had also developed a warm relationship, one that Rehnquist, at least in 1955, maintained. Unfortunately, the letter was one of a batch of Frankfurter papers stolen from his collection at the Harvard Law library sometime in the early 1970s, but from other sources, two legal scholars reconstructed the substance of Rehnquist's remarks on Jackson. In essence, Rehnquist had become critical of Jackson's powers of reasoning, his consistency, and his "going off half-cocked." They conclude that Rehnquist was sincere in his opposition to *Brown*, and that the views expressed in 1952 were his own. In 1955, he was disappointed that he was unable to persuade Jackson to dissent.[35]

When the Court reassembled in the fall of 1953, Earl Warren sat in the center chair. Fred Vinson had died. Warren was born in Los Angeles in 1891, grew up in Bakersfield, and earned his college and law degrees at the University of California, Berkeley. He served in the army during the First World War and plunged into Republican politics in Oakland after the war. His rise from county district attorney to state attorney general to three-time governor of the state was meteoric. He was a vigorous advocate of Japanese relocation during the war, a stance he later "deeply regretted" and apologized for. After throwing his support to Eisenhower at the 1952 presidential convention, he was promised the next seat on the Supreme Court. That turned out to be the center chair, and for his leadership of the Court from 1953 to 1969, he has been called the "Super Chief."[36]

35. In 1971, during the contentious nomination hearings on the appointment of Rehnquist to the Supreme Court, he wrote another letter, this time to Senator James O. Eastland of Mississippi, a supporter and founding member of the Southern Caucus. It explained once again the memo, which had surfaced and endangered his confirmation, and his views on *Brown*: "I am satisfied [from my own recollection] that the [1952] memorandum was not designed to be a statement of my views on these cases. Justice Jackson not only would not have welcomed such a submission in this form, but he would have quite emphatically rejected it and, I believe, admonished the clerk who had submitted it. I am fortified in this conclusion because the bald, simplistic conclusion that 'Plessy v. Ferguson was right and should be re-affirmed' is not an accurate statement of my own views at the time." Rehnquist also wrote in his letter to Eastland, "In view of some of the recent Senate floor debate, I wish to state unequivocally that I fully support the legal reasoning and the rightness from the standpoint of fundamental fairness of the Brown decision." Brad Snyder and John Q. Barrett, "Rehnquist's Missing Letter," *Boston College Law Review* 53 (2012): 636, 637, 639–40; Eastland letter reproduced in ibid, 633.

36. "Deeply regretted" in Earl Warren, *Memoirs of Earl Warren* (New York: Doubleday, 1977), 146; California politics: G. Edward White, *Earl Warren: A Public Life* (New York: Oxford University Press, 1982), 26–128; leadership role and reputation: Bernard Schwartz, *Super Chief: Earl Warren and His Supreme Court, a Judicial Biography* (New York: New York University Press,

From the outset, Warren was in favor of striking down segregation, but like Frankfurter, wanted the cache of a unanimous Court. Some of his leadership skills expressed themselves in the oral argument on December 7, 1953. Spottswood Robinson had joined Marshall in the rehearing of *Briggs*, the two men dividing up the response to the five questions. They presented what Greenberg called a "consolidated brief for all four of the state cases," which in Robinson's hands included 235 pages of historical evidence. Robinson included the historical research that Bickel had done for Justice Frankfurter and the evidence that a team of historians led by constitutional historian Alfred Kelly had prepared for the LDF. (While Kelly's initial reading of that history favored Davis's view, he and the other scholars found ways to reread the historical documents to reach the same conclusions as Bickel. Kelly later recalled that he had ceased to be a historian and had become a lawyer in a cause. For example, he found a way around the absence of non-discrimination clauses in the Fourteenth Amendment, by arguing that some of the amendment's supporters thought that, once ratified, it could become the basis for more sweeping anti-discrimination legislation.)[37]

Robinson presented those findings (absent Kelly's reservations) at the oral argument without interruption. Even Frankfurter was silent for a time. Robinson made the bold claim, as if he were writing the opinion of the Court, that "considering the overall evidence" of the history of the Fourteenth Amendment, it "has as its purpose and effect the complete legal equality of all persons, irrespective of race, and the prohibition of all state-sponsored caste and class systems based on race." The amendment, along with the Civil Rights Acts, were meant to counter the black codes that former Confederate states passed when they first rejoined the Union in 1865. These laws "were largely responsible for the Fourteenth Amendment." It invalidated all discriminatory state legislation. Robinson continued to refer to the "broad overall purpose of the Amendment," a kind of consonance of (the LDF) reading of the congressional debates on the amendment. The Due Process and Equal Protection Clauses "would sweep away" the black codes and all similar racially discriminatory legislation. Rather than focus on what was not in the debates on the amendment, Robinson spent a good deal of time on the discriminatory nature of the black codes preceding the amendment. He then used Pennsylvania

1983), passim; and Schwartz, *Decision: How the Supreme Court Decides Cases* (New York: Oxford University Press, 1997), 88–89.

37. Kluger, *Simple Justice*, 645; Greenberg, *Crusaders*, 182–86; Robinson, oral argument, December 7, 1953, in *Landmark Briefs*, ed. Kurland and Casper, 49A: 1–10; Kluger, *Simple Justice*, 637–41.

representative Thaddeus Stevens's speech during the debate on the black codes to connect them to the amendment. Finally, Robinson dwelt on the debates over the Civil Rights Act of 1866, again connecting that legislation to the Fourteenth Amendment. If the amendment was intended by its framers to constitutionalize the Civil Rights Act's prohibition of discrimination, then it need not have any anti-discrimination language in it. Of course, the elephant in the room was the absence of anti-discrimination language in the Civil Rights Act itself, but Robinson had done as well as anyone could have to use history in the service of desegregation.[38]

Frankfurter could wait no longer. He wanted to know what "weight is to be given, or how is [the Court] ever to deal with individual utterances of this, that, or other congressman or senator." Frankfurter would have preferred to omit any reference to the debates. Would not the opinion of Justice Samuel Miller in the *Slaughter-House Cases* (1873), that the amendment was meant to protect the rights of the freedmen, not be sufficient? Robinson was perplexed. He would happily have rested on Miller's opinion for the Court in those cases, but the Vinson Court had ordered counsel to brief the historical evidence of the debates—ironically, Frankfurter had then composed the very questions that Frankfurter now wanted Robinson to skip. "I think we get assistance" from the history, Robinson offered, on "the broad overall purpose" of Congress. But did "broad overall purpose" include desegregating the schools, Frankfurter persisted? Robinson may not have followed the justice's thinking, but Frankfurter sat back and let him continue with his historical argument that the amendment had to be understood in light of the Civil Rights Act. That the amendment would put the rights so gained "beyond the power of repeal by future Congresses."[39]

Robinson's presentation had a punctuated quality. He had a script, the historical points he wanted to make in answer to questions 1 and 2, but Frankfurter had interrupted the reading of that script, followed by Justice Reed. What Robinson, a superb courtroom attorney and a diligent student of law, lacked was the almost playful cleverness of the top law school student (even though he graduated at the top of his Howard University School of Law class and later led the school), the quicksilver ability to change topics, to read underlying meanings in questions, and to formulate appropriate replies. It was not something he needed in his Richmond, Virginia, practice or his appellate appearances. Thus, when Reed wanted to know if the absence of federal law on school segregation,

38. Robinson, oral argument, December 7, 1953, in *Landmark Briefs*, ed. Kurland and Casper, 49A: 4–5, 6, 9.
39. Id. at 10–11, 13, 14.

which might have followed from section 5 of the Fourteenth Amendment ("The Congress shall have power to enforce, by appropriate legislation, the provisions of this article"), meant anything to this case, Robinson did not have a ready answer. Congress had, as a matter of fact, passed a number of Civil Rights Acts after the ratification of the amendment. With the exception of the public accommodations section of the 1875 Civil Rights Act, struck down in the *Civil Rights Cases* (1883), all of these congressional statutes remained on the books. None of them mentioned schools or segregation, however, except, perhaps, the section of the 1875 act disallowed by the Supreme Court. Robinson summoned up the fact that during the debates, the language was changed to "no state shall" but did not explore the jurisprudence of absent words. Instead of replying to Reed, he plowed on, not getting to the gist of Reed's point. Marshall might have bantered in response to this kind of question, and Davis would have leadenly argued that Congress's refusal to legislate on the matter was another proof that it saw primary education as the business of the states. One wonders who would have understood that Reed was talking about Congress's refusal to pass an anti-lynching law? Or his own concurrence in *Screws v. United States* (1945), in which a Georgia sheriff who beat a black man to death was found not to have violated the victim's civil rights. Reed was no great friend to civil rights adjudication.[40]

Robinson's final argument went uninterrupted. He suggested that when southern states were finally returned to the Union after congressional Reconstruction (including the requirement that they ratify the Fourteenth Amendment), they did not have laws requiring segregated schools. Those came later. Thus their understanding of the meaning of the Fourteenth Amendment must have been that it barred segregation in elementary education. Those states that had earlier passed segregation laws rescinded them. "Considering the evidence overall," the amendment was regarded as antipathetic to segregation.[41]

Handling the Court's own precedents was another challenge for the LDF, for *Plessy* and *Gong Lum* still stood in their path. Instead of a chronology, Marshall opted to arrange the precedents into three groups: the most recent, the cases immediately following the adoption of the amendment, and finally the middle period, with *Plessy* thus isolated. He reassured Justice Jackson that the first group "were from this very court," further emphasizing *Sweatt* and its companion cases. By beginning with them, Marshall laid the foundations for

40. Id. at 15; Screws v. U.S., 325 U.S. 91 (1945); William M. Wiecek, *The History of the Supreme Court of the United States*, Vol. XII, *The Birth of the Modern Constitution, 1941–1953* (New York: Cambridge University Press, 2006), 658.

41. Kurland and Casper, eds., *Landmark Briefs*, 49A: 16.

arguing that the civil rights jurisprudence of the Court had evolved, and the precedents most important for it were its own. Jackson replied that the Court was pretty clear on its own precedents. Okay, Marshall rejoined, let's go to the second set, from the period immediately after ratification. That was the *Slaughter-House Cases* era, and in it, the various enforcement and the *Civil Rights Cases* under congressional acts passed between 1870 and 1875. Here was evidence that the Court and Congress agreed that the purpose of the Fourteenth Amendment was to aid the freedmen. Again Frankfurter, and now Warren, did not want to hear about those acts, the "power" of Congress in the matter; they wanted to hear about the "virtue of what flows out of the Fourteenth Amendment as such." Then why ask us to brief questions 2 and 3, Marshall must have wondered. Later, he would aver that "the question raised by this Court in June, as we understand it, requested us to find out as to whether or not class legislation and, specifically segregation, in and of itself, with nothing else, violated the Fourteenth Amendment. We have addressed ourselves to that in this brief." He concluded that the amendment barred classification and with it differential treatment of "Negroes, free or [formerly] slave."[42]

Even more to the point for Marshall, in *Strauder v. West Virginia* (1880), the Court reversed the conviction of a black man because the state, by law, barred blacks from trial juries. This violated the Fourteenth Amendment. Congress had not passed a law in the matter—the language of the amendment was sufficient for Justice William Strong to aver that the treatment of the freedmen was "practically a brand upon them, affixed by law; an assertion of their inferiority, and a stimulant to that race prejudice which is an impediment to securing to individuals of the race that equal justice which the law aims to secure to all others." Again, Frankfurter seemed unimpressed. He wanted Marshall to show how "the states lose their powers" under the amendment. Marshall took the cue. State classification of students by race or color as a proxy for race was not reasonable. Which brought him to *Plessy* and *Gong Lum*, both of which were "out of line" with *Slaughter-House* and *Strauder*.[43]

Even if Marshall was right that *Sweatt* and its parallel cases effectively isolated *Plessy*, in *Sweatt* the Court still did not overrule *Plessy*. Justice Reed reminded Marshall that *Sweatt* was decided as it was because Texas had not provided equal facilities for black law students. Marshall was reduced to reading the "thrust" of the graduate school cases rather than the letter of the

---

42. Marshall, oral argument, December 7, 1953, in *Landmark Briefs*, ed. Kurland and Casper, 49A: 20–21, 28.

43. Id. at 24–25.

Court's opinion (and its silences). "If we follow that to the logical conclusion," there was no way in which equalization could have made separate schools equal. Frankfurter interjected that Marshall was conceding that he could not base his constitutional argument on the graduate school cases. They were not actually precedent for ending all separate schools. Marshall insisted that the real issue in all of them was depriving states from "making any racial classification." Frankfurter wanted Marshall to say that equalization was "an irrelevant question." Marshall, whose caution in the graduate cases seemed at first to inhibit him, now gave in. "In this case it is irrelevant." Frankfurter agreed: "All right."[44]

Davis's oral argument followed. He adopted a folksy manner, perhaps having listened to Marshall for a while. "Few invitations" were less welcome to counsel than those to reargue a case. Unstated was Davis's belief that he had already won in the first round. Nor did he think it an act of mercy or piety on counsel's part to "increase the reading matter" a court had to consider, here some two thousand pages of briefs. As Warren was not on the bench at the time *Briggs* was first argued, Davis offered a précis of the case. Surely Warren knew the prior history; Davis merely used the opportunity to reuse his earlier notes. South Carolina, he insisted, had equalized the two school systems in the county, fulfilling the decrees of the district court and the mandate of *Plessy*. Marshall had supposedly conceded as much (he had, though he thought it was irrelevant). In fact, in the interim between the first oral argument and the present one, South Carolina had done nothing that it had promised to equalize pupil expenditures for whites and blacks.[45]

As to the five questions, Davis offered predictable answers. The abolitionists did not target segregation; they wanted only to dismantle slavery. The Radical Republicans did not dictate the terms of the Reconstruction Amendments. According to Claude Bowers, the virulently racist twentieth-century historian of Reconstruction (Davis's answer to Alfred Kelly and the LDF team), members of the Senate did not share Charles Sumner's expansive view of civil rights, the passage of Sumner's 1875 Civil Rights Act to the contrary notwithstanding. Thaddeus Stephens was "perhaps the most unlovely character in American history" and should not be held up as an avatar of anything. In the meantime, there were members of Congress (many of them Democrats, which fact Davis did not hold against them, as he was their descendent)

---

44. Id. at 27–28.

45. Davis, oral argument in *Briggs*, December 7, 1953, in *Landmark Briefs*, ed. Kurland and Casper, 49A: 31–33.

who virulently opposed every one of the Civil Rights Acts. Even those who favored the Civil Rights Acts did not speak against Jim Crow (ignoring the fact that it largely did not exist; the black codes were far more harsh, and these the majority of Congress did denounce). In his amicus brief, the "learned attorney general" (Herbert Brownell Jr.) of the United States fell "into the same fallacy."[46]

For a time, Davis was not interrupted. The justices listened politely. He must have had some sense that the tide had turned, or was turning, against his side, however. He admitted, "I see now that I underestimated the time that would be at my disposal, or overestimated my power of delivery." He shortened his historical commentary to a series of bullet points, a "catalog" enumerating each Reconstruction act's and the three amendments' provisions to demonstrate that they did not mention any bar to a state classifying students by race. To his mind, legislative silence constituted acquiescence. When advocates of civil rights tried to include schools, churches, cemeteries, and juries in the 1875 act, for example, they failed. "There isn't time to go over the stats," but even after ratification of the Fourteenth Amendment, there were four northern states that had segregated schools. Some, he did not mention, desegregated those schools after ratification. His point was not that states adopted segregation. It was that states could do as they liked with education before and after the ratification of the amendment.[47]

This brought the first question, Justice Jackson asking if Congress, under the necessary and proper clause of Article I of the Constitution, could do what Davis thought the Congress could not do under section 5 of the Fourteenth Amendment. Davis's answer was somewhat confusing; at least it confused Justice Frankfurter, who asked whether Congress could itself interpret the amendment and end segregation under the Necessary and Proper Clause. Davis was not convinced. If something was not enforceable under the amendment, it could not be brought into the amendment from another part of the Constitution. That would be to "amend the Amendment, which is beyond the power of the Court." Actually, it was not, as *Plessy* had shown. Nowhere in the amendment did the word "separate" appear. The Court had added it.[48]

46. Id. at 33–35.

47. Id. at 38–39.

48. Id. at 40–41. Neither man knew it, but they had reached a decade into the future, to the passage of the Civil Rights Act of 1964. In it, Congress restored a portion of the Civil Rights Act of 1875 struck down in the Civil Rights Cases, 109 U.S. 3 (1883). The act forbade racial discrimination in public accommodations, amusements, and other privately owned and operated businesses. The majority of the Court, John Marshall Harlan dissenting, found that the amendment only reached "state action," and discrimination of other kinds could not be curbed under

Davis doubled down on his history when he added that "the principle of stare decisis" meant that "controlling precedent preluded a construction [of the amendment] which would abolish segregation." In effect, he was telling the present Court that prior Courts' rulings denied the present Court the constitutional power to revisit the amendment and construe it in a new fashion. Frankfurter held his tongue, and Davis did not press this historically incorrect and institutionally misleading line of argument. "But be that doctrine what it may, somewhere, sometime to every principle comes a moment of repose when it has been so often announced, so confidently relied upon, so long continued, that it passes the limits of judicial discretion and disturbance." In any case, "we" meaning the states that had adopted segregation, "relied" on prior Courts' upholding separate but equal. "Who is going to disturb that situation?" Davis's passion had finally risen to the surface, matching Marshall's. "You say that is racism. Well, it is not racism." For Davis, quoting Disraeli (arguing for the morality of the English empire), averred that "no man will treat with indifference the principle of race. It is the key of history."[49]

Marshall must have listened to Davis's peroration with mixed emotions. Finally, Davis had abandoned his studied avoidance of the race issue. He had shown his true colors, and that of the makers of Jim Crow laws. The underlying issue was not an abstract idea of state sovereignty in the federal system, much less than the good of the children or the need for public order. The case did not turn on the greater knowledge and practicality of local school over the social science findings of the expert witnesses Marshall had summoned to the district court in Charleston. Segregation was first and foremost an imposed racial separation.

Marshall had a few minutes saved for rebuttal, and he offered it on December 8. Frankfurter immediately interjected: would Marshall discuss the implementation questions, numbers three through five of those posed to counsel in June. Marshall conceded that a decree ordering the end of segregation forthwith would encounter administrative problems, and that the "decree of this Court could very well instruct the lower court to take into consideration that factor, and if necessary, give to the state involved a sufficient time to meet the administration problems." One year should do it. "I can conceive of nothing administrative-wise that would take longer than a year."

---

section 5 of the amendment. In Heart of Atlanta Motel v. United States, 379 U.S. 241 (1964), the Court ruled that Congress could act under the Commerce Clause of Article I, if not section 5 of the amendment.

49. Id. at 42–43.

No one expected the high court to administer solutions in so many different local situations.[50]

The argument that there were so many black students and so few whites, with the unwanted (for Davis at least) result that whites would have to go to a formerly black school, cut no ice with Marshall. At the district court hearing in Charleston, he asked one of the witnesses for the state, a local school administrator, if his views would change if the racial composition were reversed. Even if there were a tiny number of black students, the white school would not be open to them. Why then listen to an argument that white schools would be swamped by a horde of black schoolchildren? With his dander now up, Marshall took on Davis directly. "As Mr. Davis said yesterday, the only thing the Negros are trying to get is prestige. Exactly correct."[51]

Marshall rejected the idea that some form of constitutional stare decisis barred later Courts from revisiting earlier Courts' decisions on the scope of the Fourteenth Amendment, or any other constitutional provision for that matter. As the Court had demonstrated in the political party primary cases, the Fifteenth Amendment might not mention primary elections, but it still covered the right of black voters to take part in them. Finally, "this Court has made segregation and inequality equivalent concepts." They were both constitutional wrongs. It was time to "make explicit" what the graduate school cases had held implicitly. It was the duty of the Court, not some impermissible form of judicial activism, to enforce the Fourteenth Amendment. What kind of evil "magic" had blacks and whites voting together, going to the same state university and the same college, but "if they go to elementary and high school the world will fall apart."[52]

In the final hour of oral argument, Solicitor General J. Lee Rankin explained the federal government's brief on the five questions. While President Eisenhower never came out in favor of *Brown*, his attorney general, Herbert Brownell, openly favored the end of segregation. Brownell was a Nebraskan and Yale Law graduate who helped the Republican Party regain its prominence after the New Deal. He was not, however, a conservative. After service in the New York State Assembly, he managed Tom Dewey's run for the presidency and convinced Eisenhower to seek the same office. His reward was the post of U.S. attorney general, during which he drafted the Civil Rights Act of 1957. He then returned to private corporate practice in New York City.

---

50. Marshall, oral argument, December 8, 1953, in *Landmark Briefs*, ed. Kurland and Casper, 49A: 14–15.

51. Id. at 16, 18.

52. Id. at 19, 20, 21.

He later recalled, "I very much wanted the Department of Justice to support desegregation but I knew I had my work cut out for me," for Eisenhower had to be persuaded to let the Department of Justice intervene.[53]

The Court ordinarily allows the federal government time in oral argument when it has submitted a friend of the court brief. Deputy Attorney General J. Lee Rankin reiterated the federal government's stance. Rankin was, like Brownell, a native Nebraskan and like Brownell had played a major role in the Eisenhower campaign. In oral argument he was genial and thoughtful, for example, explaining to Justice Jackson that the everyday problems of enforcement of desegregation should be handled by the district courts—a view that he would repeat when the Court was hearing from state attorneys general in prior to *Brown* II. The Court had the power, concurrent with Congress, to give teeth to the Fourteenth Amendment, and no one needed to go to history books to see "what is going on today. . . . It is a civil right to have education on the same basis as every other citizen." The Department of Justice made clear in its briefs as friends of the Court and in oral argument that "segregation in public schools cannot be maintained." Government lawyers like Brownell and Rankin regarded Jim Crow as a blot on the nation's reputation and were, in a way, the descendants of the Charles Sumners and Samuel Chases of the Reconstruction Era.[54]

In many ways, the first decision of note in the Warren Court, *Brown v. Board of Education* (1954), showed both the promise and the limitations of the judiciary in American life. A court can declare the law and decide a case, but social engineering on a broad scale may be beyond the ability of even the most determined tribunal. Warren understood this and deserves much of the credit for fashioning the approach to *Brown* and its many progeny, as well as some criticism for how the Court handled one of the most controversial cases in its history.[55]

As Justice Oliver Wendell Holmes Jr. long ago noted, hard cases make bad law. No case could have been harder than undoing at a stroke what nearly one hundred years of segregation had done in public education. The system of separate schools was rooted in the fiscal, social, and psychological life of much of the South (and some parts of the North). Justice Frankfurter's fear that courts

53. Herbert Brownell, *Advising Ike: The Memoirs of Attorney General Herbert Brownell* (Lawrence: University Press of Kansas, 1993), 190.

54. James T. Patterson, *Brown v. Board of Education: A Civil Rights Milestone and Its Troubled Legacy* (New York: Oxford University Press, 2001), 63, 117; Klarman, *Jim Crow*, 160; Kluger, *Simple Justice*, 734–35; J. Lee Rankin, oral argument, December 8, 1953, in *Landmark Briefs*, ed. Kurland and Casper, 49A: 27, 31, 32, 33–34.

55. Kluger, *Simple Justice*, 668–76; Klarman, *Jim Crow*, 290–311; Patterson, *Brown*, 46–69.

were inadequate to deal with these kinds of problems had much truth. Courts would play a vital role in the end of segregation, but there were obstacles that the best intentioned of courts could not, by themselves, overcome.[56]

When the case was first argued, in 1952, Justices Black, Douglas, Burton, and Minton favored destroying *Plessy* outright; Chief Justice Vinson and Justice Reed were reluctant to dismiss such an important precedent. Justices Frankfurter and Jackson pleaded for special arrangements so the Court could properly address what was a deeply divisive local matter. Consistent with their concern about the local passions invested in segregation, the justices (led by Frankfurter), consolidated the cases but made the lead case the Kansas lawsuit. Thus they took the southern edge off the question.[57]

After more than a little one-on-one lobbying of his brethren by Warren after the 1953 reargument, the opinion of the Court was unanimous, and Warren wrote it. From its emphasis on the importance of public schooling to American life, to the plain language that took its reasoning from one point to the next, to the forward-thinking rejection of segregation as a moral wrong, the California progressive shone through. It was a short opinion—barely ten pages— that Warren read from the bench. He reported that the historical foray into the Reconstruction congressional records could not guide the Court because that record was inconclusive. History did show that "in the first cases in this Court construing the Fourteenth Amendment, decided shortly after its adoption, the Court interpreted it as proscribing all state-imposed discriminations against the Negro race." "Separate but equal" was a later retreat from the goals of Reconstruction in general and the Fourteenth Amendment in particular.[58]

Warren and his Court read the Fourteenth Amendment simply. "What is this but declaring that the law in the States shall be the same for the black as for the white; that all persons, whether colored or white, shall stand equal before the laws of the States, and, in regard to the colored race, for whose protection the amendment was primarily designed, that no discrimination shall be made against them by law because of their color?" While this reading might be viewed as the continuation of the higher education line of cases, Warren went far beyond those precedents. He read the Fourteenth Amendment in light of the Thirteenth Amendment, following the steps that the Reconstruction Congress itself had taken to find that "the right to exemption from unfriendly legislation against them distinctively as colored—exemption from

56. Patterson, *Brown*, 56.

57. Kluger, *Simple Justice*, 617.

58. Warren lobbying: Kluger, *Simple Justice*, 699–702. Brown v. Board of Education, 347 U.S. 483, 493 (1954) (Warren, C.J.).

legal discriminations, implying inferiority in civil society, lessening the security of their enjoyment of the rights which others enjoy, and discriminations which are steps towards reducing them to the condition of a subject race."[59]

Warren opined that education was the key to success in American society. "It is doubtful that any child may reasonably be expected to succeed in life if he is denied the opportunity of an education. Such an opportunity, where the state has undertaken to provide it, is a right which must be made available to all on equal terms." Then he asked, "Does segregation of children in public schools solely on the basis of race, even though the physical facilities and other 'tangible' factors may be equal, deprive the children of the minority group of equal educational opportunities? We believe that it does.... To separate them from others of similar age and qualifications solely because of their race generates a feeling of inferiority as to their status in the community that may affect their hearts and minds in a way unlikely ever to be undone." Segregated education indelibly stigmatized black schoolchildren. In 1954 common sense revealed what in 1896 prejudice had denied: The impact in education, particularly in the lower grades, could be predicted.[60]

Warren and the Court concluded that "in the field of public education the doctrine of 'separate but equal' has no place. Separate educational facilities are inherently unequal. Therefore, we hold that the plaintiffs and others similarly situated for whom the actions have been brought are, by reason of the segregation complained of, deprived of the equal protection of the laws guaranteed by the Fourteenth Amendment."[61]

The fourth case did not come from the states. It came from the District of Columbia. In *Bolling v. Sharpe*, the Fourteenth Amendment would not apply (the district is not a state), but the Due Process Clause of the Fifth Amendment might afford black petitioners a basis for ending segregation in the district. The District Court for the District of Columbia had dismissed the petition. *Bolling* was decided the same day as *Brown* in a separate decision but with the same reasoning. John Marshall Harlan's voice in the *Civil Rights Cases* and *Plessy* had not been lost after all, despite the cacophony of racism that drowned him out at the time.[62]

In what would become something of a millstone around the neck of the otherwise simple and powerful language of *Brown*, at Warren's request, his clerk Earl Pollock added a footnote number 11 to the written opinion. The

59. 347 U.S. at 493 (Warren, C.J.).
60. 347 U.S. at 494 (Warren, C.J.).
61. 347 U.S. at 495 (Warren, C.J.).
62. Bolling v. Sharpe, 347 U.S. 497 (1954).

footnote cited studies of the psychological impact of segregation on young people. The LDF had either commissioned the studies or introduced them in the arguments, so the note was one-sided. The studies cited included "K. B. Clark, Effect of Prejudice and Discrimination on Personality Development (Midcentury White House Conference on Children and Youth, 1950)," the famous white and black dolls study showing that black children thought white dolls were "good dolls" and black dolls were not. Later critics of the Court's supposed reliance on "sociological jurisprudence" and later critics of the methodology of the doll study (no controls, no repetition) have misunderstood or exaggerated the importance of the evidence and note 11. The note and the studies were not crucial in Warren's thinking. He did not need to know what black children thought about dolls to know that forced separation was a stigma in itself.[63]

Warren's opinion did not explicitly overrule *Plessy*, a fact that had great significance. He said that the rule in *Plessy* did not apply to public education. *Plessy* was not concerned with education, though it would become the precedent on which segregation of schools was based. Instead, it concerned transportation. To overrule *Plessy* would have been tantamount to saying that all state segregation was unconstitutional. The Court would follow this path in the years to come, but for the present, it was more cautious.[64]

---

63. Jack M. Balkin, "Rewriting *Brown*: A Guide to the Opinions," in *What* Brown v. Board of Education *Should Have Said: The Nation's Top Legal Experts Rewrite America's Landmark Civil Rights Decision*, ed. Jack M. Balkin (New York: New York University Press, 2002), 50–52.

64. Thus the Court did not resurrect Justice John Marshal Harlan's dissent in *Plessy*, which, prescient for its time, was still ahead of the Court's jurisprudence in 1954. In the end, this may have made *Brown* I an easier case to decide than the long and winding road of the school desegregation cases to the high court seems to indicate. The suggestion is hinted at in David A. Strauss, "Not Unwritten after All," *Harvard Law Review* 126 (2013): 1544.

3

Making the Case for Segregation

Brown was a defeat for the segregationist lawyers, but the effort to save Jim Crow was not over—not by a long shot. There remained the question of enforcement of desegregation. The justices themselves worried about enforcement of their decision from the first moment that lawyers argued the five cases under Chief Justice Vinson and again when Warren replaced him. Frankfurter surmised that his colleagues might not be enthusiastic about the Court sweeping aside what southern legislatures and local school boards had fashioned over so many years. Warren was in favor of ending segregation and had no hesitation about the Court so ordering, but like Frankfurter and Jackson, he understood that enforcement was the real problem if the Court was to act in concert. Justice Reed was hesitant as well. According to one of Reed's law clerks at the time, Warren persuaded Reed to sign on by appealing to his patriotism and warning that he would be isolated from the rest of the Court if he dissented.[1]

In the end, Warren had his unanimous Court, but he needed to pay a substantial price for that consensus: the opinion would only rule on segregation in education and, more important, a separate implementation decision a year later would wait upon testimony from the attorneys general of the segregationist states. Warren had written that because of the "considerable complexity" involved in desegregating tens of thousands of schoolchildren in thousands of school buildings in multiple jurisdictions hitherto segregated, reargument on the compliance question was only fair to all parties. Partly at

---

1. Klarman, *Jim Crow*, 312–20; Patterson, *Brown*, 78–85; John T. Fassett, *New Deal Justice: The Life of Stanley Reed of Kentucky* (New York: Vintage, 1994), 550–75.

the urging of the newly appointed solicitor general Simon E. Sobeloff, partly because Warren was still new at the job and the senior associate justice, Felix Frankfurter, urged caution, Warren had arranged for the attorneys general of the segregation states to brief the question of enforcement. They were then to give oral argument before the Court along with Marshall and Carter for the LDF in early spring 1955.

Warren and his fellow justices had a sense of history, and they knew that not since the slavery controversy had a constitutional question so thrust the federal courts onto center stage in public opinion as civil rights after *Brown*. No imposition on the time, energy, prudence, and activity of the federal judiciary matched the long effort to implement *Brown*. What was more, civil rights' remedies elevated the federal courts to a central place in American domestic policy making, exposing the judges to considerable backlash from parties before the courts and from those in the polity who opposed not only a judicial solution to segregation, but to desegregation itself.[2]

Still, perhaps the justices had been overly cautious? The immediate response to *Brown* out-of-doors seemed acceptance of the new order. Governors in Alabama and Arkansas promised compliance. Jim Folsom of Alabama conceded, "When the Supreme Court speaks, that's the law." In some of the border states of the South, notably Kentucky and Maryland, desegregation faced protests but moved apace. In other states like Delaware, however, protests closed the schools, and local and state officials began a campaign of foot dragging. The argument of the foot draggers was that white parents were not ready to have their children sit next to black youngsters, and that if such an event were mandated, violence would ensue. It was the heckler's veto argument, and in the months after *Brown*, it gained momentum. Fervent opponents of desegregation warned of a race war. The *Jackson (MS) Daily News* ominously predicted: "Human blood may stain Southern soil in many places because of this decision. . . . [W]hite and negro children in the same

---

2. David A. Nichols, *A Matter of Justice: Eisenhower and the Beginning of the Civil Rights Revolution* (New York: Simon and Schuster, 2007), 86; Robert J. Cottrol, Raymond T. Diamond, and Leland B. Ware, *Brown v. Board of Education: Caste, Culture, and the Constitution* (Lawrence: University Press of Kansas, 2004), 183–232; James T. Patterson, *Grand Expectations: The United States, 1945–1974* (New York: Oxford University Press, 1996), 287–91, 299–310, 444, 487–505, 568–79, 593–636. The involvement of federal courts in civil rights enforcement went back to the first Civil Rights Acts of the Reconstruction Era. See, e.g., Robert J. Kaczorowski, *The Politics of Judicial Interpretation: The Federal Courts, Department of Justice, and Civil Rights, 1866–1876* (New York: Fordham University Press, 2005).

schools will lead to miscegenation . . . and mongrelization of the human race."
"Citizens councils" organized to prevent desegregation, and politicians in the
former Confederate states, calculating where the votes were, began to back-
pedal as well.[3]

Even before the rehearing of the case, Warren expected that the actual enforcement would rely on district court orders to local officials. These orders
would take the form of injunctions. Injunctions were equitable remedies going back nearly a thousand years in England. They had come with the rest of
English jurisprudence to the American colonies, thence to the federal courts,
and finally became a full partner with legal remedies (monetary judgments,
for example) under the Federal Rules of Civil Procedure in 1938. The jurisprudence of equity requires good faith by the parties. That might be presumed but was hardly true of most of the local school boards, much less of
the state governments in the South.

The southern governors, many of them with legal backgrounds, and their
attorneys general, many of whom hoped to become governors, were to become the first line of legal defense against desegregation. The district court
judges were also from the South, and they understood that racial separation
was a well-established tradition. Some would press hard for the end of segregation. Others dragged their feet. School board members and state officials
who did not obey desegregation orders could be held in contempt of court, but
what federal judge was going to send an entire school board to jail? Knowing
this, and determined not to follow the Supreme Court's lead, local and state
school boards would delay, deny, and disobey *Brown* II with ill-concealed
dodges like pupil placement and step-by-step (school-year-by-school-year)
plans, all of which would take more time for the local board to study. Finally,
members of the so-called Southern Caucus in Congress would have their say,
a "Manifesto" against court-ordered desegregation. But presuming good faith

---

3. David Goldfield, *Black, White, and Southern: Race Relations and Southern Culture, 1940
to the Present* (Baton Rouge: Louisiana State University Press, 1990), 77–78; *Jackson (MS) Daily
News*, May 18, 1954; Numan V. Bartley, *The New South, 1945–1980* (Baton Rouge: Louisiana State
University Press, 1995), 198; Klarman, *Jim Crow*, 347–49; Patterson, *Brown*, 70–85. Just how much
or how many white southerners opposed desegregation is a still unanswered question. Certainly,
"massive resistance" was "a particularly obnoxious species of popular constitutionalism," something akin to the popular defense of slavery in the later antebellum years of the South. Mark
Golub, "Remembering Massive Resistance to School Desegregation," *Law and History Review* 31
(2013): 495: "Full compliance would not and did not come until [white] southerners had themselves assumed responsibility for controlling and punishing racist violence." Belknap, *Federal
Law and Southern Order*, 228.

on the part of the state authorities, the Court reached out to the southern attorneys general for their advice and assistance.[4]

History has slighted the effective lawyering of the southern attorneys
general for their government clients. Asked to present the Court with their
views of implementation of *Brown*, they fashioned persuasive arguments for
caution and deliberation. One of the first of these was especially effective.
On October 15, 1954, Florida's attorney general Richard Ervin submitted his
state's response to the Court's invitation to answer the question of whether
the Court should allow a gradual adjustment monitored by the district panels. Ervin's stance was not be tied to *Brown* only, but to the history, traditions,
and customs of segregation. By the fall of 1954, he already had had chances to
elucidate his views on desegregation. For example, when in 1950 Virgil Hawkins, a black petitioner, sought to enter the University of Florida College of
Law, Ervin had rehearsed the arguments he would use in his *Brown* brief.
The Supreme Court of Florida bought Ervin's answer to Hawkins's plea wholesale. Ervin was indifferent to the U.S. Supreme Court's ruling in *Sweatt*:

> For further answer to the writ the respondents alleged, that the Constitution
> and statutes of the State of Florida provide that white and Negro students shall
> not be taught in the same schools but that impartial provision shall be made
> for both and that in pursuance of these requirements the State of Florida has
> established certain institutions of higher learning in the State, among which
> are the University of Florida, at Gainesville, Florida, and the Florida State Uni-
> versity, at Tallahassee, Florida, both maintained for white students, and the
> Florida Agricultural and Mechanical College for Negroes, at Tallahassee, Flor-
> ida, maintained exclusively for Negroes; that these three state institutions have
> been in operation for many years and are under the management and control
> of the Board of Control, subject to the supervising power of the State Board
> of Education, who, through a long established and fixed policy of providing
> substantially equal educational opportunities to white and Negro races alike
> have from time to time added additional schools and courses of instruction at
> each of these institutions.

The decision (that is, Ervin's brief) continued that the plan proposed—a separate but equal school for Hawkins and those similarly situated—was fully within
the guidelines of *Sipuel* and *Sweatt*. "No court in the land has ever required a

4. The breadth and skill with which southern legal authorities entered into the lists to defend segregation is surveyed in Christopher Schmidt, "Litigating against the Civil Rights Movement," *University of Colorado Law Review* 86, no. 4 (2015): 1179ff. Schmidt's contribution reminds
us that some of the litigation was reactive, but other suits were attacks against which the LDF
had to expend its resources. On the Federal Rules of Civil Procedure drafting and adoption, see
Hoffer, Hoffer, and Hull, *Federal Courts*, 298–307.

sovereign state any more than is encompassed within the plan proposed by the Board of Control in its answer." As a general rule, the state had the right, under the federal Constitution (and *Plessy*) to "adopt such methods as it find best deigned" to provide separate but equal facilities. This though the Florida court conceded that the facilities available to Hawkins to study law in Florida were "temporarily" not comparable to those of his white fellow citizens.[5]

Accounts at the time reported that the Florida legislature had appropriated ten thousand dollars for the study of desegregation by 1954, and Ervin enlisted state superintendent of education Thomas D. Bailey and eight thousand local community leaders (via questionnaires) to aid him in responding to the Court's call for state attorneys general to argue compliance with *Brown*. Providing an interpretation of the questionnaire results, among others, was young Florida State University sociologist Lewis Killian. Killian was a rising star in his profession and a key addition to Ervin's team, as events would prove. The brief's preliminary statement spanned the range of official southern responses to the first *Brown* decision. The state's response began with its claim of good faith:

> The Court will find from a study of this brief that sincere and thorough effort has been made by the Attorney General of Florida to present reasonable and logical answers to [the Court's request]. These answers are respectfully submitted by way of assistance to the court and are based upon a scientific survey of the factual situation in Florida, embracing practical, psychological, economic and sociological effects, as well as an exhaustive research of legal principles. However, in filing this brief in answer to the hypothetical questions propounded, the Attorney General is not intervening in the cause nor is he authorised to submit the state of Florida as a direct party to the instant eases. Neither can his brief preclude the Florida legislature or the people of Florida from taking my legislative or constitutional action dealing with the segregation problem.

Ervin's opening remarks were clever—as the state's chief legal officer, he was showing the Court its intent to comply, but he could not guarantee that compliance, because, after all, he was only a spokesman for the sovereign state, and its government could deal with the "segregation problem" as it wished, regardless of the Court's decision. This response hinted at the constitutional and historical foundation for resistance to federally ordered desegregation—the doctrine of states' rights.[6]

---

5. State ex rel. Hawkins v. Board of Control of Florida, 47 So.2d 608, 609, 610, 614 (1950) (Sebring, J.).

6. Amicus Brief of the Attorney General of Florida, October Term, 1954, Supreme Court of the United States, 1.

States' rights theory was as old as the republic, and it rested on the idea that the states never surrendered any of their sovereignty to the federal government or to the people assembled in the United States Congress. It made its appearance in Thomas Jefferson's and James Madison's resistance to the Federalist Party majority in Congress, during the Alien and Sedition Acts controversy of 1798–1800, in John C. Calhoun's "Exposition and Protest" during the South Carolina "nullification" controversy of 1828–33, and of course in the Secession movement of 1860–61. Although the defeat of the Confederacy and the Fourteenth Amendment seemed to put an end to the most strident states' rights arguments, the doctrine itself survived the war and Reconstruction. Indeed, murmurs and threats of nullification would rumble through pro-segregation gatherings throughout the 1950s.[7]

The gist of the remaining pages of Ervin's brief was that Florida school boards needed time and study to fulfill the objectives of desegregation. Florida was acting in good faith, a critical component of all equitable proceedings, for the state expected some form of equitable order to come down from the Court. But "coercion" of local officials was not the answer, nor was any

7. See, e.g., Forrest McDonald, *States' Rights and the Union: Imperium in Imperio, 1776–1876* (Lawrence: University Press of Kansas, 2000), 7–26 (problem of states' rights inherent in the Constitution); Timothy S. Huebner, *The Southern Judicial Tradition: State Judges and Sectional Distinctiveness, 1790–1890* (Athens: University of Georgia Press, 1999), 189–90 (states' rights and southern constitutional ideas); Sotirios A. Barber, *The Fallacies of States' Rights* (Cambridge, MA: Harvard University Press, 2013), 173–75 (arguing that modern assertions of states' rights are "pretexts" for opposition to legitimate national policies); Edward A. Purcell Jr., *Originalism, Federalism, and the American Constitutional Enterprise: A Historical Inquiry* (New Haven, CT: Yale University Press, 2007), 60–61 (advocates of states' rights sometimes change sides to strident nationalism, based on perceived interests). A strong version flavors Justice Neil Gorsuch's dissents, e.g., Artis v. District of Columbia, 583 U.S. ___ 2, 12, 18 (Gorsuch, J., dissenting): "Indeed, the Court today tells state courts that they must routinely disregard clearly expressed state law defining the appropriate length of time parties should have to sue on state law claims in state tribunals. . . . It may only be a small statute we are interpreting, but the result the Court reaches today represents no small intrusion on traditional state functions and no small departure from our foundational principles of federalism. . . . The Court's reformation of the statute introduces another problem still—one of significantly greater magnitude yet. In our constitutional structure, the federal government's powers are supposed to be 'few and defined,' while the powers reserved to the States 'remain . . . numerous and indefinite.' . . . [W]e've wandered so far from the idea of a federal government of limited and enumerated powers that we've begun to lose sight of what it looked like in the first place" (citing the *Federalist* and *Marbury* (1803) and *McElroy v. Cohen* [1839]). A milder form appears as robust and legitimate "federalism"; see, e.g., Raoul Berger, *Federalism: The Founders' Design* (Norman: University of Oklahoma Press, 1987).

attempt to "peremptorily compel school officials" to act when they did not feel ready to do so—a warning sailing fairly close to contempt of the Court.[8]

Ervin was Florida born and bred, educated at the University of Florida and its law school, and very much a product of state political alliances. Were his efforts then a product of a strong belief in the value of segregation to all parties, or some variant of political cynicism? Killian acted as a consultant as Ervin, and his staff prepared the brief. He later recalled that Ervin's personal instincts were liberal, but his political ambitions lay in the hands of the segregationists, and Ervin was not disposed to lose elective office because of *Brown*. Instead, Ervin issued "high toned" pronouncements, and when it became clear that they had fallen on deaf ears, he allowed the gradualism of "all deliberate speed" in the subsequent *Brown* II opinion to become deliberate delay. The basic law of Florida on education—that is, its Jim Crow statute—dated to 1885. How could such a long-established set of rules, understood by everyone in the school districts, be overturned overnight? The result of such a step would leave a "vacuum" in the laws. Instead, the legislature should be given time to consider a step-by-step process, which in turn would require soliciting information from all of the school districts. After all, the state had simply been in compliance with *Plessy* for so many years—another aside, this time in effect blaming the Court for segregation.

Ervin offered factual evidence to demonstrate the problem—for example, the sharp differential between white and black academic scores (itself a product of segregated school funding differentials that he did not cite) would make integrating the black and white student bodies difficult. A second surely unintended irony in the brief was his insistence that white schools were already overcrowded. Ervin even used Killian's studies of white-on-black violence to support his plea for a very cautious approach. The idea was that the problems within the black community like crime, disease, and poverty had to be solved before black children could enter white schools. Such "intangibles" needed to be taken into account before the state could act. The means for dealing with these complexities Ervin laid out in the amicus brief—create panels, study the issue, and in the meantime do nothing to desegregate the schools. Local

8. Amicus Brief of the Attorney General of Florida, October Term, 1954, Supreme Court of the United States, 43, 59; "Richard Ervin and the Gradualist Approach to Desegregation," *Florida Memory* blog, July 9, 2014, http://www.floridamemory.com/blog/2014/07/09/richard-ervin/. On the passion of the southern pro-segregation litigators, see Schmidt, "Litigating," 1184. But there is a third possibility, the "enthusiasm . . . for fighting battles" in court that animates litigators of all kinds.

option laws, which Ervin accepted, made compliance almost impossible in any case. Massive resistance in the state, encouraged by the stance of its legal authorities, had begun.[9]

Ervin responded to the "sociological jurisprudence" of footnote 11 in Warren's *Brown* opinion with what amounted to a sociology of the South. This he buttressed with citations from social scientists and educators on the importance of tradition. He did not dismiss social science, as Davis and Figg had. Instead, he countered it with his own social science evidence. This is why Killian's contribution was so important. The point was that desegregation would only be effective and safe for everyone when the hearts and minds of white folks in the South were changed. In this sociology of the South, "hardship or injury to public or private interests" must be avoided, for the white people of the South had suffered too. There was thus a tone that the South had been a victim of a long series of outside aggressions, that southern history was unique because of these, and that forced integration of the school was simply another of these harmful outside impositions on the southern way of life. It was this sense of injured pride that allowed moderates to join the "citizens councils" opposing good-faith desegregation efforts.

Perhaps unthinkingly, Ervin had reached back to a tradition begun in the antebellum period by defenders of slavery like George Fitzhugh, whose *Sociology for the South* (1854) offered an apology for southern ways that did not include any inclination to change race relations in the face of northern criticism. Ervin was not a covert defender of slavery or of the Lost Cause of secession. The comparison, if one can be made, lay in the argument for southern sensibility and good sense when it came to race. For Fitzhugh, "On all subjects of social science, Southern men, from their position, possess peculiar advantages when they undertake discussion." In defense of slavery, outside critics "overlook the protective influence of slavery, its distinguishing feature, and no doubt the cause of its origin and continuance and abuse it as mere engine of oppression." For Ervin, outside critics overlooked the protective influence of Jim Crow, with its solicitude not only for white interests but the special needs of the blacks: "the need for social engineering, time, patience, and community understanding . . . of racial differences, traditions, history, and customs."[10]

9. Lewis M. Killian, *Black and White: Reflections of a White Southern Sociologist* (Lanham, MD: Rowman and Littlefield, 1994), 84–85; Anders Walker, *The Ghost of Jim Crow: How Southern Moderates Used* Brown v. Board of Education *to Stall Civil Rights* (New York: Oxford University Press, 2009), 93–94; Brief of the Attorney General of Florida, 5, 6, 7, 8, 42.

10. Brief of the Attorney General of Florida, 69; Cobb, *The South and America since World War II*, 35–40; George Fitzhugh, *Sociology for the South; or, The Failure of Free Society* (Richmond, VA: Morris, 1854), iv, 68; Brief of the Attorney General of Florida, 91.

In the meantime, the *Hawkins* case returned to the Florida courts, and there Ervin stood figuratively at the door of the state's law school and denied Hawkins's entrance. Ervin argued for the Florida board of control in federal court three more times, winning in the district court but losing in the Fifth Circuit and the Supreme Court. The pattern—resistance in the district court to the issuance of a decree, followed by appellate reversal—would become familiar in the Fifth Circuit. Hawkins never did get to go to his home state's law school, and it did not integrate until 1961. In the meantime, Ervin went on to serve on his state's supreme court, an elective post, a reward for his defense of segregation.[11]

★

Ervin's brief and oral argument in *Brown*, as in *Hawkins*, had won ground that the LDF thought was safely theirs. When the *Brown* case was reargued, April 11–14, 1955, Maryland, Oklahoma, Texas, North Carolina, and Florida, at the invitation of the Court, presented briefs orally on enforcement. Davis no longer appeared for South Carolina and would shortly thereafter die. The state was represented by S. E. Rogers and Robert McC. Figg Jr. Figg was the attorney of record in *Briggs*'s lower court appearances. A successful Charleston lawyer, personal advisor to Governor Strom Thurmond, and well-regarded jurist, he believed that segregation was a positive good, and that its end would only come when race itself no longer mattered. Thurgood Marshall and Spottswood Robinson returned to argue for the petitioners in Clarendon County. Soboloff argued a friend of the court brief for the Department of Justice. Justice Jackson had died and his replacement, John Marshall Harlan, the grandson of the great dissenter in *Plessy*, favored desegregation. Warren read the decision of the unanimous Court on May 15, 1955. He was cautiously optimistic and welcomed the participation of the various states' legal officers. "These presentations were informative and helpful to the Court in its consideration of the complexities arising from the transition to a system of public education freed of racial discrimination. The presentations also demonstrated that substantial steps to eliminate racial discrimination in public schools have already been taken, not only in some of the communities in which these cases arose, but in some of the states appearing as amici curiae, and in other states as well." But he did not give to Marshall what he and the LDF wanted: a decree ordering that immediate desegregation begin. Instead,

11. Klarman, *Jim Crow*, 256–61; Florida ex rel. Hawkins v. Board of Control, 350 U.S. 413 (1956); Hawkins v. Board of Control, 162 F. Supp. 851 (N.D. Florida 1958); Hawkins v. Board of Control, 253 F.2d 752 (5th Cir. 1958).

he remanded the case to the district courts. "Full implementation of these constitutional principles may require solution of varied local school problems. School authorities have the primary responsibility for elucidating, assessing, and solving these problems; courts will have to consider whether the action of school authorities constitutes good-faith implementation of the governing constitutional principles. Because of their proximity to local conditions and the possible need for further hearings, the courts which originally heard these cases can best perform this judicial appraisal. Accordingly, we believe it appropriate to remand the cases to those courts."[12]

★

As the briefs and oral argument in *Brown* II demonstrated, the front line of defense of segregation in the South was the lawyering of the state attorneys general. Their representation of the case for delay was persuasive. It was also self-serving. Men like Ervin had political aspirations of their own, and the attorney general's office was one among the many stepping-stones to the governorship. The grounds for the defense lay in a collateral attack, that the LDF lawyers were stirring up litigation that would not have occurred without their intervention. In fact, black communities did not need the LDF to seek legal representation, but it was also a fact that there were few lawyers on the ground, still fewer African American lawyers, willing to represent black people in civil rights lawsuits. (If the lawsuit were not race related, for example, in criminal matters, white lawyers would be more willing to act as counsel for black defendants.) It was also a fact that black name plaintiffs in civil rights lawsuits faced retribution from white employers, neighbors, and local authorities. Standing up for their rights in court took courage, determination, and, often, outside help. But this exposed the outsiders—the LDF—to the charge of barratry (stirring up lawsuits), champerty (financing lawsuits in which one has no personal interest), and maintenance (intermeddling in a lawsuit in which one has no personal interest), among other long-outmoded common-law misdemeanors.

On their face, statutory revisions in the southern state professional codes of behavior looked like reforms meant to reduce ambulance-chasing lawyering. The effort, spurred by the attorneys general and abetted by committees of the local (all-white) bar, had, however, a different purpose. "In the middle 1950's seven southern states suddenly discovered a need to reinvigorate and extend existing champerty, maintenance and solicitation rules. The flurry of

---

12. Robert McCormick Figg Papers, South Caroliniana Library, University of South Carolina, Columbia, South Carolina; 349 U.S. at 299 (1955) (Warren, C.J.).

legislation came on the heels of the Supreme Court's decision in *Brown v. Board of Education* II in which five civil rights organizations appeared as amicus curiae. The two events were not unconnected. The action of the legislatures was a vigorous political response to the success of these organizations before the courts." With the legal authorities of the Jim Crow states, including the attorneys general, dead set against political action to end discrimination, recourse to the courts was the only avenue for redress. But the LDF lawyer who looked for a name plaintiff to forward the cause of civil rights might be condemned under these new laws.[13]

Of the seven states that in 1956 and 1957 altered their laws to prevent out-of-state chartered corporations like the LDF from seeking clients or paying for clients' legal fees, Virginia's actions were particularly thorough. The charge was led by J. Lindsay Almond, who was elected attorney general in 1948 and served until August 1957, when he launched his successful campaign for governor. Almond had argued successfully for his state in *Dorothy E. Davis, et al. v. County School Board of Prince Edward County*, until, when the case was consolidated with *Brown*, he lost. He returned to the high court at the end of 1954 with the other attorneys general and made the case for delay in *Brown* II. In the state, he privately asked for a "realistic" adjustment to the enforcement decisions, but that was not the end of his anti–civil rights lawyering. In 1956 he was one advisor in the so-called Stanley Plan (named after governor Thomas Stanley), including centralizing the administration of the public schools so that local boards could not comply with *Brown* on their own, along with the revisions of the bar code on barratry, champerty, and maintenance. Attorney David J. Mays, a consultant, helped formulate the legislation as well and represented the state in its plan to bring suits under it. Mays opposed more radical opponents of desegregation, who wanted to interpose the state government against *Brown*, it should be noted. The legislation was a model of its kind, facially neutral but deeply deceptive. Aiming for the first time at such supposedly improper conduct (although there was no evidence of a surge in prior misconduct that would require the revision of the code), Virginia broadened its improper professional conduct law. Had that law been enforced, one assumes the attorney general would have singled out LDF counsel for violations and driven the civil rights lawyers from the field. Even though they were admitted to practice in state and federal courts in the South (and in the courtroom southern lawyers had to treat the LDF lawyers

---

13. "The South's Amended Barratry Laws: An Attempt to End Group Pressure through the Courts," *Yale Law Journal* 72 (1963): 1613, 1615.

with professional civility), Virginia made clear its intent to close the courts to the LDF and its clients.[14]

The NAACP sought the aid of the federal District Court for the Eastern District of Virginia, a panel of which, in a unanimous ruling by Judge Morris Soper, a Harding appointee from Maryland, found that "it is generally known that the State Conference [of the NAACP] will furnish money for litigation if the proper need arises, but the Association does not take the initiative and does not act until some individual comes to it asking for help." The court looked behind the curtain of alleged state neutrality to find that "the five statutes against which the pending lawsuits are directed, that is Chapters 31, 32, 33, 35 and 36 of the Acts of the General Assembly of Virginia, passed at its Extra Session in 1956, were enacted for the express purpose of impeding the integration of the races in the public schools of the state which the plaintiff corporations are seeking to promote." What is more, the legislative intent, which the court could discern from the "legislative history" of the acts, was to "nullify" the high court ruling in *Brown*, and to give effect to the doctrine of "massive resistance" that political leaders in the state advocated. In court, the state presented evidence from white sheriffs in black majority counties that desegregation would promote disorder. John Patterson, the attorney general of the state of Alabama—which, as we will see, had a stake in the outcome of the case—testified that if desegregation plans went forward in Alabama, the KKK would intervene violently as it had in his state. In more restrained fashion, Almond argued that First Amendment freedom-of-speech protections claimed by the NAACP did not apply to corporations like the NAACP; that federal courts generally did not interfere with criminal statutes; and finally that the federal court should wait until the Virginia courts heard and disposed of the lawsuit.[15]

Almond's plea did not persuade Judge Soper that the legislation should stand. To be sure, "the right of the state to require high standards of qualification for those who desire to practice law within its borders and to revoke or suspend the license to practice law of attorneys who have been guilty of unethical conduct is unquestioned." But here the NAACP did not seek to make

14. David John Mays, *Race, Reason, and Massive Resistance: The Diary of David J. Mays, 1954–1959* (Athens: University of Georgia Press, 2008), 166 (Almond involvement in formulating policy); William J. Hustwit, *James J. Kilpatrick: Salesman for Segregation* (Chapel Hill: University of North Carolina Press, 2013), 61; Christopher Bonastia, *Southern Stalemate: Five Years without Public Education in Prince Edward County, Virginia* (Chicago: University of Chicago Press, 2012), 50 ("reasonable"); James E. Moliterno, *The American Legal Profession in Crisis: Resistance and Responses to Change* (New York: Oxford University Press, 2013), 73–75 (role of legislators).

15. NAACP v. Patty, 159 F. Supp. 503, 509, 511 (D.C. E.D. Va. 1958) (Soper, J.).

a profit on the litigation; instead, "it is manifest, however, that the activities of the plaintiff corporations are not undertaken for profit or for the promotion of ordinary business purposes but, rather, for the securing of the rights of citizens without any possibility of financial gain." In a prior hearing, the district court had remanded to the state courts, which upheld the legislation. Soper found that the district court had erred and again remanded to the state courts with the proviso that the legislation was "bad because, in the light of its history and of its present setting, it is seen to be a deliberate and calculated device in the guise of a tax to limit the circulation of information to which the public is entitled in virtue of the constitutional guaranties." Virginia left the teeth of the laws in place: "The activities of NAACP, the Virginia Conference, the Defense Fund, and the lawyers furnished by them, fell within, and could constitutionally be proscribed by, the chapter's expanded definition of improper solicitation of legal business, and also violated Canons 35 and 47 of the American Bar Association's Canons of Professional Ethics, which the court had adopted in 1938."[16]

It is worthwhile noting that the district court panel decision striking down portions of the Virginia law was not unanimous. Judge Charles Sterling Hutcheson dissented in part. Hutcheson believed in states' rights to this extent: "Repeatedly the Courts have discussed at length the 'deeply rooted' doctrine which has become a 'time-honored canon of constitutional adjudication' that Federal Courts do not interfere with state legislation when the asserted federal right may be preserved without such interference." In support of this proposition, he quoted dissents from Justice James McReynolds, himself a notorious opponent of black rights, that states should be left by federal courts to interpret their own laws. Hutcheson concurred with his brethren on the portions of the law left to the determination of the Virginia courts, but otherwise all the references to *Brown*, and to the witnesses the state produced, were merely "emotional" and had no place in the decision of the court. Calling a fellow judge's recital of facts "emotional" was a serious breach of judicial decorum, but the stakes for Hutcheson, a veteran opponent of civil rights, were high. He was beholden to Senator Harry F. Byrd's strongly pro-segregation and states' rights organization and had repeatedly refused to order desegregation in cases before him after *Brown* II came down. He believed that the federal courts should keep their noses out of the business of elected state legislatures, courts, and governorships. "That issue is whether the Judicial branch of the Government can sit in judgment upon

16. 159 F. Supp. 516, 531, 527 (Soper, J.); NAACP v. Button, 371 U.S. 415, 425 (1963) (quoting Virginia Supreme Court).

the collective personal motives or influences activating those charged with
the responsibility of conducting the affairs of one of the other co-ordinate
branches. If this can be done the result may be far-reaching indeed." Six years
after the litigation began, the case was before the U.S. Supreme Court, and it
found that the entire Virginia law violated the free speech rights of the civil
rights clients and their counsel.[17]

Alabama had a similar anti-solicitation law, one reason why its attorney
general was willing to appear before the federal court in Virginia, but with
the Virginia litigation throwing up a potential obstacle to the law against improper solicitation of lawsuits, the Alabama legislature had to find an alternative to constrain civil rights activists. Adapting a law concerning businesses
incorporated in other states, Alabama required the NAACP to register all of its
Alabama members. This was a kind of classification of political speech akin to
classification by color. The assumption was that public knowledge of NAACP
membership would cause locals to lose members, the members fearing economic pressure or worse from their white neighbors. (Few whites in the
South belonged to the NAACP.) The facts were simple and, on the face of
it, had nothing to do with race, civil rights, or politics. The statute requiring the NAACP, as a "foreign corporation," to register with the state was not
prejudicial, nor was it based on color. But the state used the statute to demand
that the NAACP produce its membership lists for inspection by the state attorney general's office. Attorney General Patterson filed an action on behalf of
the state that sought to enjoin the organization from conducting business in
Alabama until it produced the requested documentation. It was not inciden-
tal that Patterson was at that time a die-hard segregationist who would, two
years later, win the governorship with the support of the Klan, in part for his
role in the NAACP litigation.[18]

The NAACP refused to obey. It was adjudged in contempt of court and
was fined. The NAACP filed a petition for a writ of certiorari. The court denied the writ and dismissed the petition and instead permitted the state to
increase the fine. In a per curiam order, the Alabama Supreme Court agreed
with the state's circuit court. "It is clear, therefore, that the circuit court, in
equity, had authority to order the petitioner to disclose names, addresses and
dues paid by petitioner's members, officers, agents and employees and that

17. 159 F. Supp. 535, 537 (Hutcheson, J.); 371 U.S. 426 (Brennan, J.); Peltason, *Lonely Men*, 213;
Abraham, *Justices, Presidents, and Senators*, 134 (McReynolds on blacks).
18. Gene L. Howard, *Patterson for Alabama: The Life and Career of John Patterson* (Tuscaloosa: University of Alabama Press, 2008), 114.

the petitioner could be held in contempt of court for non-compliance with the court's order to produce."[19]

When the U.S. Supreme Court heard the case, Thurgood Marshall recognized its importance and joined with Robert Carter to argue for the NAACP. Patterson represented his state. In a unanimous opinion, Justice John Marshall Harlan lifted the veil of the state's action and found that its decision, based on a procedural nicety (the filing of an incorrect writ), was wrong on its face (the NAACP had used the proper writ) and suspect for another reason—that the state was trying to drive the NAACP's organizing efforts, including its support for the Montgomery bus boycott, into the ground.[20]

Following the sudden death of Robert H. Jackson from heart failure, Eisenhower had looked to Harlan, the grandson of the great dissenter, to fill the seat. Eisenhower had appointed him to the Court of Appeals of the Second Circuit only thirteen months earlier. Some southern senators, notably James Eastland of Mississippi, objected to the nomination to express their displeasure with the ruling in *Brown*. Nevertheless, he was confirmed by the Senate shortly in March 1955. Justice Harlan proved to be a lawyer's lawyer with a conscience, a believer in hard and careful work and the value of detail. He gained a reputation as one of the Court's ablest and most prolific writers. He was Frankfurter's natural ally. They respected one another and agreed on 80 percent of the cases. One wag went so far as to declare that Harlan, a courtly gentleman on and off the bench, was Frankfurter "without the mustard." When Frankfurter retired, Harlan became the standard-bearer of judicial restraint, federalism, and deference to legislatures, but he shared with his grandfather a concern for civil rights, especially those of African Americans, and free speech. Much respected by his brethren, he exercised great influence in the Judicial Conference of the justices. He retired in September 1971.[21]

Harlan wrote:

The Association both urges that it is constitutionally entitled to resist official inquiry into its membership lists, and that it may assert, on behalf of its members, a right personal to them to be protected from compelled disclosure by

19. Ex parte NAACP, 265 Ala. 349, 356 (1956).

20. NAACP v. Alabama ex rel. Patterson, 357 U.S. 449 (1958).

21. Tinsley E. Yarbrough, *John Marshall Harlan: Great Dissenter of the Warren Court* (New York: Oxford University Press, 1992), 92, 95–105. "Frankfurter without the mustard": quoted in David J. Garrow, *Liberty and Sexuality: The Right to Privacy and the Making of* Roe v. Wade (New York: Scribner's, 1994), 184. On the influence of Frankfurter on Harlan, see Charles Nesson, "The Harlan-Frankfurter Connection: An Aspect of Justice Harlan's Education," *New York University Law Review* 36 (1991): 179–98.

the State of their affiliation with the Association as revealed by the membership lists. We think that petitioner argues more appropriately the rights of its
members, and that its nexus with them is sufficient to permit that it act as their
representative before this Court. . . . Effective advocacy of both public and
private points of view, particularly controversial ones, is undeniably enhanced
by group association, as this Court has more than once recognized by remark-
ing upon the close nexus between the freedoms of speech and assembly. It is
beyond debate that freedom to engage in association for the advancement of
beliefs and ideas is an inseparable aspect of the "liberty" assured by the Due
Process Clause of the Fourteenth Amendment, which embraces freedom of
speech. Of course, it is immaterial whether the beliefs sought to be advanced
by association pertain to political, economic, religious or cultural matters, and
state action which may have the effect of curtailing the freedom to associate is
subject to the closest scrutiny." (citations omitted)[22]

Almond and Patterson were perhaps the best known of the executive branch
lawyers who found ways to defend segregation in court. Others were James P.
Coleman of Mississippi, a former attorney general of his state and state judge
before he was elected governor, and LeRoy Collins of Florida, elected governor in 1956, the same year as Coleman. Both men were so-called moderates
(at least by their more radical political opponents), in that they condemned
Brown, saw segregation as part and parcel of a way of life but urged law and
order, and found more subtle ways to avert the full imposition of desegregation until political necessity and pressure from the federal government made
accommodation inevitable. At the same time as they prevented their state
legislatures from passing nullification statutes, they hoped to convince the
federal courts that compliance with *Brown* merely required removing overtly
racialist language from the school laws. To this end, Collins worked closely
with Attorney General Ervin to craft the state's response to *Brown* I discussed
above. Unlike other southern governors with legal backgrounds, including
George Wallace of Alabama, a former state judge and moderate on the bench
who became far more pro-segregation in the state executive mansion, and
Ernest Vandiver of Georgia, also a lawyer, Coleman and Collins were cred-
ited with bringing about desegregation. But then, Wallace and Vandiver were
first and foremost politicians, not jurists, and they knew what they had to do
and say to gain that office. But in the interim, "these litigation tactics served
their purpose remarkably well." Later in life, like Patterson, Coleman, and

22. 357 U.S. at 458–459, 460–461 (Harlan, J.).

Collins, Wallace and Vandiver moderated their views on race and courted black voters.[23]

By the beginning of 1956, faced with such skilled and determined opposition as the southern attorneys general and the governors erected, the civil rights litigation project seemed to stall. In part, this may have been due to the infighting at the LDF, but a more important cause was the effectiveness of segregation lawyering. *Brown* II had inadvertently shifted the burden of proof in desegregation cases to the plaintiffs, while stubborn and creative litigation strategies among defendants turned delay into a legal set piece. Behind this lay the funding of southern state legislatures, well into five figures for lawyers' fees. The most able minds among segregationist and white supremacist legal fraternity eagerly joined in the enterprise. Although the LDF had won, and would continue to win at the highest levels of the judicial system, the courts were not the only lawgivers in America.[24]

✶

Theoretically in the American system of government, there is a strict separation of powers between the executive, judicial, and legislative branches. That constitutional doctrine is not always honored, however. In southern states, all three branches of government worked in close accord to protect the Jim Crow tradition, as one might expect from elective offices dependent on white supremacist voting. In the U.S. Congress, southern senators like Mississippi's James Eastland readily took to the floor of the upper house to lambaste the Court and *Brown* for the same reasons. For him, segregation was a safeguard against the pollution of the white race ("mongrelization" was his term) and the infiltration of communistic ideas into the southern heartland. Though a plantation owner, Eastland was a lawyer by training and a member of the state bar, and a politician by avocation. His rabble-rousing rhetoric was the sort that would not work well in a court of law. But it did work on the hustings, and he brought it to Congress, where it laid the template for a unified southern resistance to *Brown*.[25]

The 1955 confirmation hearings debate over the appointment of John Marshall Harlan provided an occasion for further southern anti-desegregation

---

23. Walker, *The Ghost of Jim Crow*, 5, 7, 24, 26, 43 (Coleman), 92–93, 96 (Collins); Schmidt, "Litigating," 1190, 1192.

24. Patterson, *Brown*, 94–95.

25. Maarten Zwiers, *Senator James Eastland: Mississippi's Jim Crow Democrat* (Baton Rouge: Louisiana State University Press, 2015), 36–37, 39, 45.

lawyering in the Senate. Although the hearings were relatively brief, Eastland's questions showed that *Brown*'s implementation was uppermost on his mind. He took the Court to task for amending the Constitution and assuming legislative powers. These comments were a foretaste of what was to come: a virtual rehearing of *Brown* in the Senate by a caucus of southern lawyers.[26]

Eastland's case was a political and social one, based on the notion that whites in the South shared their supremacist views with whites in the North. It was also personal in the sense that civil rights seemed an attack on the South. In hearings on *Brown* in the lower house, southern members felt similarly defensive. As Georgia representative E. L. Forrester, chair of the House Judicial Affairs Committee, wrote to Senator Richard Russell of Georgia, witnesses at civil rights hearings "directed [their testimony] against the South and against our state of Georgia." The "NAACP boys" (the derogative term "boys" was intended and both men knew its long history) "indulged in their favorite pastime of maligning the South." Forrester assumed that the NAACP was a Soviet front, or at least sympathetic to communism. They were one and all "left-wing boys." But by 1956, as northern support for *Brown* could no longer be ignored, Eastland and his cohorts assayed a different approach. In March 1956, ninety-nine members of Congress formally and forcefully breached this separation of the branches, fashioning themselves as a virtual court and issuing a virtual overruling of *Brown*. The so-called Southern Manifesto, the doppelganger of *Brown*, was the work of southern lawyers in the Senate, and its arguments encapsulated the long tradition of states' rights lawyering.[27]

Senator Strom Thurmond of South Carolina circulated a mimeographed draft of the manifesto to his southern colleagues on February 2, 1956. A second version followed a week later. This was assigned by Senator Walter George of Georgia, the senior member of the Southern Caucus, to a drafting committee headed by his Georgia colleague Richard Russell. A third draft was the work of Russell, with help from Senators John Stennis of Mississippi and Sam Ervin of North Carolina. Thurmond and Ervin were newcomers to the Senate.

26. J. Lee Annis Jr., *Big Jim Eastland: The Godfather of Mississippi* (University of Mississippi Press, 2016), 132–33. Quotations from Paul M. Collins and Laurie A. Ringhand, *Supreme Court Confirmation Hearings and Constitutional Change* (New York: Cambridge University Press, 2013), 163 (based on Harlan's own recollection).

27. *Congressional Record*, 84th Congress Second Session, vol. 102, part 4 (March 12, 1956) (Washington, DC: Governmental Printing Office, 1956), 4459–60; E. L. Forrester to Richard Russell, August 5, 1955, Richard Russell Collection, Russell Library for Political Research and Studies, University of Georgia Libraries, Athens, Georgia (hereinafter Russell Collection), box 21, folio 1.

What the senior members and their more junior colleagues had in common was legal training and practice, including experience as local judges. The last part was significant—that training and experience was all local, except for Ervin's stint at Harvard Law School.

Two more drafts circulated, and a final one was read to the Senate on March 12, 1956. For a committee effort, the job was swiftly and ably completed. It was signed by every member of the southern Senate delegation except Albert Gore Sr. of Tennessee, Estes Kefauver of Tennessee, and Lyndon Johnson of Texas. No northern member of Congress signed it, nor did anyone from Maryland, Kentucky, or Missouri, even though the latter three states had Jim Crow laws. Two Florida members of the House, four North Carolina representatives, five Tennessee representatives, led by Howard Baker, and a majority of the Texas lower house delegation, led by Speaker Sam Rayburn and Jim Wright, refused to sign. All of the signees were Democrats, save for two members of the Virginia House delegation.[28]

The drafting of the Southern Manifesto—whose actual title was the Declaration of Constitutional Principles but is here referred to by its more common name—has its own backstory, dramatic in a sense, especially as it staved off an attempt by some members of Congress to call for nullification of the *Brown* decision and other extremes, to find a more moderate, if just as unyielding, stance against Court-ordered desegregation. The conventional story of the drafting lays it in the lap of Senator Harry Byrd of Virginia, a virulent segregationist and the coiner of the term "massive resistance." Byrd was an able newspaper publisher and a senior member of the conservative coalition, but not a lawyer, and he did not see the defense of segregation in legal terms. It was political—a matter of power—and he was a veteran power broker in the Senate. As civil rights workers became more active after *Brown*, Byrd's fury grew. Clever, partisan, and efficient, he supported "the rights of states and the rights of white men," both of which *Brown* seemed to him to contravene. In that sense, his ideology was a throwback to the "old Constitution" of antebellum political leaders, in which a weak federal government left many domestic matters, including education and slavery, to the states. And Byrd was right—with the campaigns for reelection beginning a new cycle in the spring of 1956, southern defenders of segregation had to get right with their white supremacist constituents to insure reelection, or they would be out-segged by

<hr />

28. Jack Bass, *Strom: The Complicated Personal and Political Life of Strom Thurmond* (New York: PublicAffairs Press, 2005), 162–65. An able account of the drafting appears in Day, *Southern Manifesto*.

their primary opponents (the primary being the real election in the one-party South).[29]

Thurmond was new to the Senate, but not to national politics (he was the founder of the short-lived "Dixiecrat" rebellion at the Democratic National Convention in 1948) or to the segregation cause. Born in the Edgefield District of secessionist ill-fame, he was educated in the law at his father's side and soon entered politics as a county attorney and later a judge. He served with distinction in World War II, was elected governor of South Carolina during the early stages of *Briggs*, and election to the U.S. Senate followed in 1954. In 1964 he would formally depart the party of his forebears and become a Republican. In this guise, he helped the Republicans deploy the Southern Strategy, a realignment of southern white voters that persists to this day. In 1954 he was a relative neophyte in Senate politics, the opposite of Byrd. But from the first days of his senatorial career, Thurmond was no shrinking violet. He had little use for the condescension of his seniors in the upper branch. "Brash, obstreperous and shrewd," he readily took a leading role in drafting the Southern Manifesto.[30]

For the centerpiece of the manifesto, Thurmond considered calling up the specter of nullification. Nullification was an extreme doctrine by which states could refuse to enforce an act of Congress. In milder form, Georgia had employed it (albeit without much theoretical justification) to refuse to obey the Supreme Court in *Chisholm v. Georgia* (1793) and *Worcester v. Georgia* (1832). Thurmond's first draft used the term "interposition," relying on the precedent of Thomas Jefferson's secretly drafted Kentucky Resolves of 1798. Interposition claimed the power of a sovereign state to interpose itself between its citizens and an unconstitutional act of Congress. Although some southern defenders of segregation, notably the *Richmond News Leader* editor James J. Kilpatrick, beat the drum for interposition, most of his editorial peers in the South thought the idea a nonstarter. Neither interposition nor nullification was accepted constitutional law in 1956, the Supremacy Clause of the Constitution having said and the Civil War having demonstrated graphically that states could not refuse to obey federal law.[31]

29. Numan V. Bartley, *The Rise of Massive Resistance: Race and Politics in the South during the 1950s* (Baton Rouge: Louisiana State University Press, 1999), 109; Day, *Southern Manifesto*, 66–67, 68.

30. Joseph Crespino, *Strom Thurmond's America* (New York: Hill and Wang, 2012), 102–3, 105–6.

31. Typescript draft marked "Thurmond" in Richard Russell's handwriting, February 2, 1956, Russell Collection, box 27, folio 9; Hustwit, *James J. Kilpatrick*, 65. The classic version of nullification was fashioned by Thomas Jefferson in his secretly drafted Kentucky Resolves of

Thurmond's first version of the document was the most virulent, but from its inception through its many revisions, the Declaration of Constitutional Principles was not on its face a political screed. Nor did it play upon blatant racism; quite the reverse: it was high-toned, measured, and legalistic, about as distant from Thurmond's own occasional race-baiting outbursts as one could get. Thurmond did not believe in racial equality as a matter of fact or of law. The intervention of Richard Russell was the crucial moderating next step. In more than one letter, Russell claimed to be the leader of the movement to resist. Throughout his leadership of the Southern Caucus from 1954 through 1964, he declined to express racial prejudice of a base kind, however. Instead, as he confided to one Georgia friend, on December 11, 1954, "it is very difficult for any lawyer to summon any great respect for the Supreme Court as it is presently constituted," and he proudly told another that "a small group of senators under my leadership has been able to prevent" civil rights legislation from passing. He was "sorely concerned about the sword hanging over the heads of the white people of the South." It made his "blood boil." But he claimed that his opposition was rooted in the "rights of individual states which were guaranteed us by our founding fathers." These he upheld against the "specious claims of the proponents of the vicious civil rights proposals."[32]

1798. In it, a state could interpose itself between its citizens and the federal government when Congress had violated the federal Constitution. See Peter Charles Hoffer, *The Free Press Crisis of 1800: Thomas Cooper's Trial for Seditious Libel* (Lawrence: University Press of Kansas, 2011), 56, 57–58, 62, 71, 119–20. It was extended to a congressional act that violated a state's theory of the constitutional division of powers in John C. Calhoun's Exposition and Protest of 1828 (the act in question, a tariff, was unquestionably within Congress's delegated powers, but Calhoun argued that the Constitution was a compact among sovereign states, and any one of those states could assert that sovereignty when its rights were violated). See Hoffer, *Uncivil Warriors*, 27–29. Free states had in effect tried to nullify the Fugitive Slave Act of 1850 with personal liberty laws, but when the Wisconsin Supreme Court ruled in favor of such a step, the U.S. Supreme Court voided the state's decision. See Ableman v. Booth, 62 U.S. 506 (1859); Hoffer, Hoffer, and Hull, *Federal Courts*, 139–41. The idea that Congress could nullify a U.S. Supreme Court decision was a novelty, however, until it was tried with the Religious Freedom Restoration Act of 1993, but the Supreme Court voided the act for overstepping the constitutional powers of Congress in City of Boerne v. Flores, 521 U.S. 507 (1997). See Carolyn N. Long, *Religious Freedom and Indian Rights: The Case of* Oregon v. Smith (Lawrence: University Press of Kansas, 2000), 227–50.

32. Russell to R. C. Carter, December 11, 1954, Russell Collection, box 21, folio 4; Russell to Mrs. Ruby Dobyns, July 24, 1956, Russell Collection, box 21, folio 2; Russell to Mrs. Lila Benton, July 31, 1956, Russell Collection, box 21, folio 2; Russell to Samuel Robbins, August 30, 1956, Russell Collection, box 21, folio 2; John G. Stewart, "The Civil Rights Act of 1964: Strategy," in *The Civil Rights Act of 1964: The Passage of the Law That Ended Racial Segregation*, ed. Robert D. Loevy (Albany: State University of New York Press, 1997), 201.

Russell was a master when it came to crushing civil rights initiatives, but his approach to that goal was far more calculating than Thurmond's. Thurmond would have made a superb courtroom lawyer in the mold of a Lincoln or a Robert Toombs. Russell was far more like Alexander Stephens, learned and passionate only when it served him. Russell's father was a lawyer and judge, and Russell himself graduated from the University of Georgia and its law school. As governor of his native state, and from 1933 to 1971 a senator, he was regarded as a progressive and a New Dealer. Were he from New York or Wisconsin, his views on race might have been different, but he shared the white supremacist views of his white constituents. He helped block civil rights legislation in Congress, although after the Civil Rights Act of 1964 passed, he urged compliance. He was never a Dixiecrat, like Thurmond, and he never became a Republican.[33]

Above all, Russell was a legalist, defending states' rights and opposing the extension of federal power in civil rights matters. He did not oppose the extension of federal largesse, for example, in the placement of military bases in Georgia, but he was most proud of his role in preventing the implementation of civil rights. At the beginning of March 1956, as chair of the committee to which all drafts and suggestions on this project were submitted, Russell took Thurmond's idea and made it into a legal document, much as a lawyer would take the claims of a client and turn them into a document for submission to a court.

Aiding and abetting Russell were John Stennis, a former prosecuting attorney and circuit judge, and North Carolina's Sam Ervin. Stennis hoped that an appearance of moderation would reduce criticism of the South, full well expecting that white Mississippi would never voluntarily desegregate its schools. "Practical segregation" required the acquiescence of black parents along with the leadership of white school authorities. Strident racism would undermine such local compliance. Ervin was distinguished by his fidelity to the Constitution, according to his later autobiography, and that, he recalled, forced him to object to judicial policy making. In December 1954, when the second "Red Scare" and the Cold War were at their height, he was outspoken in his criticism of his fellow senator Joseph McCarthy, a stance that required courage and commitment to constitutional civil liberties.[34]

33. Gilbert C. Fite, *Richard B. Russell, Jr., Senator from Georgia* (Chapel Hill: University of North Carolina Press, 1991), 241–42, 332–33; Day, *Southern Manifesto*, 77–78.

34. Day, *Southern Manifesto*, 79–80; Joseph Crespino, *In Search of Another Country: Mississippi and the Conservative Counterrevolution* (Princeton, NJ: Princeton University Press, 2007),

The Southern Caucus was, in fine, about as varied and experienced a legal team as one could assemble in defense of states' rights and white supremacy. The end result was a brilliant if brittle and curiously opaque argument, but then, if the Southern Caucus had reason to believe that the southern attorneys general had dropped the ball, they might conclude that they were the last line of defense of white supremacy.

The idea of a southern congressional manifesto was not new, though its precedent was a chilling one. On the evening of December 13, 1860, southern congressmen gathered at Mississippi House member Reuben Davis's boardinghouse and drafted a manifesto. It read:

> To our Constituents: The argument is exhausted. All hope of relief in the Union, through the agency of committees, Congressional legislation, or constitutional amendments, is extinguished, and we trust the South will not be deceived by appearances or the pretence of new guarantees. The Republicans are resolute in the purpose to grant nothing that will or ought to satisfy the South. We are satisfied [that] the honor, safety, and independence of the Southern people are to be found only in a Southern Confederacy—a result to be obtained only by separate State secession—and that the sole and primary aim of each slaveholding State ought to be its speedy and absolute separation from an unnatural and hostile Union.

Secession conventions in the southern states soon followed and voted their departure from the Union. Representatives from them, including the signatories of the manifesto, formed the Confederate States of America.[35]

The Declaration of Constitutional Principles, styled after the Declaration of Independence, aka the Southern Manifesto, was introduced on the Senate floor on March 12 by Senator George. In Russell's final version, incorporating comments and amendments from Ervin and Stennis, the manifesto took the form of a brief of the sort that amicus curiae (friends of the court) may offer when the Court hears a case rather than a decision of the Court, Thurmond's original format. A number of such briefs accompanied the briefs of the parties in *Brown* and its companion cases. Such briefs are admitted into the record by permission of the bench. The Richard Ervin brief for *Brown* II was a different matter, as the Court had explicitly invited the attorneys general to submit such briefs in answer to specific questions. Members of Congress

18–19; Paul R. Clancy, *Just a Country Lawyer: A Biography of Senator Sam Ervin* (Bloomington: Indiana University Press, 1974), 160–64.

35. Reuben Davis, "Southern Manifesto, December 13, 1860," in Edward McPherson, compiler, *A Political History of the United States during the Great Rebellion* (Washington, DC: Philp and Solomons, 1865), 37.

could, as amici, offer such briefs, but in a constitutional case of such gravity as *Brown*, the manifesto was extraordinary, recalling its 1860 precedent.[36]

The Southern Manifesto had a preamble that Senator George offered prior to reading the document. Such preambles may be boilerplate, but this one clearly indicated the purpose of the manifesto. It was that "the increasing gravity of the situation following the decision of the Supreme Court in the so-called segregation cases, and the peculiar stress in sections of the country where this decision has created many difficulties, unknown and unappreciated, perhaps, by many people residing in other parts of the country, have led some Senators and some Members of the House of Representatives to prepare a statement of the position which they have felt and now feel to be imperative." This was an example of the heckler's veto, the same men who drafted and signed the manifesto had either actively or indirectly contributed to the stress and difficulties which they now described. But in numbers they found comfort. "I now wish to present to the Senate a statement on behalf of 19 Senators, representing 11 States, and 77 House Members, representing a considerable number of States likewise."

George's list hid as well as revealed, for some moderates had to be persuaded, some radicals had to be talked down, and many of the signers had ideas that had to be incorporated. From its outset to its final passages, the document portrayed the signers as men well versed in law, arguing a legal position, seeking to promote law and order. The document asserted that the justices of the *Brown* Court had departed from settled law; that they had misread the Fourteenth Amendment; and that the Court had brought unsubstantiated allegations of fact into a decision that should have been based wholly on law. Ironically, the manifesto exhibited some of these characteristics itself. It rested on assumptions about the facts of race relations and the likelihood of disorder that were questionable and wholly one-sided. It read prior cases as though they were carved in stone instead of products of their time and place. It cast aspersions on the motives of the other parties and the justices themselves.

The document had no legal force because it was not passed by Congress, but as an expression of the pro-segregation southern legal stance, it merits close attention. The various drafts presented in the caucus were the work of

---

36. Russell Collection, box 27, folio 9, contains drafts and comments on drafts from Sam Ervin, Price Daniel, A. Willis Robertson, John Stennis, Russell himself, and the Price Daniel/J. William Fulbright/Spessard Holland/John Sparkman "revision." All were lawyers. Robertson was the only one to introduce the race issue directly, condemning "a few zealots interested primarily in racial amalgamation," a charge that had no basis in fact much less in law.

lawyers and bear the distinct features of able lawyering. What follows is a concordance of these views, emphasizing their legal aspects. The document was also a political, social, and cultural statement. The way in which these elements were interwoven with legal arguments is what makes the following discussion such an important summary of anti–civil rights lawyering.[37]

The central theme of the final version of the document was institutional and ideological: "The unwarranted decision of the Supreme Court in the public school cases is now bearing the fruit always produced when men substitute naked power for established law." By established law the drafters turned the clock back to the founding fathers, for the broadest foundation for segregation lay in its history. "The Founding Fathers gave us a Constitution of checks and balances because they realized the inescapable lesson of history that no man or group of men can be safely entrusted with unlimited power." A discourse on the founding fathers' Constitution, possibly the contribution of Sam Ervin, recalled a world in which slavery was not only legal, but protected by the federal Constitution. In 1956 slavery was no longer the law of the land, but only because, the manifesto suggested, an amendment to the Constitution had barred it. No mention was made of the Civil War, whose concluding act required ratification of the amendment by returning southern states. "They framed this Constitution with its provisions for change by amendment in order to secure the fundamentals of government against the dangers of temporary popular passion or the personal predilections of public officeholders." One notes how carefully Russell, Ervin, and Stennis had crafted this portion of the document to omit any mention of the role of slavery in that first Constitution, or how the slave South had argued in Court (*Dred Scott*, for example) and in Congress, for the constitutional basis for slavery. As Christopher Schmidt has rightly argued, "Constitutionalism had the benefit of shifting the lines of discussion . . . to a higher plane of discourse: the language of constitutional principles."[38]

The Reconstruction Amendments surely changed all that, but initially the manifesto did not mention the Thirteenth, Fourteenth, and Fifteenth Amendments. After all, the Thirteenth and Fourteenth were the basis of the plaintiff's case in *Plessy*, and on that occasion the Court found separate but equal a perfectly acceptable formula to fulfill the intent of Congress. The historical questions briefed by all sides in the winter of 1952–53 might be "inconclusive"

---

37. While certainly not in praise of the Southern Manifesto's purpose, see Justin Driver, "Supremacies and the Southern Manifesto," *Texas Law Review* 92 (2014): 1056–57, recognizing its significance and its representativeness.

38. Day, *Southern Manifesto*, 87; Schmidt, "Litigating," 1203.

as far as the Court was concerned, but the authors of the Southern Manifesto agreed with John Davis and South Carolina that the framers of the Four-teenth Amendment in Congress did not think it disallowed racially segregated schools. Nor did the states ratifying the amendment in 1868, shortly after the secretary of state sent it to the states.[39]

The manifesto continued with Russell's version of separation of powers: "We regard the decisions of the Supreme Court in the school cases as a clear abuse of judicial power." In a system of three coordinate and sometimes com-peting branches of the federal government, as well as a system of dual sover-eignty, there would always be some wiggle room in the claim of finality. At different times in American history, the executive and Congress had asserted primacy in interpreting the Constitution. For example, President Lincoln did this throughout the Civil War, and Congress did it throughout the New Deal, but if the high court was the final authority on the Constitution, as *Brown* and prior case law suggested, what impact, what authority, in law had a con-gressional resolution? Even were the Southern Caucus a majority of Congress, and it was not, and even if the Southern Manifesto's signatories were a major-ity of Congress, and they were not, would the document have had any au-thority as law? It might of course have been persuasive, as many dissents are, or even become a majority opinion, as some dissents, notably Justice John Marshall Harlan's and Justice Hugo Black's, became. Also true, in the checks-and-balances system, Congress could impeach, try, and remove all the mem-bers of the Supreme Court. The grounds for such impeachment were hardly clear, however, particularly because the Court had not transgressed its formal authority.

According to the manifesto, the Court had disregarded its own precedents. This was Davis's argument in *Brown*, and it was a potent one. But it was a losing argument. Students in law school classes often hear their instructors' caution: you can make that argument, but it's a loser. Still, the manifesto's authors per-sisted in it. The source of this portion of the manifesto was probably Price Daniel, who made the argument in a losing cause in *Sweatt*. He returned to it on the Senate floor in 1954, after his election to that body in 1952. In a May 18, 1954, speech to the Senate, he called separate but equal a truly wise policy as well as a well-established one. Three days later, he took the floor to urge

---

39. See the discussion in Alexander Tsesis, *We Shall Overcome: A History of Civil Rights and the Law* (New Haven, CT: Yale University Press, 2008), 253; Michael W. McConnell, "Originalism and the Desegregation Decisions," *Virginia Law Review* 81 (1995): 951–52 (finding that con-stitutional scholars who agree that *Brown* cannot rest on historical intent of the framers of the Fourteenth Amendment are mistaken).

local officials to work out arrangements that protected the interests of white parents, perhaps by making school districts reflect demographic patterns—housing segregation enabling school segregation in an eerie foretaste of white flight. He did not use racial epithets, in part because that was not his style. But the Court's about-face certainly had its own precedents, discarding *Adkins v. Children's Hospital* (1923) in *West Coast v. Parrish* (1937) and *Buck v. Bell* (1927) in *Skinner v. Oklahoma* (1942).[40]

The authors of the Southern Manifesto were not blind to the wider implications of the decision, no more so than were Warren and Frankfurter. In *Brown*, Chief Justice Warren had explained why the Court had departed from some of its rulings on segregation, but he quite strikingly did not overrule *Plessy*. Had he tried, he might have lost the unanimity that was so important to him. But *Plessy* was not exactly on point—it did not involve education. The original *Brown* decision confined itself to elementary public schools. But Court watchers understood that elementary public education was the first step toward the end of Jim Crow across the spectrum. Certainly the LDF lawyers thought so, and along with the signers of the manifesto, they were right. It was this prospect, as much as the ground lost to Jim Crow in elementary education, that made *Brown* so dangerous in the segregationists' eyes.[41]

But Warren's refusal to overrule *Plessy* did not undermine *Brown*. He did not have to justify his handling of precedent, because those precedents were the Court's own. In *Brown* the Court had cases before it on which it had jurisdiction. It heard arguments on them and then decided them. The only grounds for challenging the decision within established constitutional canon was the class-action nature of the certification. Because the cases were class actions, they applied to all state-mandated segregation of elementary schools. This, too, was a power (of classifying cases as class actions) that Congress had given to the Court when Congress approved the Federal Rules of Civil Procedure in 1938, along with its periodic later amendments. All of this meant that the manifesto's citation of *Plessy* was a losing argument.[42]

Russell knew this and added to the document an institutional component. In effect, he and his confreres were arguing "in the alternative." In modern

40. Price Daniel, address to the Senate, May 18 and May 21, 1954, 83rd Cong., 2nd sess., *Congressional Record*, 100: 6742, 6743, 6750.

41. See, e.g., Bruce Ackerman, "Concurring," in *What Brown Should Have Said*, ed. Balkin 119: "Education is not enough. The Constitution confers other privileges of national citizenship and extends its exigent demands for equal protection and due process into many other spheres of life."

42. On this grant in the Rules Enabling Act of 1934, see Hoffer, Hoffer, and Hull, *Federal Courts*, 301–10.

constitutional pleading, one does not have to rest one's case on a single strand of precedents or doctrine. One can even make conflicting and self-contradicting arguments, in the hope that one or more of them is a winner. Here Russell proposed a political science argument, that the decision allegedly "climaxes a trend in the Federal Judiciary undertaking to legislate, in derogation of the authority of Congress, and to encroach upon the reserved rights of the States and the people." Russell did not associate these rights with minority rights, the classical Madisonian version of the argument. Minority rights, he knew, typically meant black people's rights, and he regarded the rights of the majority—whites—as the rights that needed protection.[43]

Here, the rights of the people were actually the customs of the whites, and these were not national; they were sectional. In this sense, Russell was arguing the same sociology of the South as Richard Ervin and Ervin's predecessors. As Stennis and Sam Ervin offered suggestions, the document became a truly southern one, with Russell as its compiler rather than a sole author or editor. The manifesto also gained a patina of non-partisanship, accusing the Court rather than individual justices of seeking power, subverting the Constitution, and trampling on southern (whites') rights.

At this point, the manifesto began to shadow the *Brown* decision, adopting point by point Davis's argument in *Briggs v. Elliot*. The question was whether education, (presumably) left to the states by the original federal Constitution, was somehow nationalized by the Fourteenth Amendment. "The original Constitution does not mention education. Neither does the 14th Amendment nor any other amendment." The Court had asked the parties in *Brown* to research the debates surrounding the Fourteenth Amendment to see if legislative intent could supply what the text of the amendment omitted. Obviously, the latter was not going to itemize the activities of states that fell under the Due Process and Equal Protection Clauses. Congress might, but the provisions of the Civil Rights Act of 1875 that attempted to fill this gap were overturned by the Court in the *Civil Rights Cases* of 1883. The manifesto concluded, contrary to the Court in *Brown*, that "the debates preceding the submission of the 14th Amendment clearly show that there was no intent that it should affect the system of education maintained by the States." Obviously,

43. On James Madison's argument for minority rights' protection in the Constitution, see *Federalist*, no. 10, November 22, 1787, from which Russell might have argued in the manifesto, as he did in private correspondence, that the pro–civil rights forces were a faction, and factions were dangerous to the rights of a minority. "By a faction I understand a number of citizens, whether amounting to a majority or minority of the whole, who are united and actuated by some common impulse of passion, or of interest, adverse to the rights of other citizens, or to the permanent and aggregate interests of the community." *New York Packet*, Friday, November 23, 1787.

the authors could not ignore the Fourteenth Amendment forever. That would not be very good lawyering, but bringing it in as a negative drained it of significance. The manifesto also denied that the Jim Crow laws were the sort of "state action" to which the Court had later confined the amendment's reach.[44]

Further shadowing of the *Brown* I decision—based on the historical findings submitted by the attorneys general in their briefs in the summer and fall of 1954—followed. "The very Congress which proposed the amendment subsequently provided for segregated schools in the District of Columbia." This was the same attempt at legislative intent analysis as Davis and the other respondents' counsel attempted in the 1953 oral argument, and which the Court found inconclusive as evidence of congressional intent. The manifesto did not offer alternative facts; it merely interpreted which historical facts were relevant. "When the amendment was adopted in 1868, there were 37 States of the Union. . . . Every one of the 26 States that had any substantial racial differences among its people, either approved the operation of segregated schools already in existence or subsequently established such schools by action of the same law-making body which considered the 14th Amendment." In other words, when there was a significant black population, a kind of critical mass, the state governments and their agencies adopted a regime of racial segregation. In a sense, this argument was circular, claiming that existence of segregation was a legal basis for segregation when the question was whether segregation was legal at all. Whatever the logical strength of the argument, as history it was plausible. The assumption was that former slaves, newly emancipated by the Thirteenth Amendment, did not attend schools, period, except where these were created for them after the war.

The legal fact of segregation Russell then folded into the historical fact of segregation. "As admitted by the Supreme Court in the public school case (*Brown* v. *Board of Education*)," the doctrine of separate but equal schools "apparently originated in *Roberts* v. *City of Boston* (1849), upholding school segregation against attack as being violative of a State constitutional guarantee of equality." This constitutional doctrine began in the North, not in the South, and it was followed not only in Massachusetts, but in Connecticut, New York, Illinois, Indiana, Michigan, Minnesota, New Jersey, Ohio, Pennsylvania, and other northern states until they, exercising their rights as states through the constitutional processes of local self-government, changed their school systems. "In the case of *Plessy* v. *Ferguson* in 1896 the Supreme Court expressly declared that under the 14th Amendment no person was denied any

---

44. On the continuing debate over this, see Stephen G. Calabresi and Michael W. Perl, "Originalism and *Brown v. Board of Education*," *Michigan State Law Review* (2014): 429–571.

of his rights if the States provided separate but equal facilities. This decision
has been followed in many other cases." There was no doubt that the Court
in 1896 had accepted, if not supported, school segregation.

Whether or not formal legal arrangements—in particular constitutional
interpretations, dictate habits, traditions, and ways of life—belonged here is
a subject resistant to generalization. Insofar as these top-down rules affect
ordinary people's conduct, they usually reflect what already exists. That is,
the law follows custom. Jim Crow was based on law, was imposed on a largely
disempowered minority, and was maintained by violence (lynching, for example) as well as by law. The Southern Manifesto's sociological theory was
the antithesis of the sociological theory in *Brown*, proving that the manifesto's
authors' dismissal of the social science in *Brown* did not deter them from
resorting to social factoids when these supported their views. "This interpretation, restated time and again, became a part of the life of the people of
many of the States and confirmed their habits, traditions, and way of life. It is
founded on elemental humanity and commonsense, for parents should not
be deprived by Government of the right to direct the lives and education of
their own children." The invocation of both local autonomy and tradition
was not especially southern. One could find it in the customs and culture of
the many regions of the nation. It often elided the suppression of minorities,
however, as the "life of the people" was not inclusive and diverse, but exclu-
sive and homogenous. The opposite view was characteristic of urban localities, where many different cultures met. The South, however, was at this time
still not heavily urbanized and, more important, its politics remained a rural
character.

The manifesto then returned to the thesis that only through explicit amendment could segregation be dismantled, understanding that no such amendment could gain the three-fourths majority necessary for ratification. "Though
there has been no constitutional amendment or act of Congress changing
this established legal principle almost a century old, the Supreme Court of the
United States, with no legal basis for such action, undertook to exercise their
naked judicial power and substituted their personal political and social ideas
for the established law of the land." This was the closest that the manifesto
came to revealing the strong personal animus that Russell felt toward Warren
and the Court. There was a pervasive sense of defensiveness in the document,
a sense that defended a South under attack by outside forces. Stennis's original draft insisted that there was "no political, moral, or legal basis for such
action, except the naked power of nine men." Russell muted the absolutism of
the language to read "no constitutional amendment or Act of Congress" but
left in the "naked power of nine men."

Was this a conspiracy against the South by outsiders? On the Court when *Brown* was first heard, Black was from Alabama, Clark was from Texas, and Vinson and Reed were from Kentucky, but Vinson was replaced by Warren, and the rest of the Court were from northern states. Perhaps more important, the litigants, the black schoolchildren of Virginia and South Carolina, were just as southern as Russell. The sense in which the black citizens of the South were made invisible by segregation (literally as well as figuratively) was a fact that Russell and his peers could not ignore. "This unwarranted exercise of power by the Court, contrary to the Constitution, is creating chaos and confusion in the States principally affected. It is destroying the amicable relations between the white and Negro races that have been created through 90 years of patient effort by the good people of both races. It has planted hatred and suspicion where there has been heretofore friendship and understanding." In fact, this peace between the races was not entirely amicable, for neither side was easy in it, and the violence that one side imposed on the other, along with the police regime that actually condoned the violence, and occasionally took part in it, gave the lie to the notion that friendship and understanding underlay Jim Crow. One thus has to ask if the authors of the manifesto came to the table with "clean hands." When one wants a court to do equity, one has to prove that one is not guilty of offenses against the peace. Russell knew all about the lynchings, including those not far from his home outside of Athens.[45]

The manifesto sounded the alarm that outside agitators would be responsible if disorder erupted because of desegregation. "Without regard to the consent of the governed, outside mediators are threatening immediate and revolutionary changes in our public schools systems. If done, this is certain to destroy the system of public education in some of the States." The manifesto's peroration was a call to action against "the explosive and dangerous condition created by this decision and inflamed by outside meddlers." It consisted of a series of three bullet points: "We reaffirm our reliance on the Constitution as the fundamental law of the land. We decry the Supreme Court's encroachment on the rights reserved to the States and to the people, contrary to established law, and to the Constitution." But "we commend the motives of those States which have declared the intention to resist forced integration by any lawful means." Finally, a warning to the North: "We appeal to the States

45. See, e.g., George C. Wright, "Growing Up Segregated," in *Understanding the Little Rock Crisis: An Exercise in Remembrance and Reconciliation*, ed. Elizabeth Jacoway and C. Fred Williams (Fayetteville: University of Arkansas Press, 1999), 45–46; Clarence L. Mohr, "General Introduction," in *New Encyclopedia of the South*, ed. Clarence L. Mohr (Chapel Hill: University of North Carolina Press, 2011), 17: 21–22.

and people who are not directly affected by these decisions to consider the
constitutional principles involved against the time when they too, on issues
vital to them may be the victims of judicial encroachment." Many of these
points resonated with the states' rights language of the nineteenth century—
for example, Russell's own belief that "a solemn protest by a sovereign state
of the invasion of its rights and powers by federal government" was fully con-
sonant with American constitutional law. Other inclusions reflected an even
earlier version of constitutional thinking, in particular, "the substitution of a
government of men for established law," a version of John Adams's aphorism
"a government of laws, and not of men"[46]

The final lines had, if not fully intended, something of a concession that
the South did not represent the rest of the nation. "Even though we constitute
a minority in the present Congress, we have full faith that a majority of the
American people believe in the dual system of government which has enabled us to achieve our greatness and will in time demand that the reserved
rights of the States and of the people be made secure against judicial usurpa-
tion." Leave us alone, it pled. "We pledge ourselves to use all lawful means to
bring about a reversal of this decision which is contrary to the Constitution
and to prevent the use of force in its implementation." The unreality of this
penultimate prescription was itself suggestive of facts not at hand. No force
had been assayed in the effort to end segregation. No federal troops or marshals appeared at the doors of southern schools. In fact, just the opposite had
occurred. The Court had left implementation in the hands of district federal
judges, whose opinions in many cases mirrored those of the school officials
involved. With the exception of some border states, the speed of desegregation had been so deliberate as to amount to judicially enabled delay. Why then
the reference to the use of force?

The answer lay in history, or rather the manifesto authors' perception of
history. Reconstruction was very much alive in the minds of pro-segregation
leaders. They understood that Jim Crow was part of the redemption of the
South, and that it was only possible when federal troops were removed from
the former Confederate states in 1877. William Faulkner's much-repeated adage that the past is never dead, it's not even past was true of the South. The
Southern Manifesto can thus be read as a response to a "second" Reconstruction as much as to *Brown*.[47]

46. John Adams, in his draft for the Massachusetts Constitution, 1780, in *Works of John Adams*, ed. Charles Francis Adams (Boston: Little, Brown, 1851), 4:230.

47. On civil rights movement as a "second" Reconstruction, a term introduced by C. Vann Woodward in the 1960s, see J. Morgan Kousser, *Colorblind Injustice: Minority Voting Rights*

Hence the deeper meaning of the final lines, written first by Thurmond, then modified by Russell, that captured the ideal of a separate South shared by all of the draftsmen and signers: "In this trying period, as we all seek to right this wrong, we appeal to our people not to be provoked by the agitators and troublemakers invading our States and to scrupulously refrain from disorder and lawless acts." In 1956 there were no "agitators and troublemakers" infiltrating the South. Freedom riders and federal voter registrars were five years in the future, and federal troops would appear in Little Rock in 1957. Rather, it was the shame of the Lost Cause and the anxiety of the unfinished revolution of Reconstruction that infused the manifesto and energized the drive to resist desegregation.

If the manifesto is any indication, the southern anti–civil rights lawyers looked to the past, just as the civil rights lawyers of the LDF looked to the future. But the invocation, repeated throughout the former, was one of "lawful means," not a call to nullification or interposition, although these were the very terms that earlier drafts, particularly those Thurmond crafted, deployed. Russell prudently edited these terms out of the final version, recognizing that they had been steps toward secession.

Lawful means was a creative, lawyerly answer to the deeply imbedded idea of the problem South. Neither conveniently altered memories nor aggressive depictions of the southernness of the framers of the Constitution and of the early nation could erase the fact that the South had problems in the aftermath of the Civil War. Was not making war on the U.S., if not secession itself, an act of treason? Many in the North still regarded it so in 1956, as veterans in blue had regarded it after 1865. Attempts to employ the rituals of reconciliation (veterans on both sides shaking hands across the stone wall at Cemetery Hill, for example) made for popular images of reconciliation, but could not quiet the lingering notion that the South was the problem child of the reunified nation. Poverty (demonstrated by the Public Works Administration's photographic tours of the rural South in the 1930s), diseases peculiar to the South like pellagra and hookworm, and widely circulated photographs of lynching (a popular southern postcard industry) undermined the South's vaunted white supremacy. The Lost Cause and Jim Crow segregation were inseparable because without Jim Crow the Lost Cause was finally lost, along with it the white South's claim to superiority. No one knew or felt this more

---

and the Undoing of the Second Reconstruction (Chapel Hill: University of North Carolina Press, 2000), 2ff. Kousser was Woodward's student at Yale. Faulkner's adage appeared in his *Requiem for a Nun* (1950; repr., New York: Vintage, 2013), 73.

keenly than men who supposedly represented the best in the white South, like Russell.[48]

The draft returned to the committee, and then to the Southern Caucus on March 1. As copies circulated to members of the caucus, some weighed in with calls for moderating the language, while others wanted to rewrite portions of the document themselves. As unity was of utmost importance, again a shadow version of Warren's efforts to promote unanimity on the *Brown* Court, overt racism was removed. A new version, the one published and seen in public, resulted, although Russell later insisted that the changes to his document were "only cosmetic." Even the so-called moderates supported the continuation of separate school systems. In later years, individual members of the caucus backtracked, trying to portray themselves as reluctant defenders of the status quo, or advocates of gradualism, though the historical evidence does not support anything like this backpedaling.[49]

Thurmond was the first to take the floor of the Senate to defend the Southern Manifesto, given time to expound on it by Majority Leader Lyndon Johnson of Texas. Johnson understood both the mandate of civil rights, a mandate too long waiting for congressional imprimatur in his personal opinion, and the language of his southern peers, who regarded the civil rights leaders and activists as little more than outside agitators and borderline subversives. Thurmond proclaimed the presentation of the manifesto on the Senate floor to be a "historic event" and called for support from "all the people who love the Constitution." He and the other signers wanted above all to "avoid any disruption of the harmony which has existed for generations between the white and Negro races . . . by outside agitators." Looking ahead to inevitable civil rights initiatives in the Congress, he warned against "disregard for established doctrine," although the established doctrine was now *Brown*. But that doctrine was merely "legislation by judicial decree" and so did not count. His final comment reflected once more the pervasive defensiveness that had run through the entire drafting process, and perhaps went all the way back to the Lost Cause. For "the white people of the South are the greatest minority in this nation."[50]

48. Brian Matthew Jordan, *Marching Home: Union Veterans and Their Unending Civil War* (New York: Norton, 2014), 100; David W. Blight, *Race and Reunion: The Civil War in American Memory* (Cambridge, MA: Harvard University Press, 2001), 286, 356; W. Fitzhugh Brundage, *The Southern Past: A Clash of Race and Memory* (Cambridge, MA: Harvard University Press, 2005), 9–10, 272–74.

49. Day, *Southern Manifesto*, 97–98.

50. Laura Kalman, *The Long Reach of the Sixties: LBJ, Nixon, and the Making of the Contemporary Supreme Court* (New York: Oxford University Press, 2017), 9, 10, 16 (Johnson straddles); Robert M. Caro, *The Years of Lyndon Johnson IV: The Passage of Power* (New York: Knopf, 2012),

Collective lawyering by anti–civil rights counsel differed from the strategizing and preparation of the LDF lawyers in *Sweatt* and *Brown* I and II. The LDF team was filled with strong personalities, but it had a leader in Marshall and a common goal. The Southern Caucus had many would-be leading counsels, and though Russell, Stennis, Ervin, and Thurmond were not running against one another, they were not disposed to let any of their number dictate to the others (though each thought that he was the leader of the others). Thus the Southern Manifesto read like a compilation rather than a brief, indulged in personal accusations (without naming names to be sure), and bounced back and forth between calls for resistance and pleas to keep order. It was not incoherent, but neither was it as powerful as a single author's work might have been.

What further undercut its force as a legal argument was the way that it was perceived from its inception. Russell insisted and his coauthors agreed to moderation in tone and careful parsing of argument. Their reputation as statesmen and their professionalism as lawyers were at stake. But these same qualities of tone and argument were dysfunctional in profound ways. Charles Fairman—a conservative law professor whose credentials as a legal historian were excellent (having just finished a definitive history of the Civil War and Reconstruction Era Courts for the Oliver Wendell Holmes Jr. Devise)—was asked by the *Harvard Law Review* editors to write the foreword to the Court's 1956 coming term. He focused his essay on the "Attack on the Segregation Cases" under way in Congress, and from the outset made clear that the attack's use of history was flawed. "Without restraint," southern members of Congress reasserted old and discarded versions of "states' rights" doctrine, a "delicate" historical subject was mangled in the rush to reargue *Brown* on the floor of Congress. In the end, however, it was the "ultimate spiritual values" that the *Brown* Court upheld, that mattered most to Fairman. In effect, his article was an answer to Vinson's hesitation rather than the manifesto, though Fairman clearly wanted a "calm" to prevail and the Court to be free from the caterwauling of its critics. A document meant to be high-sounding, to Fairman and other intellectuals seemed little more than losers' sour grapes.[51]

Fairman found the manifesto wanting in its lack of respect to a coordinate federal government institution. Other critics saw it as a failed lament for white supremacy. White supremacy is a powerful prejudice that has survived

---

76 (Johnson courts Russell but looks for black votes); Strom Thurmond, speech in the Senate, March 12, 1956, *Congressional Record*, 84th Cong., 2nd sess., 3949–3950.

    51. Charles Fairman, "The Attack on the Segregation Cases," *Harvard Law Review* 70 (1956): 83, 85, 87, 92, 94.

civil rights drives, the liberalization of the academy, and the election of an African American to the nation's highest office. Indeed, in the subsequent years, it resurfaced in a successful presidential campaign and as a theme in the administration of the Donald Trump presidency. The better angels of our nature as a people do not allow us to accept the supremacy of any race, ethnicity, or color. However, insofar as the Southern Manifesto was directed to southern white audiences, it hardly needed more than a few code words to evoke white supremacist sympathy, and for the same reason it was hardly news. It may have received wide attention and general support, but massive resistance was already well under way. Indeed, some politicians in the Deep South were calling for the impeachment of the justices and the nullification of the decision. Insofar as it was directed to northern audiences, the manifesto's relative moderation on race might have concealed its true purpose. There is little evidence that the manifesto changed anyone's minds in the North, although some civil rights leaders, including A. Philip Randolph, were worried that it had. Thus moderation—though rigorously self-imposed by lawyers like Russell, thinking of the manifesto as a legal document—actually weakened its force.[52]

Last but hardly least, the manifesto failed as a legal document. The arguments of both sides in the graduate school cases and *Brown* were clearly legal. They were presented in courts, to judges, and the parties accepted the courts' decisions or appealed to higher courts. As former attorney general Herbert Brownell wrote in response to the manifesto, "Every contention which the Manifesto asserts was treated in lengthy briefs and carefully considered by the Court. It would be superfluous to add to what was so eloquently and persuasively said by the Court." Of course, Brownell was a party at interest, as the federal government was friend of the court on the appellants' side. As he hinted, the manifesto should have been read as a political statement rather than a legal brief. In the Deep South, it was cheered by political leaders as a statement of their resolve and offered to their voters as a political platform. Individual signers thought that their political future depended on where they stood on it. Southern newspapers recognized this. Even those few editorial writers who supported some version of desegregation conceded that

52. C. Vann Woodward, "The 'New Reconstruction' in the South: Desegregation in Historical Perspective," *Commentary*, June 1, 1956 (a response to the manifesto); Andrew Edmund Kersten, *A. Philip Randolph: A Life in the Vanguard* (Lanham, MD: Rowman and Littlefield, 2007), 94; Simon Hall, *1956: The World in Revolt* (New York: Pegasus, 2016), 72–73 (white supremacy well understood by white southerners); Paul Oberst, "The Supreme Court and States' Rights," *Kentucky Law Journal* 48 (1959): 73; Driver, "Supremacies," citations at 1070–71. Note that Driver disagrees with the authors he cites and claims that the manifesto was aimed at non-southern audiences. Whether this is true or not, its white supremacist foundation was clear.

the Caucus members supported the Court only when they thought it was right for them—in other words, when its politics were theirs. In the North it was decried for the same reasons. Perhaps most damaging, the manifesto was never fully or truly validated by any court in the nation. And that is where the next stage of lawyering would be taking place.[53]

For if the defenders of segregation wanted to keep the end of Jim Crow at bay, they must find ways to win in the district courts of the South. Did they have a chance to win? No. But they had a chance to delay the inevitable for generations, and to that goal they directed their energies.

53. Herbert Brownell, "The United States Supreme Court: Symbol of Orderly, Stable and Just Government," *American Bar Association Journal* 43 (1957): 538; Jay Jenkins, "Vote Margins a Show of Strength—Those Who Failed to Sign Manifesto Turned Out of Office by Tar Heels," *Atlanta Constitution*, June 3, 1956, 5E; Roscoe Drummond, "Southern Manifesto Ignores Precedent," *Atlanta Constitution*, March 19, 1956, 4; Anthony Badger, "The South Confronts the Court: The Southern Manifesto of 1956," in *The Constitution and Political Policy in U.S. History*, ed. Julian E. Zelizer and Bruce J. Schulman (University Park: Pennsylvania State University Press, 2009), 127–42; Day, *Southern Manifesto*, 97–107.

4

They Had a Dream

Martin Luther King Jr.'s 1963 invocation of a dream in which sons of the former slaves and sons of the former masters would sit down at the same table as equals would have made a fitting conclusion to the struggle for desegregation. If it had happened, the table might have sat in the well of a federal courtroom. A flood of civil rights cases came to federal district and courts of appeals in the Fifth, Eighth, and Tenth Circuits in this period. The relief promised in *Brown* II required the good-faith efforts of public school boards and local and state officials. Federal district court judges, charged with managing enforcement of the *Brown* decision, had an array of equitable powers to insure compliance. The principal weapon was the injunction, which parties ignore at peril of contempt citations, fines, and incarceration.[1]

The transition to a unitary school system could have gone relatively smoothly. The goal was clear. But the spirit of many localities, led by pro-segregation politicians and abetted by anti–civil rights lawyering, was unwilling. In their New York City headquarters, the LDF was frustrated at the snail's pace of change, perhaps watching the way that the city's school board delayed implementation of the decision in *Brown* II. In 1960 long years of litigation lay ahead for desegregation forces, inevitable in light of the stance of the Court in *Brown* II that individual judges must hear and determine individual cases in their districts, taking local considerations into account.[2]

---

1. Portions of this chapter were taken from Hoffer, Hoffer, and Hull, *Federal Courts*, 365–92. Permission to reuse (with changes) from Oxford University Press is gratefully acknowledged.

2. Brown v. Board of Education, 349 U.S. 294 (1955); Klarman, *Jim Crow*, 316; Christopher W. Schmidt, *The Sit-Ins: Protest and Legal Change in the Civil Rights Era* (Chicago: University of

Was an alternative to *Brown* II possible—that is, could the Court have concluded its original decision with the order that it be implemented in every state and public school system that was segregated by law? Analysis of the thinking of several of the justices, including both those who felt strongly that Jim Crow was wrong and those who vacillated, shows that Chief Justice Warren would have been hard put to get unanimity without the promise that the conditions in different districts would be given a fair hearing. The result was another round of argument and another decision. That year's delay may have been sufficient for massive resistance to gain momentum. What is more, it is not clear who would monitor compliance were it not the district courts, and if they were given the task, that they would have been as willing to countenance delay as some turned out to be. After all, the inferior courts were created as part of the federalist compromises of the founding era, and that meant that local interests and conditions would influence the judgments of district courts. Added to which, the district court judges were almost always drawn from the local bar and brought with them to the federal bench the attitudes and sympathies of the local power structure—a Jim Crow power structure.[3]

Nevertheless, after *Brown* II, plaintiffs in the federal courts chipped away at the massive resistance of the segregationist South. Lower federal court judges there did not always press hard for good-faith compliance with *Brown* II. Federal judges are lawyers. With only a few exceptions, they practiced law before they were called to the bench. Most, but not all, practiced in the district on whose bench they would sit. As advocates for clients, they saw the law from their clients' point of view. As judges, their perspective had to be broader. Judging has been the subject of much commentary from those on and off the bench from the time that courts first appeared. Moses and Caesar had their critics and champions. In more recent years, judges have written elegantly of the process. The classic essay was New York Court of Appeals judge Benjamin Cardozo's 1920 Storrs Lectures at Yale, later published as *The Judicial Process*, wherein he lifted the veil of formalist jurisprudence to reveal that "the work of deciding cases goes on every day in hundreds of courts throughout the land. Any judge, one might suppose, would find it easy to describe the process which he had followed a thousand times and more. Nothing could be farther from the truth. Let some intelligent layman ask him to explain: he will not go very far before taking refuge in the excuse that the

Chicago Press, 2018), 48–49; Jeanne Theoharris, *A More Beautiful and Terrible History: The Uses and Misuses of Civil Rights History* (Boston: Beacon, 2018), 37.

3. Hoffer, Hoffer, and Hull, *Federal Courts*, 34–40 (compromises to lawsuit local interests in Judiciary Act of 1789).

language of craftsmen is unintelligible to those untutored in the craft. Such an excuse may cover with a semblance of respectability an otherwise ignominious retreat. It will hardly serve to still the pricks of curiosity and conscience." In fact, the judge looked at the legal precedents, the black letter law (statutes and codes), and then, though s/he might not be as free as Cardozo to admit it, introduced the times and place, along with the judge's own values and experience. For law in hard cases was not found on the walls of some Platonic cave. "Within the confines of these open spaces and those of precedent and tradition, choice moves with a freedom which stamps its action as creative. The law which is the resulting product is not found, but made. The process, being legislative, demands the legislator's wisdom." Federal judge Richard Posner, who has studied Cardozo's own judging, added that "what is reasonable or sensible will often depend on moral feelings, common sense, sympathies, and other ingredients of thought and feeling." The law does not "make" the judge do anything, although in some cases the law is so clear and the case so easy that it may seem so. The desegregation cases were anything but clear and easy, however, as Warren explained in *Brown* II.[4]

Open defiance to the courts of appeals in their circuit or the Supreme Court is rare for district judges, but it did happen in the school cases. The vast majority of district judges came from the region in which they sat, shared its values, and valued its customs. Southern whites opposed to desegregation expected southern federal district judges to share their views and slow if not stop the process of desegregation. For most of these judges, it was genuinely hard to take a wrecking ball to the well-mortised wall of segregation. If they did, they faced ostracism from their own social set and threats of violence from segregationist vigilantes, as had Judge Waring. All knew what none would say: Jim Crow was a social system as well as a legal one, designed to keep the black minority in its place—at the bottom of society. Some even actively denounced *Brown*. Judge Timmerman of South Carolina, for example, openly condemned the NAACP for spreading "poisonous propaganda," but then he was defending the state's governor, his son.[5]

4. Benjamin Cardozo, *The Judicial Process* (New Haven, CT: Yale University Press, 1922), 9, 115; Richard Posner, *Reflections on Judging* (Cambridge, MA: Harvard University Press, 2013), 4, 6.

5. Peltason, *Lonely Men*, 4–5, 8, 9, 10; Charles L. Black Jr., "The Lawfulness of the Segregation Decisions," *Yale Law Journal* 69 (1960): 421–30. This point is not limited to civil rights litigation, although it provided the most numerous examples of what may be called district court judicial nullification. See, e.g., Chad Westerland, Jeffrey A. Segal, Lee Epstein, Charles M. Cameron, and Scott Comparato, "Strategic Defiance and Compliance in the U.S. Courts of Appeals," *American*

In a number of cases, federal judges in southern judicial districts approved local plans featuring delay in their implementation. Sometimes the delay poorly camouflaged the local board's intention to resist desegregation. Rarely, it also openly revealed a similarity of outlook between the judges and the school authorities. Perhaps the overriding motivation for these judges was not localism or racism, so much as a conservative judicial philosophy. They simply doubted that courts were the best engines for fundamental social change. In 1957 the Dade County (Miami) School Board had no desire to desegregate its schools. District court judge Joseph Patrick Lieb refused to force it to comply. According to Judge Lieb, "It is deemed by the Board that the best interest of the pupils and the orderly and efficient administration of the school system can best be preserved if the registration and attendance of pupils entering school commencing the current school term remains unchanged. . . . [U]ntil further notice the free public school system of Dade County will continue to be operated, maintained and conducted on a nonintegrated basis." Black parents brought a lawsuit. The judge found no grounds in the lawsuit for his court to order the school board to act. The Court of Appeals for the Fifth Circuit reversed and remanded. The state came up with a complicated pupil placement plan that required individual parents to petition the board for placement of their student in a particular school. Individual school boards then delayed ruling on the petitions. The parents again turned to the district court, and Judge Lieb found the pupil placement plans were an adequate remedy. "The Court finds that the Florida Pupil Assignment Law enacted by the Legislature of Florida since the filing of this lawsuit meets the requirements of such a plan and the demands of the plaintiffs. . . . No reference whatever is made in the Act to consideration of race or color of the pupils." Again the Fifth Circuit reversed and remanded.[6]

What was Judge Lieb's thinking? Sometimes historians infer a jurist's motivations in a particular case by probing his or her own memoirs, along with

---

Journal of Political Science 54 (2010): 891–905; Charles A. Johnson, "Law, Politics, and Judicial Decision Making: Lower Federal Court Uses of Supreme Court Decisions," *Law and Society Review* 21 (1987): 325–40.

6. Gibson v. Board of Public Instruction, 246 F.2d 913, 915 (5th Cir. 1957); Gibson v. Board of Public Instruction, 170 F. Supp. 454, 457 (D.C. S.D. Fla. 1958) (Lieb, J.); Gibson v. Board of Public Instruction, 272 F.2d 763 (5th Cir. 1959). On the judge who refuses to follow the dictates of the higher court, see, e.g., Jeffrey Brand-Ballard, *The Limits of Legality: The Ethics of Lawless Judging* (New York: Oxford University Press, 2010), 3–11. In this case, one cannot presume that Lieb misunderstood the precedent. He simply thought it wrong and refused to follow it.

candid interviews, oral histories, or personal papers of a more general nature. Lieb left little of this. A single notice in the digital collection at the University of South Florida depicts a small bear of a man who left St. Paul, Minnesota, to gain a law degree at Georgetown, and in Washington, D.C., almost immediately entered government service with the FBI, followed by a long stint as an assistant U.S. attorney in Miami. In Tampa, he married and settled into a private law practice. To his "Irish good humor" and his gentlemanly ways, he added a prodigious taste for hard work, both in his practice and later as a judge. Unlike many who traveled this course, he was not a Democrat, but neither was he, like Parker and Timmerman, born and bred in Jim Crow. Had he had grown to sympathize with the dominant ways of his adopted home? Had the political and legal establishment in south Florida, its lawyers standing before him in court representing the segregated school districts, made him one of their own after Eisenhower chose him for the district court in 1955? Was it social acclimatization, a natural conservatism, or some other reason that he denied petitioners' pleas in both Dade County cases? Lieb's opinion was rooted in the narrowest of readings of the command "all deliberate speed" in *Brown* II. It was deferential to state laws clearly intended to delay or deny desegregation. He was not deterred when the Fifth Circuit overturned his decisions in increasingly stentorian language. In 1962, he was redeployed to the newly created Middle District of Florida, and there, with the Kennedy administration's Department of Justice and the Court of Appeals watching over his shoulder, he ordered integration of the schools notwithstanding the Florida pupil placement laws.[7]

The step-by-step plans many Deep South school boards adopted to delay actual desegregation passed muster in more than just Lieb's court. Indeed, they were acceptable to what may now seem to be a surprising number of district court judges. In one Georgia case, district judge Frank A. Hooper not only allowed the Atlanta school board an additional two years to put a twelve-year plan in place, he told the LDF attorney for the petitioners, Constance Baker Motley, that he put as much stress on the "deliberate" as on the "speed" in *Brown* II. Motley regarded him as a "conservative" judge, but his deference to the Atlanta school board was as much social (he and they came from the same schools, neighborhoods, and social set) as legal. Hooper was

7. Morison Buck, "Joseph P. Lieb: Gentleman, Gentle Judge," 1-1-1990, Digital Collection, Florida Studies Center Publications. Lieb was a well-known conservative. Thomas Tobin, "Where Are They Now?" *St. Petersburg, Tampa Bay Times*, May 21, 2003, sptimes.com/2003/05/21/Tampabay/Where_are_they_now.shtml.

a close friend of Richard Russell, and out-of-doors suggested that he had no problem with gradualism.[8]

But Hooper was no pushover for segregationists. He ordered the desegregation of his home city's parks, buses, and hospitals, and he told future governor Lester Maddox that he was in contempt of court when he refused to allow black folks to eat at his Pickrick Cafeteria in Atlanta. Though in 1957 he dismissed Horace Ward's application for admission to the University of Georgia School of Law (Ward had applied in 1950 and dropped the suit, was then enrolled at Northwestern School of Law, and would join Hooper on the federal bench some years later), Hooper made clear that "it is now well established that the authorities in control of the operation of any state-supported law school in this country may not refuse admission to any person solely on account of race and color." Hooper would later order the University of Georgia to admit black students.[9]

What was Hooper's thinking? He was born in Americus, Georgia, went to Georgia Tech, and received his law degree from Atlanta Law School, after which he clerked for Walter F. George in the state's court of appeals. He then served in the state House of Representatives, on the court of appeals, and taught law at his alma mater. Truman appointed him to the federal bench in 1949. Hooper's conservatism was a matter of style and personal commitment. No one was going to push him faster than he wanted to go, but when push came to shove, Hooper was not going to let anyone disobey the U.S. Supreme Court, including Governor Vandiver (who threatened to shut down all the public schools rather than obey *Brown*) or the state's legislature when they threatened to do what Vandiver could not (they changed the Georgia flag to include the stars and bars of the Confederacy instead).[10]

One could find, thus, a certain picaresque quality in Hooper's ruling in the Atlanta school cases. He opined, "This Court is under no duty, nor does it have the power, to order integration, but it is compelled to enjoin racial discrimination. It is not the function of the Court to suggest to defendants how such discrimination can best be eliminated, but the plan must originate with the defendants and be submitted to the Court for approval." There was

8. Constance Baker Motley, *Equal Justice under Law: An Autobiography* (New York: Farrar, 1999), 143; Peltason, *Lonely Men*, 131–32.

9. Ward v. Regents of Georgia University System, 191 F. Supp. 491, 492 (1957) (Hooper, J.).

10. Brown-Nagin, *Courage to Dissent*, 312–13; Kevin Michael Kruse, *White Flight: Atlanta and the Making of Modern Conservatism* (Princeton, NJ: Princeton University Press, 2005), 228; Charles Zelden, *Thurgood Marshall: Race, Rights, and the Struggle for a More Perfect Union* (New York: Routledge, 2013), 98–99.

deference to the local board, but in addition, there was deference to a kind of thinking about courts and change. "Nothing said by the Court during the trial of this case was intended to be an expression of opinion by the Court as to the plan, but the Court did assume, and now assumes, that any plan submitted would contemplate a gradual process, which would contemplate a careful screening of each applicant to determine his or her fitness to enter the school to which application is made." When faced with the prospect that the state government would prefer to shut down the schools than desegregate them, however, he wrote: "It was and is, the feeling of the Court that the people of Georgia through their chosen representatives in the Legislature should be allowed to make the important decision as to whether they would prefer the closing of their schools on one hand, to the gradual desegregation of the schools on the other hand, pursuant to the Plan under consideration."[11]

Not every southern-born and -bred district court judge had Hooper's wry sense of humor or his recognition of the inevitability of change in southern life after *Brown*. The Louisiana Parish school boards were recalcitrant when it came to desegregation, and efforts by the Fifth Circuit to mandate effective desegregation ran into opposition not only from the local officials, but from one of the district judges. In *Hall v. West* (1964), Fifth Circuit Court of Appeals judge John Minor Wisdom admonished the lower court judge Elmer Gordon West for a "startling, if not shocking, lack of appreciation of the clear pronouncements of the Supreme Court and this Court during the past year which make it perfectly plain that time has run out for a district court to temporize for the purpose of making accommodations." Judge West was born in Massachusetts, but after service in the U.S. Navy removed to Louisiana. There he attended Louisiana State University's law school (where he and classmate future U.S. senator Russell Long won the moot court competition) and opened a practice in Baton Rouge. A Democrat, he was appointed to the federal bench by John F. Kennedy in 1961. One cannot ascribe to him a born-and-bred liking for segregation, but, like Lieb, something about southern ways appealed to West. West resented his decisions being overturned and thought it a matter of personal honor to respond. "However, in this most unusual case, since the opinion rendered by the Court of Appeals is so injudiciously couched in personal terms, and is so written as to directly, and by clear implication accuse me, personally, of refusing to accept my responsibilities as a Judge of this Court, of wasting precious judicial time, of acting in an 'unusual' and 'shocking' manner, and even intimating that I have, in some way, acted unethically in the handling of this case, I would be a poor judge

---

11. Calhoun v. City of Atlanta, 188 F. Supp. 401, 404, 411 (N.D. Ga. 1959) (Hooper, J.).

indeed, and less than a man, if I were to let such an obvious attack on my personal integrity go unnoticed." Judge West's response sounded much like the antebellum southern honor code, in which a gentleman publicly insulted was required to challenge his opponent to a duel—unless an apology was forthcoming. None was in this case. Judge West nevertheless ordered the school board to bring in a plan.[12]

The effort to end Jim Crow through court action was hard going, and one senses that the judges in the desegregation cases found them difficult to manage even with the best of intentions. Mississippi, for example, presented the federal courts with twenty-nine individual cases by the end of 1968, in each of them local and state officials respectfully asking for more time. The same problems occurred in the Fourth Circuit, where Virginia massive resistance delayed compliance. In a few school districts—for example, Richmond—compliance came early. There school board chair Lewis F. Powell Jr. insisted that the public schools stay open and desegregation begin. The result was "token" integration based on residential segregation, for dropping legal barriers to desegregation left residentially segregated school districts in place. Still, in vain Powell tried to convince U.S. senator Harry Byrd to abandon his vehement opposition to all desegregation. Powell's stand may have influenced newly elected governor Almond's decision to reopen the public schools in the rest of the state (Prince Edward County's remained shuttered for five years, with a private "academy" open only to white students) and assay gradual accommodation to the Court's orders. Almond told Senator Byrd that as governor he could not and would not defy federal law. Almond did not advocate wholesale desegregation, however, as we have seen.[13]

Even the judges in the Fifth Circuit who interpreted *Brown* II in the fullest sense of *Brown* I, and pressed school boards for desegregation forthwith, did

12. W. Lee Hargrave, *LSU Law: The Louisiana State University Law School from 1906 to 1977* (Baton Rouge: Louisiana State University Press, 2004), 115; Hall v. West, 335 F.2d 481, 484 (5th Cir. 1964) (Wisdom, J.); Hall v. St. Helena Parish School Board, 233 F. Supp. 136 (D.C. E.D. La. 1964) (West, J.).

13. Robert A. Pratt, *The Color of Their Skin: Education and Race in Richmond, Virginia, 1953–1989* (Charlottesville: University of Virginia Press, 1993), 34–36; James E. Ryan, *Five Miles Away, A World Apart: One City, Two Schools, and the Story of Educational Opportunity in Modern America* (New York: Oxford University Press, 2010), 47–48; J. Lindsay Almond Jr., Oral History Interview, February 7, 1968, transcript in John F. Kennedy Oral History Program, p. 4; Matthew D. Lassiter and Andrew B. Lewis, "Massive Resistance Revisited: Virginia's White Moderates and the Byrd Organization," in *The Moderates' Dilemma: Massive Resistance to School Desegregation in Virginia*, ed. Matthew D. Lassiter and Andrew B. Lewis (Charlottesville: University of Virginia Press, 1998), 6–9; Green v. County School Board of New Kent County, 382 F.2d 338 (4th Cir. 1967); Green v. County School Board of New Kent County, 391 U.S. 430 (1968).

so with some sense that the parties' disagreements were not going to be resolved in court any more than they were in the community. It was thus the
exceptional judge who pressed for full compliance from the outset. Among
these, J. Skelly Wright of the Eastern District of Louisiana, including the city
of New Orleans, led the way. New Orleans—with its diverse population of African Americans, Creoles, Italians, Irish, and other ethnically proud groups—
was always different from the rest of the Deep South. Wright grew up in the
city and attended both Loyola College and Loyola University College of Law.
The natural rights philosophy of the Jesuits made its mark on him, as did
teaching American history in high school. When he was named to the district
court bench, in 1949, he already had a strong moral sense that segregation was
wrong. In 1951, he ordered desegregation at LSU, and after *Brown* he pushed
for the end of segregated schools in New Orleans. The city, disregarding
Brown, put up all manner of objections to the lawsuit. Wright knocked them
down one after another: "In their first preliminary defense, the defendants say
that this action is in effect a lawsuit against the State of Louisiana, which has
not consented to be sued, and therefore, this court is without jurisdiction. But
a lawsuit against officers or agents of a state acting illegally is not a lawsuit
against the state." The city's counsel found an error in the pleading. Wright
refused to dismiss on that ground. "The objection . . . even if well taken, would
not result in a dismissal of the action, but only in the giving to the plaintiffs
time to amend." A third, equally feeble objection followed: "Defendants also
move to dismiss on the ground that no justiciable controversy is presented by
the pleadings. This motion is without merit. . . . The defendants admit that
they are maintaining segregation in the public schools. . . . If this issue does
not present a justiciable controversy, it is difficult to conceive of one." Last but
not least, the city argued that the black parents had not exhausted their administrative remedies. Wright had heard that one already: "As a practical matter, plaintiffs here have exhausted their administrative remedies. They have
petitioned the Board on three separate occasions asking that their children be
assigned to nonsegregated schools. The Board not only has refused to desegregate the schools, but has passed a resolution noting the existence of the present
lawsuit." He would brook no nonsense, and his opinion was devoid of arcane
nuance. Do it, he ordered. His efforts brought him and his family social ostracism and death threats, and in 1962 President Kennedy named Wright to the
D.C. Court of Appeals bench, removing him from the front lines in Louisiana.
Wright died in 1988, honored by his peers and his many clerks.[14]

14. Earl Benjamin Bush et al., Plaintiffs v. Orleans Parish School Board et al., Defendants,
138 F. Supp. 337, 340, 341 (E.D. La. 1956) (Wright, J.); Patricia Wald, "J. Skelly Wright," in *Yale Bio-*

Judge Frank Johnson Jr. of the Middle District of Alabama may have owed his appointment to patrons in the Republican Department of Justice and friends in the old-line Democratic organization, but from the moment of his appointment in 1955, he showed a streak of pragmatic activism, coupled with a sure sense of social justice, in fashioning his desegregation decrees. Early in his life, he developed a sense of the casual injustice with which the white establishment treated black citizens. In law school in Tuscaloosa, his lodestar was Justice Harlan's dissent in *Plessy*. In case after case coming from Birmingham and Montgomery city schools, Johnson developed a style of creative and expeditious injunctive relief that would mark much later district court management of desegregation. He would retain hands-on supervision, making it easier for all parties, even those who dragged their feet, to know what they had to do. He faced the same harassment and threats of violence as other southern judges who confronted segregation, and with every threat, every disingenuous plea for more time, his conviction that the time had come for an end to the injustice grew stronger.[15]

Whether chiding or abetting the district judges, the Fifth Circuit Court of Appeals bore the brunt of the civil rights legal campaign, its judges crying out, "When, oh when, shall the task be done?" A leader had emerged among them—"General" Elbert Tuttle. Alongside Judge John Minor Wisdom and Judge Richard Taylor Rives (the only Democrat among the three), Tuttle demanded compliance from foot-dragging local boards, but it was not merely a respect for the rule of recognition that motivated him. Born in California, educated in Hawai'i and New York, Tuttle was a newspaper reporter, a World War II combat veteran (at the age of forty-eight reaching the rank of brigadier general), and one of Attorney General Brownell's liberal Republican cadre of lawyers when President Eisenhower tabbed him for the Fifth Circuit in 1954. Tuttle made no bones about his opposition to segregation when *Brown* was decided. Indeed, he optimistically assumed that the decision's opponents would "fall in line." He had hoped for a "forthwith" order from the Supreme Court in 1954 and was disappointed that the Court allowed delay in compliance. Tuttle's distinguished service on the Fifth and then the

graphical Dictionary, ed. Newman, 605–6; Arthur S. Miller, *A Capacity for Outrage: The Judicial Odyssey of J. Skelly Wright* (Westport, CT: Greenwood, 1984), 71ff.

15. Tony A. Freyer and Timothy Dixon, *Democracy and Judicial Independence: A History of the Federal Courts of Alabama, 1820–1994* (Brooklyn: Carlson, 1996), 215–42; Jack Bass, *Taming the Storm: The Life and Times of Judge Frank M. Johnson, Jr., and the South's Fight over Civil Rights* (Athens: University of Georgia Press, 2002), 52–53; Tinsley E. Yarbrough, *Judge Frank Johnson and Human Rights in Alabama* (Tuscaloosa: University of Alabama Press, 1981), 49.

new Eleventh Circuit continued until his death in 1996, a mere ninety-nine years old.[16]

If one case best depicted Tuttle's approach to the law, it would be his response to the challenge that segregationists made to the Civil Rights Act of 1964. Some of the provisions of the act concerning public accommodations appeared to resemble the very same provisions of the Civil Rights Act of 1875 struck down by the Supreme Court in the *Civil Rights Cases* (1883). Here, the challenger was the Heart of Atlanta Motel. When the motel owner's counsel sought injunctive relief against the imposition of the statute, Tuttle wrote for the three-judge district court: "Title II declares the right of every person to full and equal enjoyment of the goods, services and facilities of any hotel or motel which provides lodging to transient guests if it contains more than five rooms for rent or hire." The motel was one of the largest in the state capital, often hosted out-of-state guests, and so was fully in the stream of interstate commerce. The commerce clause of Article I thus applied, allowing Congress to require the motel to house all guests in a non-discriminatory manner. Tuttle concluded: "Heart of Atlanta Motel, Inc. . . . together with all persons in active concert or participation with them, are hereby enjoined from . . . [r]efusing to accept Negroes as guests in the motel by reason of their race or color." The general had spoken—an order in plain terms and easily understood.[17]

The Fourth and Fifth Circuits judges were not the only ones to deal with nationally noticed desegregation cases. The city of Little Rock, Arkansas, sat at the southern end of the Eighth Circuit. Following *Brown* II, Fayetteville, the seat of the University of Arkansas central campus, desegregated its schools. It seemed that Arkansas was ready to desegregate quietly. The case would ordinarily have landed in the lap of Judge Thomas C. Trimble, but he recused himself. His son was representing the school board. Judge John Miller approved a plan for the city of Little Rock that featured phased desegregation from the high school down to the first year of elementary school. He was no friend to *Brown* and preferred the go-slow plan that the school board had adopted before the NAACP filed suit, but he resisted calls for no action and ordered the plan initiated. The Eighth Circuit Court of Appeals heard the

16. Anne Emanuel, *Elbert Parr Tuttle: Chief Jurist of the Civil Rights Revolution* (Athens: University of Georgia Press, 2011), 153, 158.

17. Civil Rights Cases, 109 U.S. 3 (1883); Heart of Atlanta Motel, Inc. v. United States, 231 F. Supp. 393, 395, 396 (D.C. N.D. Ga. 1964) (Tuttle, J.). The Supreme Court upheld the panel in Heart of Atlanta Motel, Inc. v. U.S., 379 U.S. 241 (1964).

plan and agreed. But the state courts intervened, barring the plan, and local resistance, spurred by Governor Orval Faubus, led to violence. The Eastern District of Arkansas was short of judges, and the chief judge of the circuit, Archibald K. Gardner, following the course laid out in the Judiciary Act of 1922, designated Ronald Davies, of the District of North Dakota, to temporary service in the district. "I didn't even know what case I would get when I was ordered to go down there," he recalled in 1987. The desegregation case fell to him. He decreed that the state courts had no jurisdiction in the matter and ordered the school board to implement its plan forthwith. Violence outside of the high school and inside its classrooms did not deter nine black students from entering the school, in part because President Eisenhower sent soldiers of the 101st Airborne Division to patrol inside and outside Central High School. The court of appeals backed Davies.[18]

With Davies returning to North Dakota, the school board, citing the violence, then petitioned District Judge Harry J. Lemley, the next federal judge to preside over implementation of the plan, to delay implementation of the plan for three years, and he acceded to their request. Lemley had "roots in the South," according to the local newspaper, and after holding hearings in the summer of 1958, he determined that "the pattern of Southern life" embedded in separation of the races needed more time to change. The court of appeals refused to back down. Newly seated court of appeals judge Marion Matthes wrote for a divided panel: "a plan of integration, once in operation . . . suspended because of popular opposition thereto, as manifested in overt acts of violence . . . the fires, destruction of private and public property, physical abuse, bomb threats, intimidation of school officials, open defiance of the police department of the City of Little Rock by mobs." This was a perfect example of the heckler's veto, and it could not defeat a legal commitment to genuine desegregation. Chief Judge Gardner dissented. He had been sitting on the court of appeals since 1929 and was familiar with state- and local-mandated segregation of schools. "Having in mind that the school officials and the teaching staff acted in good faith and that the school officials presented their petition for an extension of time in good faith," a delay should be granted. A "cooling off" period would allow the school board to implement

18. Francis Lisa Baer, *Resistance to Public School Desegregation: Little Rock, Arkansas, and Beyond* (New York: LFB Books, 2008), 25; Jeffrey Morris, *Establishing Justice in Middle America: A History of the United States Court of Appeals for the Eighth Circuit* (Minneapolis: University of Minnesota Press, 2007), 162–69; Michael Molyneux, "Ronald Davies, 91, Who Issued Little Rock Order, Is Dead," *New York Times*, April 21, 1996.

the plan in good order, he judged. He did not address the possibility that if violence could derail a plan in 1958, a resumption of violence could derail it at any time thereafter.[19]

A unanimous Supreme Court upheld Matthes's ruling in *Cooper v. Aaron* (1958). When the board decided to close the school, Judge Miller, once more managing the case, heard petitioners seeking an injunction to keep the schools open and found the law closing the schools unconstitutional. He ordered them reopened. Other Arkansas cities reluctantly, even grudgingly, opened their public school doors to all their children.[20]

When the Supreme Court finally dropped the "all deliberate speed" formula in *Green v. County School Board of New Kent County, Virginia* (1968), courts of appeals told district judges that all deliberate speed was no longer acceptable. One grade at a time was no longer acceptable. The end of "all deliberate speed" accelerated desegregationists' return to the courts. By 1970 the Court of Appeals for the Fifth Circuit, stretching from Miami to El Paso, had become the busiest in the nation, with civil rights and voting rights cases leading the way. Appeals had increased twelvefold from 1960 to 1964, and doubled again by 1970. According to the Administrative Office of the Federal Courts Director's annual report, the Fifth Circuit had 2,014 filings, leading the next circuit, the Second, by nearly 700 filings. The Fifth had fifteen appeals court judgeships, leading the Ninth Circuit, the next highest, by two judges. After Congress increased its judgeships to 26 in 1978, the difficulty of operating an appellate court that size led its judges to petition Congress to split the circuit in two, thus creating a new Eleventh Circuit, consisting of Alabama, Georgia, and Florida, with a new court of appeals. Congress complied in 1980. The New Fifth Circuit comprised the districts of Mississippi, Louisiana, and Texas.[21]

While school boards and federal judges were jousting, civil rights advocates were making advances on other fronts, though none came easily. Aiding

19. Tony Freyer, *Little Rock on Trial:* Cooper v. Aaron *and School Desegregation* (Lawrence: University Press of Kansas, 2007), 133, 144–46; Cooper v. Aaron, 163 F. Supp. 13 (D.C. E.D. Ark. 1958); 257 F.2d 33, 37, 39 (8th Cir. 1958) (Matthes, J.); 257 F.2d at 41 (Gardner, J.).

20. Cooper v. Allen, 358 U.S. 1 (1958); Freyer, *Little Rock*, 210–11.

21. Harvey C. Couch, *A History of the Fifth Circuit, 1891–1981* (Washington, DC: Judicial Conference of the United States Courts, 1984), 148–49; Deborah J. Barrow and Thomas G. Walker, *A Court Divided: The Fifth Circuit Court of Appeals and the Politics of Judicial Reform* (New Haven, CT: Yale University Press, 1988), 55–61, 123, 224–51; Cynthia Harrison and Russell R. Wheeler, *Creating the Federal Judiciary*, 3rd ed. (Washington, DC: Federal Judicial Center, 2005), 26.

and abetting their efforts were LDF and local NAACP lawyers and, most importantly, African American suitors willing to take their chances in court. On December 1, 1955, Rosa Parks refused to leave the "Whites Only" section of a city bus in Montgomery, Alabama. Her arrest for violating the city ordinance became the starting point for a remarkable movement in American history. The NAACP had been looking for another test case to challenge state-required segregation, and the respectable secretary fit the bill. Soon local civil rights activists organized a bus boycott with the support of neighborhood black churches, including one led by Dr. Martin Luther King Jr. The eloquent, spiritual Atlanta-bred King modeled the movement he was soon to lead on that of Mohandas K. Gandhi, whose nonviolent resistance policies helped gain India independence from Britain. Founded in 1957, King's Southern Christian Leadership Conference (SCLC) joined the Congress of Racial Equality (CORE) and the NAACP in organizing against the white supremacist South.[22]

The end of the bus boycott came when a federal court ruled that segregation on the buses violated the Equal Protection Clause of the federal Constitution. In *Browder v. Gayle* (1956), a case that tested *Plessy* directly, court of appeals judge Richard T. Rives, writing for himself and Judge Frank Johnson on the three-judge court, found that all of the plaintiffs had standing to bring the lawsuit and that they satisfied the Federal Rules criteria for a class action. (Again, note that when plaintiffs sought an injunction preventing the state from relying on its own law, the district court judge could order a three-judge panel.) Bus drivers for the city had ordered the plaintiffs to the back of buses merely following Alabama law. That law conferred on the bus drivers the authority to segregate the seating. The court brushed away the argument that state court remedies should be sought and only when denied should the case be heard in federal tribunal. If the grounds for the lawsuit lay in federal law or the U.S. Constitution, there was no need for plaintiffs to exhaust state remedies. Segregation in public facilities may have had the sanction of custom, but "there is, however, a difference, a constitutional difference, between voluntary adherence to custom and the perpetuation and enforcement of that custom by law." Judge Rives had struck at the heart of Justice Henry Billings Brown's justification for equal but separate car assignments in Louisiana's Separate Car Act. Citing an array of cases from the 1940s and 1950s, the court

22. Maurice Isserman and Michael Kazin, *America Divided: The Civil War of the 1960s*, 2nd ed. (New York: Oxford University Press, 2004), 30–32; Patterson, *Grand Expectations*, 400–405.

found that *Plessy* no longer applied. "We cannot in good conscience perform our duty as judges by blindly following the precedent of *Plessy*" when "under the later decisions, there is now no rational basis upon which the separate but equal doctrine can be validly applied to public carrier transportation within the City of Montgomery and its police jurisdiction."[23]

Rives was born and would die in Montgomery. He read law and practiced law there until his appointment to a seat on the Court of Appeals for the Fifth Circuit in 1951. Courtly, respected, he had "never lost sight of his roots" in rural Alabama. He knew what customs prevailed there, but his duty as a judge and his sense of fairness dictated that separate but equal had no place in public accommodations.[24]

District judge Seybourn Lynne dissented. Like Rives, his attachment to soil and the customs of Alabama ran deep. His grandfather had served in the army of the Confederate States of America, then started a law firm, in which Lynne's own father and the future judge practiced. Having taken part in the state courts' refusal to provide the kinds of remedies that plaintiffs sought in *Browder*, he offered a segregationist reading of *Brown*: "It seems to me that the Supreme Court therein recognized that there still remains an area within our constitutional scheme of state and federal governments wherein that doctrine [of separate but equal] may be applied even though its applications are always constitutionally suspect." Given his reading of the relative recency and reticence of Chief Justice Warren's refusal to overturn *Plessy* outright, Lynne worried that "a comparatively new principle of pernicious implications has found its way into our jurisprudence. Lower courts may feel free to disregard the precise precedent of a Supreme Court opinion if they perceive a 'pronounced new doctrinal trend' in its later decisions." But Lynne judged that a significant passage of time, not recent jurisprudential fashions, should convince trial court judges to abandon long-held opinions about the law and race relations. "I would dismiss the action on the authority of *Plessy v. Ferguson*." Seven years later, Lynne ordered Alabama governor George C. Wallace to admit the African American students that he refused to allow entrance to the state university. "I love the people of Alabama," he said, but he insisted that the law of the land came first. "I know many of both races are troubled and like Jonah of old, are 'angry even unto death,' " he wrote. "My prayer is that all

23. Donnie Williams and Wayne Greenhaw, *The Thunder of Angels: The Montgomery Bus Boycott and the People Who Broke the Back of Jim Crow* (Chicago: Chicago Review Press, 2006), 212–21; Browder v. Gayle, 141 F. Supp. 707, 713, 717 (D.C. M.D. Ala. 1956) (Rives, J.).

24. Barrow and Walker, *A Court Divided*, 15–16.

of our people, in keeping with our finest tradition, will join in the resolution that law and order will be maintained."[25]

In the meantime, King's inspirational message spread to college campuses. In Greensboro, North Carolina, on February 1, 1960, four freshmen from the North Carolina Agricultural and Technical State University initiated a sit-in at a Woolworth's lunch counter reserved for whites. In subsequent days, they were joined by others, including students from a local women's college. White supremacists brandishing Confederate flags attacked them, drawing international media attention to the protest. As the practice spread to other cities throughout the South, so did the confrontations and the boycott of those establishments that refused to serve African Americans. Violent segregationist responses to the sit-ins enabled segregationist state governors like Georgia's Vandiver to order the arrest of those participating in sit-ins in Atlanta. The state legislature followed Vandiver's lead, passing legislation criminalizing sit-ins. Florida's LeRoy Collins, like Vandiver a lawyer, was the exception—he decried the sit-in as a tactic but saw the moral principle behind the trespass. "Change must come and the South must accept it." In April of that year, African American students from across the South meeting in Raleigh, North Carolina, followed the advice of experienced civil rights activist Ella Baker and formed their own organization independent of SCLC, CORE, or the NAACP—the Student Non-Violent Coordinating Committee (SNCC). Although some lunch counters continued to segregate well into 1965, despite the Civil Rights Act of 1964, the Greensboro Woolworth lunch counter relented on July 25, 1960.[26]

Unwilling for the slow process of litigation in federal courts to work its way through segregationists' intransigence or, more likely, to gain national attention for the Civil Rights Movement, in the spring of 1961, SNCC members participated in a CORE-planned challenge to the still-segregated interstate buses. Called the Freedom Rides, the two buses' riders encountered violent attacks by Ku Klux Klan members and their sympathizers in local law enforcement. At first, federal judges in Mississippi, on the Fifth Circuit, and the Supreme Court were reluctant to provide habeas corpus relief to the freedom riders, jailed by local police, until the petitioners had exhausted their appeals to the state courts (according to the rule applied to convicts in state prisons). Judge Sidney Mize of the Southern District of Mississippi decided instead

25. 141 F. Supp. at 718, 720, 721 (Lynne, J.); Douglas Martin, "Seybourn Lynne, 93; Ruled in Civil Rights Case," *New York Times*, January 12, 2000.

26. Isserman and Kazin, *America Divided*, 33–34; Schmidt, *The Sit-Ins*, 102–3, Collins quoted on 104.

to order a moratorium on freedom rides, although the constitutionality of such an order restricting interstate commerce was arguable. Judge Mize was born in Mississippi, educated in Mississippi, and practiced in Gulfport, Mississippi, before President Roosevelt appointed him for the Southern District of Mississippi bench. A per curiam decision from the U.S. Supreme Court and an order from the attorney general integrated the buses officially, but the violent confrontation over integration in the South would last throughout the 1960s.[27]

Shortly thereafter, Judge Mize denied James Meredith's request for an order admitting him to the University of Mississippi. Meredith was fully qualified, but Mize ruled that "the management and control of the University of Mississippi and all other state institutions of higher learning in the State of Mississippi is vested in the Board [of Regents]." Apparently, federal law stopped at the Mississippi state line. The admissions officer who refused to allow Meredith to register testified that, in his opinion, Meredith was not a citizen of the state. Mize agreed. "The overwhelming weight of the testimony is that the plaintiff was not denied admission because of his color or race. The Registrar swore emphatically and unequivocally that the race of plaintiff or his color had nothing in the world to do with the action of the Registrar in denying his application. An examination of the entire testimony of the Registrar shows conclusively that he gave no consideration whatsoever to the race or the color of the plaintiff when he denied the application for admission and the Registrar is corroborated by other circumstances and witnesses in the case to this effect."[28]

The Fifth Circuit overturned Mize's decision with the somewhat exasperated comment that the judge should know what everyone else knew. "A full review of the record leads the Court inescapably to the conclusion that from the moment the defendants discovered Meredith was a Negro they engaged in a carefully calculated campaign of delay, harassment, and masterly inactivity." The law had barred black Mississippians from attending Ole Miss, but Judge Mize "held, 'there is no custom or policy now, nor was there any at the time of the plaintiff's application, which excluded Negroes from entering the University.' This about-face in policy, news of which may startle some people

27. Raymond Arsenault, *Freedom Riders: 1961 and the Struggle for Racial Justice* (New York: Oxford University Press, 2006), 367 (denial of habeas corpus relief), 507 (general inaction of federal courts); Isserman and Kazin, *America Divided*, 34–35; Patterson, *Grand Expectations*, 468–71.

28. Meredith v. Fair, 199 F. Supp. 754, 757 (D.C. S.D. Miss. 1961) (Mize, J.).

in Mississippi, could have been accomplished only by telepathic communication among the University's administrators, the Board of Trustees of State Institutions of Higher Learning. As the trial judge pointed out in his opinion, 'nearly every member of the Board of Trustees, testified unequivocally and definitely that at no time had the question of race of a party ever been discussed at a meeting of the Board of Trustees or at any other place and that so far as the Board of Trustees was concerned, all policies and regulations were adopted and followed without regard to race, creed or color.'" The court of appeals did not deal with the hidden issue—how officials of the state government could swear under oath in a federal court to what they knew to be a falsehood. While perjury was a federal as well as a state offense, the more significant and insidious fact was that Jim Crow and racism had undermined what had been the most sacred of all the steps in giving testimony—the oath. At the trial on the merits, Judge Mize again did not question the sworn testimony of officials to what everyone knew and what was on the face of the older law a series of falsehoods. But that was not the end of the bad faith shown not only by the university but by the district court judge. For he mischaracterized Meredith's suit as one requiring a jury rather than an equitable remedy (the injunction), continually offered scheduling reasons for delaying the hearing, and finally agreed with the state that the case would be delayed until the state's counsel was feeling better. On the fifth circuit, Judge John Minor Wisdom corrected Judge Mize. "We draw the inference that not a few of the continuances and the requests for time in which to write briefs were part of the defendants' delaying action designed to defeat the plaintiff by discouragingly high obstacles that would result in the case carrying through his senior year. It almost worked."[29]

But again the three-judge panel was not unanimous. Judge Dozier Adolphus DeVane dissented from Judge Wisdom's majority ruling. Judge DeVane was a Florida-born corporate attorney, a Democrat appointed to the Northern District of Florida bench in 1943 by President Roosevelt. He was briefly a county attorney before World War I, but spent most of his legal career representing railroads and telephone companies in Florida and in the District of Columbia. While he found that much of Judge Wisdom's concerns were well-grounded, he gave Judge Mize (not the state of Mississippi) the benefit of the doubt on one of the admissions office's stated grounds for denying Meredith admission. "The one defense that leads me to dissent is the fear expressed by the appellees [the state] that Meredith would be a troublemaker if permitted

29. Meredith v. Fair, 305 F.2d 343, 344, 352 (5th Cir. 1962) (Wisdom, J.).

to enter the University of Mississippi." According to DeVane, Judge Mize sat across the bar from Meredith and his attorneys while Judge Wisdom only had the trial transcript. "Judge Mize heard the case, observed appellant throughout the trial and reached the definite conclusion from appellant's testimony, his conduct and other testimony that was offered that Meredith would be a troublemaker if permitted to enter the University." One notes in passing the future conditional of both Mize's and DeVane's logic—the potential danger. This is the same logic as the Old English definition of the crime of seditious libel. Such criticism of the crown had the pernicious tendency to undermine support for the government. So, too, Meredith's litigiousness might be taken as evidence that he would be a troublemaker. "Under such circumstances, the opinion of Judge Mize is entitled to more weight than any conclusion that could be reached by Court of Appeals Judges where their opinion is based upon a cold, printed record of the facts at issue. . . . In my opinion Judge Mize was correct in finding and holding that appellant bore all the characteristics of becoming a troublemaker if permitted to enter the University of Mississippi and his entry therein may be nothing short of a catastrophe." In fact, nothing in Meredith's conduct outside of the courtroom suggested that he was likely to make trouble. He never had any run-ins with the law previously. But if all the civil rights activists were classed by Jim Crow jurisprudence as troublemakers, and if Meredith's persistence in the face of all of the obstacles erected by the university, the state, and Judge Mize was considered proof of the likelihood that he would continue to agitate for fair treatment, then Mize and DeVane might be right.[30]

One parallel to resistance to desegregation of schools and public facilities was the agonizingly slow desegregation of the federal bench. President Eisenhower made no African American nominations for the federal bench. In fact, at least one of his nominees to the Fifth Circuit Court of Appeals, in 1955, Benjamin F. Cameron of Mississippi, was an avowed segregationist, and another, G. Harrold Carswell, tabbed in 1958 for the Northern District of Florida, had made inflammatory racist remarks during a campaign for a congressional seat from Georgia ten years earlier. Other potential nominees, like Solicitor General Sobeloff, whose role in promoting desegregation was well known, were blocked for a time by southern senators. Sobeloff himself would gain a place on the Court of Appeals for the Fourth Circuit in 1956, his credentials among the Maryland members of the bar (he was chief judge of Maryland's highest court, the court of appeals, from 1952 to 1954) and his

---

30. 305 F.2d at 362 (DeVane, J.)

service as U.S. solicitor general (from 1954 to 1956) outweighing any animus among southern senators for his support of civil rights. On the Court of Appeals for the Fourth Circuit, he played a vital and positive role in assuring the root and branch dismantling of school segregation, reversing the course that Chief Judge Parker had piloted for the circuit. But the bottom line was that none of these nominees was an African American.[31]

By contrast with all his predecessors, save Truman, President John F. Kennedy named African Americans to highly visible judicial posts. His appointees—James Parsons, Wade McCree Jr., and Thurgood Marshall—were all well known in civil rights circles, although political payback played a major role along with the aim of diversifying the bench. The president was aware of the importance of the African American vote in northern cities, and his choices can be seen in that light.[32]

All three African American choices were highly qualified. Parsons was an assistant U.S. attorney for the Northern District of Illinois when President Kennedy toured Chicago with him. Kennedy kept a promise to the Chicago Democratic machine, and Parsons was nominated to the Northern District of Illinois and confirmed in the first year of the new administration. When Parsons joined the bench, its judges had courtesy memberships in the Union League Club, an elite cultural and social organization. When the board of the club denied Parsons membership, all his colleagues resigned theirs and with him joined the rival Standard Club.[33]

With Chicagoland gaining a federal judge of color, political pressure from Detroit grew for McCree. He was serving as a judge in a Michigan circuit court, in Detroit, when Kennedy selected him for the District Court for the

31. John M. Spivack, "Richard Taylor Rives and Benjamin F. Cameron: The Varieties of Southern Judges," *Southern Studies* 1 (1990): 225–41; John W. Dean, *The Rehnquist Choice: The Untold Story of the Nixon Appointment That Redefined the Supreme Court* (New York: Simon and Schuster, 2002), 20; Morton L. Wallerstein, *The Public Career of Simon E. Sobeloff* (Boston: Marlborough House, 1975); Sanford J. Rosen, "Judge Sobeloff's Public School Race Decisions," *Maryland Law Review* 34 (1974): 498–531.

32. Nicholas Andrew Bryant, *The Bystander: John F. Kennedy and the Struggle for Black Equality* (New York: Basic Books, 2006), 116ff. (need for black votes), 120ff. (civil rights bills in the Senate), 174ff. (civil rights as Kennedy policy).

33. Richard Cahan and Marvin Aspen, *A Court That Shaped America: Chicago's Federal District Court from Abe Lincoln to Abbie Hoffman* (Evansville, IL: Northwestern University Press, 2002), 144. Of course, Parsons had—had to have—the support of the Mayor Richard Daley machine in Chicago and Illinois senator Paul Douglas. Every federal judgeship in the Northern District of Illinois had their stamp of approval in these years. Joseph C. Goulden, *The Benchwarmers* (New York: Ballantine, 1976), 119–20.

Eastern District of Michigan. In 1966 he was named to the Court of Appeals for the Sixth Circuit by President Johnson. He resigned that seat in 1977 to serve as President Jimmy Carter's solicitor general, and when Carter's term ended, McCree accepted a professorship at the University of Michigan Law School.[34]

Thurgood Marshall was lead counsel for the LDF when Kennedy asked him to serve on the Court of Appeals for the Second Circuit. The nomination took some courage on Kennedy's part, for southern Democratic congressmen had little love for this toughminded grandson of a former slave. The appointment to the Second Circuit doubled his income but removed him from the advocacy of the cause he valued so highly. Despite a nearly yearlong confirmation fight, bespattered with the vitriol of southern Democrats, he gained Senate approval. None of his ninety-eight majority opinions were overturned by the Supreme Court. When Johnson made him solicitor general, he solidified his reputation as one of the nation's ablest civil rights advocates, winning fourteen of nineteen cases. Many of those cases protected the landmark civil and voting rights legislation of the Johnson presidency. In 1967, Johnson chose Marshall for the Supreme Court. Confirmation followed a month and half later.[35]

Next, Johnson selected A. Leon Higginbotham for the Eastern District of Pennsylvania in 1964. His nomination was confirmed within a month. Although that space of time was not unusual for candidates, the fact that confirmation was not prolonged by southern senators' delaying tactics, as was Hastie's and Marshall's, was a novelty. Higginbotham was in private practice in Philadelphia at the time, but had served in various state official capacities. President Jimmy Carter's choice of Higginbotham for the Court of Appeals for the Third Circuit went just as swiftly through the Senate. Higginbotham was an articulate student of slavery and the law, of racism in American history, and of the long road ahead to genuine racial equality. He would retire in 1993 and join the faculty at Harvard Law School.[36]

Another of the Johnson choices was Constance Baker Motley, the first female African American to sit on the federal bench. Motley had been a key

34. Goldman, *Picking Federal Judges*, 129–30, 183–84.

35. William Domnarski, *Federal Judges Revealed* (New York: Oxford University Press, 2008), 117–18; Mark V. Tushnet, *Making Constitutional Law: Thurgood Marshall and the Supreme Court, 1961–1991* (New York: Oxford University Press, 1997), 11–12 (Second Circuit confirmation), 18–19 (solicitor general); Thurgood Marshall, *Supreme Justice: The Writings and Speeches of Thurgood Marshall* (Philadelphia: University of Pennsylvania Press, 2003), 147.

36. A. Leon Higginbotham, *Shades of Freedom: Racial Politics and Presumptions of the American Legal Process* (New York: Oxford University Press, 1996), 3–17.

member of Marshall's LDF team and had argued the Atlanta schools desegregation case before Judge Hooper. Senator James O. Eastland of Mississippi,
chair of the judiciary committee, held up her confirmation hearings for
months. She recalled that President Johnson refused to send any names for
judgeships to the Senate until he relented. Joining her was Spottswood Robinson III, a veteran of the LDF and the Prince Edward County segregation
case. Robinson would serve in the District Court (1964) and later the Court of
Appeals (1966) for the District of Columbia. The desegregation of the federal
judiciary was picking up speed.[37]

In the meantime, Jack Greenberg and the LDF team were trying to push
the rock of desegregation up the hill of local southern resistance. The pupil placement plans and step-by-step grade plans were not desegregating
schools. The LDF lawyers went back to court to ask the district court judges
to prod the defendants. Fourth Circuit Court of Appeals judges like Albert V.
Bryan of Virginia and Clement Haynsworth of South Carolina sympathized
with the local authorities. Bryan served as a Virginia district court judge from
1947 until his elevation to the Fourth Circuit in 1961. He sat on the three-judge
panel that rejected the LDF desegregation lawsuit in Prince Edward County,
in 1951. At the time the LDF counsel knew they had little chance of winning
in front of three lifelong Virginia conservatives. Haynsworth's legal degree
was from Harvard Law School, but he joined the Court of Appeals for the
Fourth Circuit in 1957, when massive resistance was still the mantra of pro-
segregation. The threat of violence hung in the air in South Carolina, and
federal judges could take heed of what happened to Judge Waring when he
broke ranks with his colleagues on civil rights issues. Though not particularly
enamored of Strom Thurmond or his allies, Haynsworth was a strict con-
structionist, a believer in judicial restraint, and a Republican; these, added to
his South Carolina roots, made him an unlikely avid desegregationist.[38]

In *Dillard v. School Board of Charlottesville* (1962), Bryan and Haynsworth
showed how a sophisticated version of the anti-desegregationist argument
could be retrofitted seven years after *Brown* II. Greenberg and James Nabrit Jr.
sought aid from the bench against a city pupil placement plan that only allowed a handful of black students' transfers from residentially segregated
schools. Haynsworth's dissent from the en banc order finding the plan violated
Brown II, crafted by him and circuit judge Bryan, essentially thumbed its nose

37. Motley, *Equal Justice under Law*, 215–16; Mark V. Tushnet, *Making Civil Rights Law: Thur-good Marshall and the Supreme Court, 1936–1961* (New York: Oxford University Press, 1994), 72ff.

38. Kluger, *Simple Justice*, 486–87; Ernest F. "Fritz" Hollings, *Making Government Work* (Co-lumbia: University of South Carolina Press, 2008), 141–46.

at *Brown*. "This is to argue, also, that by leaving [all-black] Jefferson School the white children create segregation there. With equal reason it may be argued that the colored children in departing from the other schools caused segregation there. All of these contentions wrongly ignore three vital considerations: the fairness of the entirety of the [transfer] plan; the Fourteenth Amendment does not guarantee a student an integrated school to attend; and the 'segregation' here is not the result of plan but of individual choices of individual students. In law there has been no discrimination, for the Negro child has not been denied any privilege through policy, usage, law or regulation. If there has been a deprivation, it is—solely, actually and not capriciously—the result of the geographical location of his residence. This is a consideration understandably overlooked by the Court in the generality of its statement that the infrequency of Negro attendance in 'white' schools is itself proof of discrimination." The southern anti-desegregation jurists had found the near-perfect answer to *Brown* II—residential resegregation. White flight could do what massive resistance could not—resegregate the schools. Aided by federal policies that overtly or covertly gave preferential treatment to white workers and families in housing projects, and by the decision of builders like the Levitt brothers to exclude blacks from new single-housing developments, white relocations became a hallmark of postwar residential patterns. But the dissent did more. It returned to Justice Brown's view of the constitutional protection for social choice in *Plessy*. "The transfer rule is simply a means of permitting a child to express his wishes. Surely, to allow a child such an option—even though his wishes be based on racial grounds—is not unconstitutional. Allowing expression by both races so far as practicable—with equal opportunity—of their preferences in a personal matter has not in any degree been precluded by the Supreme Court in its efforts to solve the school problem or in any other field. The Court has merely ruled against enforced separation of persons of different races by reference to objective criteria. Never has the Court denied the exercise of the personal tastes of the races in their associations." The other members of the court disagreed, and Charlottesville was told to pick up the pace.[39]

*

More lawsuits at the district level, more victories at the appeals levels, more local pressure for the end of Jim Crow, and, finally, Congress acted. A watered-

39. Dillard v. School Board of Charlottesville, 308 F.2d 920, 925, 926, 927 (1962) (Haynesworth, J.); Richard Rothstein, *The Color of Law: A Forgotten History of How Our Government Segregated America* (New York: Liveright, 2017), xii ff.

down Civil Rights Act in 1957 had been a victory for the Southern Caucus, but the Kennedy Civil Rights Act, after Kennedy's assassination, in the hands of President Lyndon Johnson, was both far-reaching and had enforcement provisions. In particular, Title III and Title IV authorized the Department of Justice to bring lawsuits on behalf of those denied access to public accommodations and Title IX provided federal assistance, including intervention in lawsuits based on the Equal Protection and Due Process provisions of the Fourteenth Amendment. Senator Ervin might rumble about violations of the basic principles of federalism and indifference to the Constitution, but those arguments, already rehearsed in the Southern Manifesto, no longer persuaded anyone outside of the caucus. J. Lister Hill of Alabama, a legalist like Ervin, explained the full constitutional implications of the bill in what was perhaps the most well-organized of all the filibuster speeches. As if in a courtroom that he and the caucus presided over, the jury box filled with his white constituents, he told the Senate on March 23, 1964, not to bow to any "rash and expedient action to satisfy the demand of any particular group at any particular hour." This was the lesson of Madison's *Federalist* No. 10—not to let a faction in control of the executive and judicial branches also control the legislative branch. Worse, the bill was "too sweeping," an overreach of government that would "trample on established rights of a majority of Americans" and "drastically change the system of laws." Hill was right about the impact of the Civil Rights bill in ways that even its most ardent supporters could not have foreseen. It would change American public and private life profoundly. But his accompanying fear that it would "destroy the constitutional liberties, freedom, and . . . safeguards fundamental to our form of government" was itself overboard. In fact, it simply put Congress on record as supporting what the federal courts were already doing. His fear that it would promote a "mammoth federal government" was similarly unjustified, for the New Deal and World War II had already accomplished far more of that than the Civil Rights bill would. Return to the Constitution of 1787 he urged, or to Pilgrims, or the American Revolution. Anywhere but to the excesses of Reconstruction. He cited William Blackstone and Joseph Story as if they were contemporary students of individual liberty, ignoring Blackstone's defense of the authority of Parliament and crown and Story's view of the federal government in *Prigg v. Pennsylvania* (1842). Perhaps inspired by Hill's history lesson, Strom Thurmond joined with the Alabaman in a kind of constitutional colloquy, each man asking and answering the other about the limitations of the Fourteenth Amendment and the way in which the *Civil Rights Cases* (1883) were still good precedent, barring the public accommodations provisions of the bill. But the

Senate was not a virtual law school classroom, and such back and forth soon gave way to the roll call vote.[40]

The story of the Civil Rights Act of 1964 and the Voting Rights Act of 1965 was not the end of the southern anti–civil rights lawyering, but proof that law and legal reasoning had given way to politics pure and simple. Men like Russell might want to gird themselves in the armor of states' rights constitutionalism as they had in 1956, but as Senator Thurmond conceded, civil rights legislation was "a political fight and we are losing it because we are not matching political power with political power." The increasing use of war metaphors, references to the Civil War defiance of the solid slave South, and even the invocation of the Lost Cause were not designed to win in a courtroom. Although it is certainly arguable to regard the states' rights/constitutional limitations public rhetoric of the lawyers on the Southern Caucus as a "code," concealing racist attitudes, the private language of the anti–civil rights lawyers matched their public pronouncements. The key shift was not from legalism to racism—it was from law to politics. They now conceded that legal arguments would not suffice. They could not win the virtual court battle in the Senate any more than they could win it in the federal courts. Although one theme in their filibuster against the bill was its supposed violation of constitutional principles, this time only they were engaging in rote constitutional pleading. Similarly, the Jim Crow school district lawyers' tactic of strategic retreat, allowing delay and permitting only piecemeal accommodation to the desegregation orders, was also failing in the Senate. Thurmond, Russell, and the other lawyers in the caucus warned their constituents that the day of reckoning was coming. Delay and compromise would not stop the passage of the Civil Rights Act of 1964.[41]

✦

Four days before the Senate vote on the Civil Rights Act of 1964, Russell proposed to amend the bill by giving the attorney general the power to attack

40. Hill, March 23, 1964, *Congressional Record*, 88th Cong., 2nd sess., 5956, 5957, 5958, 5959; Thurmond, in ibid., 5958, 5959.

41. Thurmond, quoted in Keith M. Finley, *Delaying the Dream: Southern Senators and the Fight against Civil Rights, 1938–1965* (Baton Rouge: Louisiana State University Press, 2008), 245, 246 ("code"), 249, 256 (failure of delaying tactics), 258–59 (argument based on constitutional principles). Bruce Ackerman, *We the People*, Vol. 3: *The Civil Rights Revolution* (Cambridge, MA: Harvard University Press, 2014), 231 ("the popular mandate for Brown, so vividly demonstrated by the Civil Rights Act of 1964") continues the triumphal liberal account of the act—a Second Reconstruction theme.

de facto segregation. Although he had proposed it cynically, knowing it had no chance of success and wanting simply to show the hypocrisy of northern advocates of civil rights, it was prescient. For when the legal combat for civil rights turned north, NAACP studies revealed that school district lines were routinely drawn to isolate black students in black-only schools. Efforts by local groups and the NAACP brought mixed results. In some cases, like New York City, residential segregation in the schools after *Brown* actually made school segregation worse. In other cases, like Manhasset on Long Island, district courts framed orders that led to substantial progress in integration. *Blocker v. Board of Education of Manhasset, New York*, heard in the Eastern District of New York, involved two elementary schools in the district, one 100 percent black and the other 99 percent white, because the attendance areas were drawn along racial lines. Robert Carter represented the parents of the black children. The court ordered the school board to present a plan for desegregating the schools, even though they were not segregated by law. Judge Joseph Zavatt reported that the board "maintain that the neighborhood school policy of the District is color blind; that it operates equally upon all children within each attendance area, regardless of race or color; that the racial imbalance in the Valley area is a fortuitous circumstance due solely to the pattern of housing within the District for which they are not responsible; that, therefore, they are under no duty to change attendance area lines or modify their present attendance rules." He was not convinced. A Long Island native and a lifelong Republican, he had practiced law on the Island for thirty years before he was named to the bench in 1957, and he must have known exactly how such school boards operated. "To argue, as do the defendants, that Negro residents have come to the Valley voluntarily and segregated themselves is to ignore the actualities."[42]

The judge considered the real-world impact of de facto segregation on the learning of the black children, the ways in which the board had dodged, delayed, and explained the facts by arguing that the black children simply had inferior intelligence, and concluded that *Brown*'s reasoning did apply—de facto segregation was as harmful as de jure segregation. Where segregation imposed a constitutionally impermissible harm, desegregation was a mandated remedy. Although local schools had some advantages to the children, the supposed advantage of a homogeneous school population did not outweigh the

---

42. Blocker v. Board of Education, 226 F. Supp. 208, 212, 218 (1961) (Zavatt, J.); Theoharris, *A More Beautiful and Terrible History*, 42–44.

disadvantages to minority students and the white majority created by segregation. Zavatt hinted that he saw through the board's thinly veiled attempt to gerrymander the attendance lines in order to do in fact what *Brown* barred in law. "Were the Board to take such action today would it not be reasonable to regard it as a rather ingenuous device to separate the races, protestations to the contrary notwithstanding?" In cases like *Blocker*, it was the ability of civil rights lawyers to gather facts as well as garner local support from community leaders to press for integration. But the avidity with which some northern school boards tried to maintain segregated schools—for example, in Detroit— suggested that the Southern Caucus's hope for support in the North was not entirely without basis.[43]

In the meantime, die-hard segregationists did not surrender. Instead, they assayed collateral attacks on the front-line advocates of civil rights. John Patterson and Alabama were involved in a wide variety of cases of this type. One of them was *Dixon v. Alabama*, a challenge to the due process–less expulsion of six Alabama State University students for seeking service at the segregated lunchroom of the state capitol. Called to explain why he and the state board of education had voted to expel the students, without telling them why or giving them a hearing, Patterson told the district court judge Frank Johnson:

> The action taken by the State Board of Education was—was taken to prevent—to prevent incidents happening by students at the College that would bring—bring discredit upon—upon the School and be prejudicial to the School, and the State—as I said before, the State Board of Education took— considered at the time it expelled these students several incidents, one at the Court House at the lunch room demonstration, the one the next day at the trial of this student, the marching on the steps of the State Capitol, and also this rally held at the church, where—where it was reported that—that statements were made against the administration of the School. In addition to that, the—the feeling going around in the community here due to—due to the reports of these incidents of the students, by the students, and due to reports of incidents occurring involving violence in other States, which happened prior to these things starting here in Alabama, all of these things were discussed by the State Board of Education prior to the taking of the action that they did on March 2 and as I was present and acting as Chairman, as a member of the Board, I voted to expel these students and to put these others on probation

43. 226 F. Supp. 218, 224 (Zavatt, J.); Carter, *Matter of Law*, 176–77; Patterson, *Brown*, 186–87; Joyce A. Baugh, *The Detroit School Busing Case:* Milliken v. Bradley *and the Controversy over Desegregation* (Lawrence: University Press of Kansas, 2011), 86–91.

because I felt that that was what was in the best interest of the College. And the—I felt that the action should be—should be prompt and immediate, because if something—something had not been done, in my opinion, it would have resulted in violence and disorder, and that we wanted to prevent, and we felt that we had a duty to the—to the—to the parents of the students and to the State to require that the students behave themselves while they are attending a State College, and that is [*sic*] the reasons why we took the action that we did. That is all.

The Fifth Circuit found that the students were entitled to due process hearings, at which they could defend their actions, and for this purpose ordered the case remanded to the district court for rehearing. In the process the court set the precedent for due process rights for students disciplined or expelled at public colleges and universities. Patterson's reasoning—that peaceful sit-ins and other civil rights demonstrations might lead to violence, and at the very least called into question the reputation of the school, the state school board, and, by implication, the government of the state—was one of the arguments commonly used against immediate desegregation of schools. It was the argument that Judges Mize and DeVane used to bar James Meredith's admission to Ole Miss. Such arguments of the bad tendency variety, where no actual danger was present and demonstrators were not the cause of violence, were well rehearsed in freedom of speech cases long before Jim Crow came under attack. They were examples of the inextricable linkage of politics and law in cases where the state imposed arbitrary and discriminatory discipline on its citizens exercising constitutional rights.[44]

The sit-in cases were not part of the original LDF plan for desegregation, as they did not focus on education, but one of the by-products of the civil rights revolution was to engage a cadre of African American college students in the larger project of equality before the law. While some of this energy was spent on integrating campuses across the country, the students also led in movements like the voting registration drive and the desegregation of public accommodations. The role of African American students in the Student Non-Violent Coordination Committee and other "bottom-up" reform movements in the early 1960s was in many ways as vital to the second stage of the civil rights revolution as the continuing contributions of the Southern Christian Leadership Conference, the Congress of Racial Equality, and of course the NAACP. The sit-ins, while outside the central focus of this book—on segregation in education—remind us that much of the

44. Dixon v. Alabama, 294 F.2d 150 (5th Cir. 1961) (Rives, J.).

impetus for the civil rights revolution came from "below," that is, from ordinary people who saw and challenged injustice, often at a palpable cost to
themselves in employment, physical safety, and, in some tragic cases, life
and limb.[45]

45. See, e.g., Schmidt, *The Sit-Ins*, 79, 180; but also see Goluboff, *Lost Promise*, 269 (impetus
from below unsuccessful in work-related cases). I believe that the bottom-up story is not the
rival of the top-down story of LDF lawyering, nor even a parallel story, for over time the two
were intertwined. The civil rights lawyers and sympathetic courts stood just outside of the lunch
counters, ready to aid students harassed by segregationist law and law enforcement. Thurgood
Marshall argued Boynton v. Virginia, a prequel to the sit-in cases, before the Supreme Court in
1960, and in a 7–2 decision written by Justice Black, the Court found that the ICC Act's provision
for non-discrimination in interstate travel facilities barred Virginia from segregating interstate
railroad terminal dining rooms. 364 U.S. 454 (1960). In Burton v. Wilmington Parking Authority,
365 U.S. 715 (1961), a 6–3 majority found that a privately owned restaurant in a public parking
facility was within the ambit of the Fourteenth Amendment's Equal Protection Clause. Justice
Tom Clark, who had dissented in Boynton, wrote for the majority. Garner v. Louisiana was the
first of the sit-in cases, an appeal from conviction of the sit-ins for criminal trespass. Jack Greenberg argued for the appellants. Justices Black and Frankfurter, stalwarts against segregation in
Brown, here dissuaded their brethren from a broad constitutional ruling, over the objection of
Justice Douglas, who wanted the Court to reach for the constitutional issue. Chief Justice Warren wrote for a unanimous Court that the arrests and prosecutions violated the students' due
process rights. 368 U.S. 167 (1961). In a series of cases the following years, Greenberg pleaded for
a broad statement of the students' rights to speech and assembly; while U.S. solicitor general Archibald Cox, reflecting President Kennedy administration's go-slow civil rights policy, asked the
Court for minimalist rulings in favor of the appellants. The states attorneys general wanted the
property rights (and the segregation policies) of the restaurant owners protected. Schmidt,
The Sit-Ins, 130–31. The Court complied with Cox's wishes, finding that municipal ordinances
mandating segregated eating were sufficient to trigger the "state action" provision of the Fourteenth Amendment. My point is that even if the sit-ins were not planned or organized by the bar,
the LDF and the legal system protected the constitutional rights of the students.

5

Whose Victory? Whose Defeat?

In the desegregation cases, total victory for the civil rights lawyers would mean a regime of legal equality. Success for the defenders of segregation would be the retention or the re-creation of a traditional system of racial separation. By the first decades of the 1970s, true victory—integrated school systems—had proved elusive for the civil rights lawyers. Defenders of separate schools had found legal ways to maintain separation, admittedly at some cost to their core values of stability and order, side steps to which judges assented.[1]

Ironically, segregation lawyering won extra innings when civil rights lawyers turned their sights on de facto segregation in the North. There they found the reservoir of racialist attitudes that the Southern Caucus had suspected. The civil rights lawyering indirectly enabled southern advocates of separate schools to claim they had been right all along. Pro-segregation lawyers could not prevent the death of Jim Crow—the legal regime of segregation—but by taking their cause north, along the way abandoning the specifically and uniquely regional justification for segregation, they could defend separation of the races in court. Once de facto segregation was clearly a national issue, the old argument against segregation—that it reflected a bygone time of southern racial animus by which the South defined its Lost Cause—faced a different and ironically far more widely justified response.

The essence of the LDF's school cases against segregation was that a child should not be denied the chance to attend a school in his or her neighborhood.

---

1. The very outcome that Derrick A. Bell warned about when he cited the depth of the evil of racism in the American social fabric. See Bell, "Dissenting," in *What* Brown *Should Have Said*, ed. Balkin, 185–200.

When the civil rights crusade turned north, it found that vicinity coupled it-self to socioeconomic status. In the South, poor and rich often lived in close proximity. Not so in the North. Black children went to inferior schools that were overwhelmingly black because that is where the parents lived. The LDF aim had to become integration. That was the essence of the *Blocker* case on Long Island discussed above. Such discrepancies were surmountable, largely through inter-city, inter-county, or inter-district busing to achieve mixed-race school populations. That stretched the idea of neighborhood schools. Surely such court-ordered remedies as Judge Joseph Zavatt insisted on had geograph-ical limits. The two cases in which advocates of integration and defenders of de facto segregation came at the end of our period, in the Charlotte-Mecklinburg combined school district in North Carolina and in the Detroit school system in Michigan. In the latter, the battle to end de facto segregation in a northern school district did for the South what all its pro-segregation oratory, dilatory tactics, and threats to close down all public education could not. It was only necessary for white parents to migrate far enough away from centers of black population to reinstitute a legally defensible regime of separate schools.[2]

In the mid-1960s, "virtually all blacks in Charlotte [North Carolina] were still attending all-black schools." District judge James B. McMillan was not satisfied with the school board's compliance or with his predecessor's view that the board had done enough. Though a North Carolinian born and bred and new on the federal bench, he recalled that the litigation "educated" him about the realities of white southern resistance to *Brown*. With the help of Dr. John Finger, an expert on the subject of education administration, Mc-Millan ordered a comprehensive busing plan. "This is political dynamite and will cause a real commotion. But let's go ahead," he told Finger. In *Swann v. Charlotte-Mecklenburg* (1970), they did. "The School Board, after four oppor-tunities and nearly ten months of time, have failed to submit a lawful plan (one which desegregates all the schools). This default on their part leaves the court in the position of being forced to prepare or choose a lawful plan. . . . The intention of this order is to put on the Board the full duty to bring the schools into compliance with the Constitution as above outlined, but to leave maximum discretion in the Board to choose methods that will accomplish the required result. However, it is directed that leave of court be obtained before making any material departure from any specific requirement set out herein. The court will undertake to rule promptly on any such requests

2. Rothstein, *Color of Law*, 122, 153–54 (federal policy); Beryl Satter, *Family Properties: Race, Real Estate, and the Exploitation of Black America* (New York: Henry Holt, 2009), 177–78 (Chi-cago local politics).

for deviation from prescribed methods." Prompted by Judge McMillan, the school board "aggressively" pursued the goal of desegregation. In the southern district of Texas, Judge Woodrow B. Seals began to take an active role in the desegregation of Corpus Christi schools. He consulted directly with lawyers and witnesses, gathering information on the district, found busing a law-suitable remedy to end de facto segregation, and "announced an ambitious" busing scheme for Corpus Christi and stayed involved in the process to insure compliance with his orders.[3]

Meanwhile, in the North, massive white flight from city school systems to suburbs, for example, could undo the fairest-minded desegregation plans. In Detroit, where longtime residential segregation had led to de facto school segregation in the city, black families sought integration of the city's schools. White flight, however, had taken many wealthier white families outside the city limits. In *Bradley v. Milliken* (1971) (on appeal *Milliken v. Bradley*), federal judge Stephen Roth, a Kennedy appointee who had been a refugee from communist Hungary, presided over a forty-one-day bench trial. The lawsuit pitted the city, in the person of student Ronald Bradley, against Governor William Milliken. In the meantime, a plan for busing children across districts was approved in Pontiac, Michigan, and the *Swann* opinion came down. Roth found that the state had failed to provide equal educational opportunities to the inner-city children, in effect using districting to re-create de jure segregation. "The City of Detroit is a community generally divided by racial lines. Residential segregation within the city and throughout the larger metropolitan area is substantial, pervasive and of long standing. Black citizens are located in separate and distinct areas within the city and are not generally to be found in the suburbs. While the racially unrestricted choice of black persons and economic factors may have played some part in the development of this pattern of residential segregation, it is, in the main, the result of past and present practices and customs of racial discrimination, both public and private." After consultation with the parties, he fashioned a comprehensive regional busing plan. What was more, he continued over the course of three more years to refine and enforce the remedy. In the name of the white families who had left the city to avoid sending their children to Detroit schools, the state of

3. Green v. School Board of New Kent County, 391 U.S. 430 (1968) (freedom of choice plans not acceptable step toward genuine desegregation); Swann v. Charlotte-Mecklenburg Bd. of Ed., 311 F. Supp. 265, 267, 270 (W.D. N.C., 1970) (McMillan, J.); Bernard Schwartz, *Swann's Way: The School Busing Case and the Supreme Court* (New York: Oxford University Press, 1986), 3–4, 14–18, 19; Davison M. Douglas, *Reading, Writing, and Race: The Desegregation of the Charlotte Schools* (Chapel Hill: University of North Carolina Press, 1994), 245–46.

Michigan fought back. It stood behind the concept of neighborhood schools and regarded the city limits as the proper limit of any busing plan involving the city's children. On appeal, it won its case.[4]

In Nashville, Tennessee, the effort to desegregate the public school system began in 1956 and finally resulted in a comprehensive busing plan for the Davidson County school district. It was fashioned by district judges William E. Miller and his successor, L. Clure Morton. Miller, a native Tennessean and 1955 Eisenhower appointee, had managed the litigation in the traditional fashion, hearing and determining motions after his original order to the district to desegregate. He struck down a statewide parent preference plan that did not compel integration, but allowed a "grade-a-year" plan that in effect maintained a dual system of schools through the 1960s. At the end of the decade, Judge Miller ordered the district to prepare a busing program. Judge Morton was not happy with the plan, however, and called on experts from the U.S. Department of Health, Education, and Welfare to assist him in achieving racial balance in the metropolitan public schools. Morton was a Nixon appointee, a longtime Republican, and a close friend of Republican senator Howard Baker. He was determined to see that the schools desegregated. The new plan featured ratios and zones to insure that no school had a majority of minority students. The result was fury coming close to violence by anti-busing parents. Two students of the case found that "all this activity was directed at one man, Judge L. Clure Morton." Deputy federal marshals guarded the personal safety of the judge as he worked to insure the success of the plan. White flight took the form of parents sending their children to private schools, effectually resegregating public education. Black parents responded by condemning busing and calling for increased funding for schools, once again almost entirely black, in black neighborhoods.[5]

Other judges faced even more vexing difficulties as they tried to manage the desegregation remedies they had ordered. Judge W. Arthur Garrity in the district of Massachusetts wrestled with a hostile Boston City Council, a candidate for mayor who was running on a platform of civil disobedience,

---

4. Thomas Sugrue, *The Origins of the Urban Crisis: Race and Inequality in Postwar Detroit* (Princeton, NJ: Princeton University Press, 1996), 63–86; Baugh, *Detroit School Busing Case*, 88–118, 127–30; Bradley v. Milliken, 338 F. Supp. 582, 586–587 (D.C. E.D. Mich., 1971) (Roth, J.); Milliken v. Bradley, 418 U.S. 717 (1974) (de jure state segregation can only be proven when there is evidence of prior or present intent to impermissibly segregate).

5. Kelley v. Board of Education of the City of Nashville, 159 F. Supp. 272 (D.C. M.D. Tenn. 1958); Richard A. Pride and J. David Woodard, *The Burden of Busing: The Politics of Desegregation in Nashville, Tennessee* (Knoxville: University of Tennessee Press, 1985), 54–65, 71, 168.

and an enraged Irish community in South Boston that simply refused to integrate its schools. The Boston city schools imbroglio became national news. Unable or unwilling to move to the suburbs as the white parents of Detroit had, South Boston white residents mobilized massive resistance to the Garrity plan. Garrity might have had divided loyalties, as he was the handpicked choice of the Boston Kennedy clan, which derived much of its political clout from Boston's Irish population, but he was a man of strict moral conscience and fidelity to the rule of law. When it fell to him to manage desegregation of the Boston schools, he appointed masters in equity to aid him, including a former attorney general of the state, a former justice of the state supreme court, and a former U.S. commissioner of education. In *Morgan v. Hennigan* (1974), his seventy-four-page densely detailed opinion combined tables and statistical findings, resembling a social science monograph. Unlike Roth in *Milliken*, Garrity did not extend the ruling to the surrounding communities: "The court denied a motion of the city defendants to join numerous cities and towns around Boston as defendants, partly on the ground that the proposed defendant cities and towns had not been charged by the plaintiffs with contributing to the violation of their constitutional rights." But he found that the open enrollment and controlled transfer plans earlier inaugurated by the city school board were inadequate remedies for the pervasive fact of continuing segregation. Busing was the answer. "Southie won't go" was the response of anti-busing activists, along with anonymous promises to murder the judge. Ostracized by former friends, reviled by his fellow city citizens, Garrity nevertheless arranged for the plan to cover the entire city and prepared to supervise its implementation.[6]

Garrity could not reverse the flight of white Bostonians to almost entirely white surrounding communities. As one study of the impact of the desegregation fight in Southie concluded, "Today, segregation across school districts, rather than within them, poses challenges that are more resistant to legal or judicial approaches. Over the years, an insidious form of educational gerrymandering has built invisible and arbitrary borders that separate poorer districts serving mostly students of color from adjacent districts serving more affluent children who benefit from greater resources. These stark borders lock students into—or out of—opportunity. This shifting geography of segregation makes legal remedies more difficult to implement and many districts

6. J. Anthony Lukas, *Common Ground: A Turbulent Decade in the Lives of Three American Families* (New York: Knopf, 1985), 222–51; Morgan v. Hennigan, 379 F. Supp. 410, 416 (D. C. D. Mass., 1974) (Garrity, J.).

have given up the fight to desegregate altogether, pursuing goals of increasing teacher diversity instead."[7]

The burden of managing remedies sometimes had a profound impact on the judges. Not only did it absorb much of their time, but it also altered the way that they looked at desegregation. Judge McMillan's background in rural North Carolina had not made him sympathetic to the plight of black city schoolchildren, but reviewing the facts did. Judge Roth was initially skeptical of the arguments that the Legal Defense Fund of the NAACP made, but as the evidence he acquired began to mount, his views changed. He became far more responsive to the plight of the inner-city school children and to the efforts of the city school board to provide the parents with truly integrated schools. Judge Garrity would have preferred some other remedy than city-wide busing, but the facts he had gathered left him no choice.[8]

After watching nearly twenty years of the Little Rock School District's attempts to avoid integration, including drawing school district lines to keep the neighboring Pulaski Special School District overwhelmingly white, Judge Henry Woods—a Little Rock, Arkansas, native appointed to the district bench by President Carter—recused himself from further involvement in the case. His last decree had ordered a unitary or consolidated school district, but it was overturned by the Eighth Circuit's judgment that consolidation was not constitutionally warranted. His regret and dismay were palpable in his final opinion. "In my years as district judge in this difficult case involving the three school districts in Pulaski County, I have attempted to oversee the implementation of positive desegregation plans which would benefit all children in the public schools. To that end, I have sought the help of the most progressive and able persons in this country. . . . Whatever the plan finally mandated by the Court of Appeals, those who take as their part delay and obstruction will have won. For those people, delay is victory, regardless of the cost to the school children or to a community economically stagnant because of the 'school mess.'" The judge had seen the future, or at least a portion of it, for in later decisions the Court struck down plans in Louisville, Kentucky, and Seattle, Washington, to end de facto school segregation.[9]

7. Thomas Maffai, "A 40-Year Friendship Forged by the Challenges of Busing," *The Atlantic*, November 17, 2016, https://www.theatlantic.com/education/archive/2016/11/a-40-year-friendship-forged-by-the-challenges-of-busing/502733; Jonathan Kozol, *The Shame of the Nation: The Restoration of Apartheid Schooling in America* (New York: Crown, 2005), 230–31.

8. Baugh, *Detroit School Busing Case*, 88–90, 114–16; Lukas, *Common Ground*, 251.

9. Jack Bass, *Unlikely Heroes* (New York: Simon and Schuster, 1981), 19; Little Rock Sch. Dist. v. Pulaski County Special Sch. Dist., 740 F. Supp. 632, 633, 636 (D.C. E.D. Ark. 1990) (Woods, J.);

*

One could argue that anti–civil rights lawyering won more than one court battle in the years after *Brown*, but had its jurisprudential foundation been similarly successful? One should not make short shrift of southern jurisprudence by describing it as a mere delaying tactic. Older arguments based on states' rights had failed, but in the course of their defense of Jim Crow, members of the Southern Caucus were not without examples of innovative thinking. Although primarily concerned with the defense of a traditional way of life, their arguments hinted at other constitutional doctrines that would gain far wider use.

The first was the doctrine of freedom of association or freedom of choice. The First Amendment's right to peaceably assemble may seem about as far away from segregation as one can travel, and indeed it was the freedom of association that the first black codes denied by regarding gatherings of blacks in public places as vagrancy. Jim Crow itself, insofar as it denied to blacks the right to join white organizations, was a denial of freedom of association, as Alexander Bickel made clear in his *Least Dangerous Branch*: segregation "denied the Negro's freedom of association, with the inevitable consequence of keeping him in a situation of permanent inferiority." At the same time, Bickel conceded that "we do not wish to force all whites to use only the public (integrated) schools and other facilities." The suppression of black demonstrations against segregation was another denial of freedom of association, but turned on its head, it can be viewed as the right to deny membership or belonging to unwanted individuals or groups. In a kind of catch-22, there was no easy exit from this loop.[10]

Although the first Supreme Court articulation of the doctrine of freedom of association came in favor of the NAACP, freedom-of-choice arguments also played out in school resegregation cases. The Los Angeles consolidated school district was but one of many successful efforts of integration opponents. The argument of Proposition 1, a coalition effort to amend the California Constitution to bar the state from imposing school integration on local

Meredith v. Jefferson County Board of Education, 551 U.S. 701 (2007); Parents Involved in Community Schools v. Seattle Board of Education, 551 U.S. 701 (2007).

10. See, e.g., Risa L. Goluboff, *Vagrant Nation: Police Power, Constitutional Change, and the Making of the 1960s* (New York: Oxford University Press, 2016), 116; Herbert Wechsler, quoted in Horwitz, *Transformation of American Law*, 267; Kimberly Johnson, *Reforming Jim Crow: Southern Politics and the State in the Age before Jim Crow* (New York: Oxford University Press, 2010), 13; Bickel, *Least Dangerous Branch*, 60.

school boards, ran something like this: we are not opposed to civil rights, but we do insist on a color-blind Constitution. That means color cannot be taken into account in where school boards place schools. Residential segregation, based on socioeconomic conditions (primarily the cost of housing), thus re-segregated schools de facto without de jure segregation. The proposal won by a two-thirds vote in the state, and effectively undid busing and other initiatives to balance racial composition of the schools.

The California Supreme Court did not find that the proposition violated the federal constitution, as it was in line with *Milliken* and other U.S. Supreme Court cases on busing. In *Crawford v. Los Angeles Board of Education* (1982), the high court agreed that Proposition 1 did not violate the Equal Protection Clause. Perhaps equally important, it raised freedom of choice to a privileged position among the rights guaranteed by the federal Constitution. Justice Lewis Powell, long associated with the battle over desegregation of the Richmond city schools (whose school board he had led, at one time), wrote for the Court (Thurgood Marshall alone dissenting), "Proposition I does not inhibit enforcement of any federal law or constitutional requirement. Quite the contrary, by its plain language the Proposition seeks only to embrace the requirements of the Federal Constitution with respect to mandatory school assignments and transportation. . . . The benefits of neighborhood schooling are racially neutral."[11]

Marshall was not persuaded. "In my view, these principles inexorably lead to the conclusion that California's Proposition I works an unconstitutional reallocation of state power by depriving California courts of the ability to grant meaningful relief to those seeking to vindicate the State's guarantee against *de facto* segregation in the public schools." The majority voice expressed in the referendum and ratified by the state supreme court was a macro version of freedom of choice—that parents should be able to send their children to neighborhood schools even when neighborhoods were racially homogeneous. The argument that the Southern Caucus had made for the white majority's freedom of choice in the segregated South echoed in the racially diverse far West.[12]

11. NAACP v. Alabama ex rel. Patterson, 357 U.S. 449, 460–461 (1958); see also Sweezy v. New Hampshire, 354 U.S. 234, 250 (1957) (recognizing First Amendment protection to participate in political organizations). The irony is hinted at in Margaret E. Koppen, "The Private Club Exemption from Civil Rights Legislation: Sanctioned Discrimination or Protection of Right to Associate," *Pepperdine Law Review* 20 (1993): 650. On Los Angeles, see Daniel Martinez Hosang, "The Changing Valence of White Racial Innocence," in *Black and Brown in Los Angeles: Beyond Conflict and Coalition*, ed. Josh Kun and Laura Pulido (Berkeley: University of California Press, 2014), 115–42; Crawford v. Los Angeles School Board, 458 U.S. 527, 535, 544 (Powell, J.).

12. 458 U.S. 555 (Marshall, J.).

In *Hurley v. Irish-American Gay, Lesbian and Bisexual Group of Boston* (1995), the U.S. Supreme Court majority adopted a permissive view of exclusion that was eerily parallel to the argument for Jim Crow public accommodations and echoed *Crawford*. In a Boston St. Patrick's Day parade, the organizers, the "council," sought to deny the LGBT group from marching. The Massachusetts Supreme Judicial Court found that the denial violated the group's free speech rights. The U.S. Supreme Court heard the case on appeal and, writing for the unanimous Court, Justice David Souter found that the judicially forced inclusion of the gay and lesbian marchers violated the First Amendment rights of the organizers. The fact that the city of Boston, a public agency of the state, permitted the parade and cleared the streets for it did not impose a Fourteenth Amendment Equal Protection sanction on the organizers' refusal, for the city, after 1947, no longer sponsored the event, ceding control to a private body. As a private association, they could exclude individuals or groups whose values did not comport with their own. "The issue in this case is whether Massachusetts may require private citizens who organize a parade to include among the marchers a group imparting a message the organizers do not wish to convey. We hold that such a mandate violates the First Amendment." Inclusion by judicial writ violated the freedom of association of the organizers. Because the parade was an "expressive" event, the LGBT marchers were not simply part of a procession going from one place to another (hence entitled to use the public streets), but wanted to express LGBT pride in an event whose organizers rejected those values. "Rather like a composer, the Council selects the expressive units of the parade from potential participants, and though the score may not produce a particularized message, each contingent's expression in the Council's eyes comports with what merits celebration on that day." The LGBT marchers simply were a discordant fit. How might the same argument have been made for excluding black students from attending white schools, when the values and traditions of the two races were so different, as different as "oil and water," according to Florida senator Spessard Holland during the debate over the Civil Rights Act of 1964? Was not the freedom of association a part of the Ninth Amendment and thus "fundamental" to life in America? One might of course attempt to distinguish freedom of association in the public school cases from parades by private organizations, but the shift in primary education in segregated districts from public to quasi-private academies shows how potent the freedom-of-association argument could be on the ground.[13]

13. Hurley v. Irish-American Gay, Lesbian and Bisexual Group, 515 U.S. 557, 569, 574 (1995) (Souter, J.); Richard J. Ellis, *Judging the Boy Scouts of America: Gay Rights, Freedom of Association,*

A second constitutional novelty touched on in the filibusters against the Civil Rights Act of 1964 further demonstrated the innovative potential of anti–civil rights lawyering. It would later be termed original intent. Members of the Southern Caucus explained that fidelity to constitutional principles required fidelity to the "intentions of the framers" of the Constitution, in particular, the Article I, section 2 provision that states would determine qualifications for voters. The Civil Rights Act supposedly subverted that intention by discarding the system of checks and balances (giving more power to the executive branch and the federal courts) and the system of federalism (shifting power away from the states). While this was not a dire deviation from the founders' views, it had some merit as a matter of fact. Federal enforcement of the public accommodations and voting rights provisions of the act was a significant step toward a national legal regime. Southern legalists proclaimed that the Court, and now Congress, had violated the principles of the Constitution from the moment that *Brown* was announced, but the measuring rod for those principles had been unclear until Sam Ervin insisted that the framers' intent must govern the interpretation of the Constitution.[14]

In 1985 Attorney General Edwin Meese III adopted this stance. In an address to the American Bar Association, Meese reviewed recent Court decisions and concluded, "It seems fair to conclude that far too many of the Court's opinions were, on the whole, more policy choices than articulations of constitutional principle. The voting blocs, the arguments, all reveal a greater allegiance to what the Court thinks constitutes sound public policy than a deference to what the Constitution—its text and intention—may demand." This was precisely what the Southern Caucus had contended in the Southern Manifesto. But Meese had a further contribution to constitutional jurisprudence. "A jurisprudence seriously aimed at the explication of original intention would produce defensible principles of government that would not be tainted by ideological predilection. This belief in a Jurisprudence of Original Intention also reflects a deeply rooted commitment to the idea of democracy. The Constitution represents the consent of the governed to the structures and powers of the government. The Constitution is the fundamental will of the people; that is why it is the fundamental law." Although Meese was not arguing that desegregation be rolled back and Jim Crow be reinstalled as southern

---

and the Dale *Case* (Lawrence: University Press of Kansas, 2014), 75–76 ("fundamental"), 223–26 (freedom of association after *Dale*). See also Boy Scouts of America v. Dale, 530 U.S. 640 (2000); "oil and water": Spessard Holland, April 13, 1964, quoted in Finley, *Delaying the Dream*, 264.

    14. Finley, *Delaying the Dream*, 258.

law, his contention that the majority of the South, its white voters, had not consented to judicially imposed desegregation or to congressionally imposed equal access to public accommodations bore an eerie similarity to the legalism of the Southern Caucus in 1964. The correspondence, in political context, was not, however, eerie, for one could argue that the Republican Party of 1985 owed its resurgence to the support of the white South. One can easily hear Sam Ervin saying what Meese said in conclusion, "It is our belief that only . . . the sense in which laws were drafted and passed provide a solid foundation for adjudication. Any other standard suffers the defect of pouring new meaning into old words, thus creating new powers and new rights totally at odds with the logic of our Constitution and its commitment to the rule of law."[15]

The connection between the Southern Caucus's invocation of original intent and the U.S. attorney general's exposition of the doctrine of original intent ran through a federal judge, W. Brevard Hand. A southern-born and -educated intellectual on the bench, Alabaman Hand's most famous contribution to the idea of original intent was his opinion in *Wallace v. Jaffree* (1982). Jaffree sought injunctive relief from Governor George Wallace and the Alabama state law provision for a period of silence for religious prayer in public schools. Precedent for the petitioner was *Engel v. Vitale* (1962), *School District of Abington v. Schempp* (1963), and other U.S. Supreme Court decisions barring such religious practices under the Establishment Clause of the First Amendment. Wallace, whose role in the civil rights cases was clearly in accord with the Southern Caucus, and the Alabama legislature did what the caucus had wanted to do—refuse to obey *Brown* II. Judge Hand did in his courtroom what the caucus tried to do with the Southern Manifesto—provide alternative grounds for deciding who should and who should not determine what happened in the classroom. In the first hearing of the case, in the process of allowing a temporary injunction against the implementation of the Alabama law, Judge Hand explained, "The background of this country and its laws is one based upon the Judeo-Christian ethic. It is apparent from a reading of the decision law that the courts acknowledge that Christianity is the religion to be proscribed. Webster defines religion as 'a cause, principle, system of tenets held with ardor,' or 'a value held to be of supreme importance.' The religions of atheism, materialism, agnosticism, communism and socialism have escaped

15. Attorney General Edwin Meese III, Speech Before the American Bar Association, Washington, DC, July 9, 1985, available at https://www.justice.gov/sites/default/files/ag/legacy/2011/08/23/07-09-1985.pdf.

the scrutiny of the courts throughout the years, and make no mistake these are to the believers religions; they are ardently adhered to and quantitatively advanced in the teachings and literature that is presented to the fertile minds of the students in the various school systems."[16]

In the end, Hand granted the petitioners' plea for an injunction against the Alabama law, but when he heard the case on its merits, he went further: "The establishment clause was intended to apply only to the federal government. Indeed when the Constitution was being framed in Philadelphia in 1787 many thought a bill of rights was unnecessary. It was recognized by all that the federal government was the government of enumerated rights. Rights not specifically delegated to the federal government were assumed by all to be reserved to the states. Anti-Federalists, however, insisted upon a bill of rights as additional protection against federal encroachment upon the rights of the states and individual liberties." History, the history of the framers according to the judge, showed Hand that the First Amendment did not empower the federal courts to interfere in states' rights, including the right to establish a religion or promote it. "The prohibition in the first amendment against the establishment of religion gave the states, by implication, full authority to determine church-state relations within their respective jurisdictions." The basis for this history in the courtroom was the framers' intent. "The intent of the framers of the first amendment can be understood by examining the legislative proposals offered contemporaneously with the debate and adoption of the first amendment. For instance, one of the earliest acts of the first House of Representatives was to elect a chaplain. . . . In sum, while both Madison and Jefferson led the fight in Virginia for the separation of church and state, both believed that the first amendment only forbade the establishment of a state religion by the national government."[17]

In case anyone had missed the point, Judge Hand made it crystal clear—the Supreme Court had erred in its Establishment Clause jurisprudence. "The interpretation of the Constitution can be approached from two vantages. First, the Court can attempt to ascertain the intent of the adoptors, and after ascertaining that attempt apply the Constitution as the adoptors intended it to be applied. Second, the Court can treat the Constitution as a living document, chameleon-like in its complexion, which changes to lawsuit the needs of the times and the whims of the interpreters. In the opinion of this Court, the only proper approach is to interpret the Constitution as its drafters and

---

16. Jaffree v. James, 544 F. Supp. 727, 732 (S.D. Ala. 1982) (Hand, J.).

17. Jaffree v. Board of Commissioners, 544 F. Supp. 1104, 1114, 1117 (S.D. Ala.) (1982) (Hand, J.).

adoptors intended." It was the same argument that John W. Davis made in reargument of *Brown*; the only novelty was the original intent phraseology.[18]

The weakness of freedom of association, original intent, and other southern constitutional contributions to the jurisprudence of civil rights was that they were haphazardly and inconsistently argued by members of the Southern Caucus and other defenders of southern separatism. Instead of evolving into a serious conversation about the reach and limits of federal authority, southern anti–civil rights legalism in the years after 1964 became increasingly shrill and repetitive in its assertions that black agitators and radicals, with their left-wing allies, were driving the civil rights movement. Over and over, opponents of desegregation embraced tropes of racialism that undercut any credibility that freedom-of-association and original-intent doctrinal contentions might have had. Instead, anti–civil rights lawyers became historians, comparing their struggle to retain southern rights to the Civil War's secessionists, whose last-ditch battles the Russells and Ellenders refought in their minds and their speeches. The same arguments, decorated in different colors but garbed in the same cloth, had already lost in the courts—the Southern Manifesto and the filibuster against the Civil Rights Act of 1964—but southern lawyers clung to them. The only difference between 1954 and 1964 was a sense of impending doom. In that light, more and more of the racism underlying the southern legal case showed itself. Instead of rose-colored accounts of white-black relations absent outside agitators, southern constitutionalism bewailed the mongrelization of the nation and its laws. As Strom Thurmond stormed during the Civil Rights Act of 1964 debates, "It looks like the Negros have our country by the throat." That kind of language would have had no place in a court of law, but by this time Thurmond and his allies in Congress had abandoned the legalist side of the battle.[19]

All of which begs the question of why the southern legalists could not develop better or at least a fresher response to civil rights lawyering. One tantalizing answer may be that the southern mind, to borrow a phrase from students of southern literature and culture, was rich and innovative in the antebellum period, modern in its melding of political economy and social structure, and

18. 544 F. Supp. 1126 (Hand, J.); Leonard W. Levy, *The Establishment Clause: Religion and the First Amendment* (New York: Macmillan, 1986), 233; Melvin Urofsky, *Religious Freedom: Rights and Liberties under the Law* (Santa Barbara, CA: ABC-CLIO, 2002), 100.

19. Thurmond, March 8, 1964, private correspondence, quoted in Finley, *Delaying the Dream*, 268–69; but see Schmidt, "Litigating," 1106–7 (southern defenders of Jim Crow still looked to the courts to rally their forces).

expansive in its vision for the future. The Civil War and subsequent economic and cultural stagnation dimmed these visions. With Lincoln's untimely demise, as the foremost southern historian of Reconstruction lamented, the prospect of true reconciliation died. When New South intellectuals reformulated the mind of the South in the twentieth century, they looked backward to a time before the late unpleasantness. The arguments of the "Fugitive" literary movement (named after their short-lived literary magazine) were poetically cogent. As the twelve authors of *I'll Take My Stand* introduced their work, "Nobody now proposes for the South, or for any other community in this country, an independent political destiny. That idea is thought to have been finished in 1865. But how far shall the South surrender its moral, social, and economic autonomy to the victorious principle of Union? That question remains open. The South is a minority section that has hitherto been jealous of its minority right to live its own kind of life. The South scarcely hopes to determine the other sections, but it does propose to determine itself, within the utmost limits of legal action. Of late, however, there is the melancholy fact that the South itself has wavered a little and shown signs of wanting to join up behind the common or American industrial ideal." The vibrancy of the new southern mind lay in its self-conscious conservatism. "The younger Southerners, who are being converted frequently to the industrial gospel, must come back to the support of the Southern tradition. They must be persuaded to look very critically at the advantages of becoming a 'new South' which will be only an undistinguished replica of the usual industrial community." In a less sentimental vein, North Carolina newspaperman W. J. Cash lamented that "the evidence for the vast survival of these [racial] emotions is plain."[20]

But when the South's best legal minds turned to defense of segregation after *Brown*, southern spokesmen could no longer claim that the South was unique. So long as the South was a separate place, its sense of self inspired a distinctive culture, but after World War II, the South came to look like the North. Commercialization, urbanization, and even the interstate highway system made southern landscapes and soundscapes similar to those throughout the rest of the country. The southern difference was just about gone and, with it, the peculiar sensibility that empowered the southern imagination. While caucus filibusterers might take hardly concealed delight in the prospect of white northern racism coming to their aid, the reverse was true—whites in

20. O'Brien, *Conjectures of Order*, 1:46; Claude G. Bowers, *The Tragic Era: The Revolution after Lincoln* (New York: Houghton Mifflin, 1929), 4; *I'll Take My Stand: The South and the Agrarian Tradition* (New York: Harper, 1930), 3; Wilbur J. Cash, *The Mind of the South* (New York: Knopf, 1941), 301.

the South were beginning to accept the inevitable. Jim Crow was dying. The "lesson was sinking in." In the process, the "mystique with which Americans have always surrounded the South has begun to vanish."[21]

One may also explain the intellectual impoverishment of southern legal thought by comparing its morphology in 1964 to that of the antebellum southern legalism. The conservatism of the latter was rooted in the "old Constitution," the pre–Civil War idea that the federal government had very limited powers, and the domestic law of the states governed almost all everyday activities. At that time, southern lawyers' ideal "republican social order" paralleled the ideal of good government—that is, a truly republican government should not touch the liberties of free men. Southern religion, social thought, and view of race relations was of a piece in this intellectual configuration. Agitation like abolitionism, the work of outsiders to the South, imperiled not only the South's peculiar institution of slavery, it imperiled the old Constitution as well. Antebellum southern conservative legalism thus had a coherence and contemporary relevance. Even Lincoln in his First Inaugural Address seemed to bow to it. By contrast, the conservatism of 1964 rested on a barely concealed racism. That was out of step with southern professions of constitutional principle, as the Constitution no longer enshrined racial classification. Denied the legitimacy of its constitutional visions, southern thinking seemed a shriveled remnant of its former self.[22]

*

Who had won? Who had lost? After over twenty-five years of lawyering, the LDF faced an America in many ways as divided as it had always been. Federal housing politics and private development projects, combined with white families' decisions to relocate away from black populations, had re-created segregation. It was no longer legal, that is, imposed on both races by state law, but it was just as real, and one of many ironic twists to the civil rights story. In a new kind of resegregation of school districts tellingly called "secession," heavily white neighborhoods, supported by state laws, seceded from the surrounding counties and created their own overwhelmingly white public school systems. While federal trial courts have established without doubt that the purpose of these secessions was to reinstitute racial separation, they have thus far refused to order an end to secession. As a result, these miniature

21. Cobb, *The South and America since World War II*, 102; Belknap, *Federal Law and Southern Order*, 231–32; Howard Zinn, *The Southern Mystique* (New York: Knopf, 1964), 3.

22. Eugene Genovese and Elizabeth Fox-Genovese, *The Mind of the Master Class* (New York: Cambridge University Press, 2004), 65; Hoffer, *Uncivil Warriors*, 26–38.

public school districts, added to the largely racially segregated private schools that dot the same southern landscape, have once again left minorities to their own devices in segregated schools.[23]

The basis for the early victories of the LDF—that the target was the states and their county or municipal agencies, and thus the Fourteenth Amendment state action doctrine applied—was also the basis for their defeats in later years. That is, by targeting public entities like school systems that separated children by race, the civil rights lawyers inadvertently immunized private parties from lawsuit. Thus when individual parents elected to move beyond school districts to escape integration, there was no basis for legal action. Had the LDF done what the attorneys for Homer Plessy tried to do, that is include the Thirteenth Amendment badge of servitude argument, they might have had grounds to use federal power against private discriminators. Courts intervene in private law disputes all the time. Common law and statute both provide monetary remedies for private misconduct. Courts can also offer injunctive relief. The labor cases of the 1940s had set some parameters for such lawsuits, but even in them there had to be some tie to public entities. The LDF had brought private actions and public interest into close accord, but close accord was not perfect alignment. In any case, the LDF did not pursue this line of argument, and white flight was safe from the long arm of integration.

The civil rights lawyers had won the larger battle. They had won the war of ideas. No longer would racism be enshrined in American constitutional law. Perhaps that was enough. Perhaps not. For plaintiffs seeking racial justice, winning the war of ideas may be a hollow victory. At the very least, civil rights lawyering had carried *Brown* from a mere declaration of rights hesitantly enforced on a recalcitrant minority to the standard by which the very soul of a nation could be measured.

23. Nikole Hannah-Jones, "Dividing Lines," *New York Times Magazine*, September 10, 2017, 42–43. See, e.g., Stout v. Jefferson County (Alabama) School Board, Cas. 17-12338 (N.D. Ala. 2017).

6

Legal Academics and Civil Rights Lawyering

In one corner of the post-*Brown* lawyers' world, the intellectual contest over the legitimacy of *Brown* continued unabated throughout the period from 1954 through the 1980s. In law reviews, law professors wrangled over Chief Justice Warren's reasoning in *Brown* and the limits of desegregation law. Was desegregation the goal of a color-blind Constitution; or did the remedy for Jim Crow require more far-reaching steps? As the case became iconic in American constitutionalism, how should law teachers treat it in their classrooms? Did an academic have to be a supporter of *Brown* to gain federal judicial office?[1]

One might integrate the legal academics' role into the body of the narrative. However, the law professors did not play quite the same part in the story as the litigators. (There were exceptions, of course, as there always are to such generalizations, like Burke Marshall, of the Civil Rights Division of the Department of Justice and Yale Law School.) But in the main, the disjoint between academic discourse and the give-and-take of the litigation was almost entirely complete. True, the law school professoriate was hardly the most progressive academic cadre in the first half of the twentieth century; but even the academic lions of early twentieth-century law reform—Roscoe Pound at Harvard Law School, William O. Douglas and Charles E. Clark at Yale Law School, William Draper Lewis at the University of Pennsylvania Law School, and Karl Llewellyn at Columbia Law School, to name a few—did not step directly into the fray over civil rights for minorities. The 1960s saw a shift in the elite law professoriate to the left, but the younger proponents of law reform, like their

---

1. "Getting right with *Brown*": among many others, Michael J. Gerhardt, *Constitutional Theory: Arguments and Perspectives* (Newark, NJ: Matthew Bender, 2007), 238.

intellectual predecessors, did not sit at the civil rights plaintiffs' table. Perhaps the culture of academia militated against such activism? Did offices filled with books, small armies of adoring third-year law students, and ivy-covered walls insulate law professors from the world of tar-papered shacks, unpaved roads, and hostile local police in the everyday life of southern blacks? Did the canon of "excellence in teaching and mastery of the doctrines and theories of one's subject matter" in the classroom constrain the professors? Prior to the Civil Rights Era, few law schools taught civil rights law, much less prodded faculty to engage in civil rights litigation. As Yale Law School's Owen Fiss recalled, many years later, "I entered Harvard Law School at a time [in 1961] when civil rights and the *Brown* ruling made only fleeting appearance in the curriculum, and even then not in an especially favorable light." Howard University School of Law was the exception that proved the rule. By the middle 1960s, however, civil rights law was becoming a part of every major law school curriculum.[2]

Perhaps one reason why even professors sympathetic to the civil rights movement did not walk into the courtroom ready willing and able to launch Socratic dialogue on *Brown* is the same reason why it makes sense to discuss legal academics in a separate chapter. In a 1992 talk to the students and faculty at the University of Michigan Law School, his alma mater, Judge Harry T. Edwards hinted at the reason he thought why legal educators had not taken up civil rights lawyering. A former law professor himself, a product of the civil rights revolution, he had overcome race prejudice to advance in his career. So when the judge spoke about civil rights, legal education, and the role of professors, he knew whereof he spoke. And what he said was that the professoriate was addicted to doctrine, and doctrine did not win lawsuits.[3]

It was a general phenomenon, for which Edwards sounded the tocsin: "For some time now I have been deeply concerned about the growing disjunc-

2. Susan Edgerton and Paul Farber, "Dreaming the Academy," in *Imagining the Academy: Higher Education and Popular Culture*, ed. Susan Edgerton, Gunilla Holm, Toby Daspit, and Paul Farber (New York: Routledge, 2005), 4–5; American Association of Law Schools, "Statement of Good Practices by Law Professors," in *AALS Handbook* (Washington, DC: AALS, 2003), 95. Civil rights law in law schools: Owen Fiss, *Pillars of Justice: Lawyers and the Liberal Tradition* (Cambridge, MA: Harvard University Press, 2017), 4; Stevens, *Law School*, 234.

3. Harry T. Edwards, "The Growing Disjunction between Legal Education and the Legal Profession," *Michigan Law Review* 91 (1992): 34, 37; F. Michael Higginbotham, "Harry Thomas Edwards," in *African American Lives*, ed. Henry Louis Gates Jr. and Evelyn Brooks Higginbotham (New York: Oxford University Press, 2004), 266–68. Law professors moving to the left: John O. McGinnis, Matthew A. Schwartz, and Benjamin Tisdell, "The Patterns and Implications of Political Contributions by Elite Law School Faculty," *Georgetown Law Journal* 93 (2005): 1167–202; Tor Krever, "Law on the Left: Interview with Duncan Kennedy," *Unbound: Harvard Journal of the Legal Left* 10 (2015): 6–7.

tion between legal education and the legal profession." The "so-called elite" law schools were emphasizing "abstract theory" instead of giving the next generation of practitioners the tools they needed to practice law "ethically." The law reviews and course descriptions were overflowing with "impractical" notions, of little use to practitioners, including those with civil rights lawyering on their agenda. As law professor Deborah Rhode revealed in a personal account, ordinary people were not likely to read anything in a law review (to which one might add understand much of anything either). Was that the root of the problem—the canon of legal scholarship, linked to the limitations of law school student editors' reviews? Articles in these journals were the extensions of law school teaching methods: spotting issues rather than revolving them; seeing all sides of the issue rather than the one, right, side; rewarding nuance, cleverness, and complexity over straightforward argument of the sort that the LDF adopted. As one astute observer concluded, "Much of the legal scholarship published in law reviews in modern times does not appear to be intended to be relevant to the day to day concerns of practitioners and judges." So it was with the subject of school desegregation in the law reviews.[4]

To be sure, with so much of the legal and political community focused on civil rights litigation in the period 1950 to 1975, law professors and law students could hardly have missed what was happening in the courts of the South and the corridors of Congress. Typical of those who applauded *Brown* in the law reviews, Paul G. Kauper celebrated the return of the voice of John Marshall Harlan I in a *Michigan Law Review* report soon after the decision was announced. "History" marched with the Court, he opined. Much loved in the legal community, much respected for his service to the law school and civic organizations, and deeply imbued with a sense of moral purpose, Kauper was an advocate for civil liberties and prison reform. He passed away in 1974, but his 1954 essay was all he had to say about desegregation. He added that improvement in the lot of minorities must come from within the higher sympathies of good men, not be forced by judicial fiat. Also typical was Marshall Becker's piece in the *Nebraska Law Review* that noted, without further comment, that *Brown* "nullified" (note the choice of doctrinal terminology)

---

4. Edwards's remarks in Ronald K. L. Collins, "On Legal Scholarship: Questions for Judge Harry T. Edwards," *Journal of Legal Education* (2016): 641; Deborah Rhode, "Professional Reputation and Public Service: An Unfinished Agenda," in *The Paradox of Professionalism: Lawyers and the Possibility of Justice*, ed. Scott L. Cummings (New York: Cambridge University Press, 2011), 154; Thomas L. Fowler, "Law Reviews and Their Relevance to Modern Legal Problems," *Campbell Law Review* 47 (2001): 47; Richard A. Posner, "Against the Law Reviews," *Legal Affairs*, November/December 2004, https://www.legalaffairs.org/issues/November-December-2004/review_posner_novdec04.msp.

state statutes requiring segregation in schools, but did not reach other forms
of segregation. It was the limitations of the decision that were most important. Such references to *Brown* notwithstanding, what is most striking is the
relative paucity of law review pieces on such a momentous decision. It was as
if the academics were holding their breath, waiting to see how desegregation
played out in the courts and in the school districts.[5]

*

A few legal academics personally involved in the effort to desegregate the schools
had more to say. Frankfurter's former law clerk and a future law professor,
Alexander Bickel, played a key role in the Court's deliberations then and after.
After which a few in the law professoriate fully weighed in, led by Columbia's
Herbert Wechsler. During the battle for the school cases, men like Charles L.
Black Jr. of Yale Law School and Louis H. Pollak of Penn Law responded to
Wechsler, as did Bickel. The studied silence of the southern law academy was
broken when its numbers rushed to defend segregated law schools, a phalanx
that only a few southern law professors were willing to fight.

Supreme Court justice's clerkships are highly competitive. The clerks are
recent law school graduates, generally from the top-tier schools, and they assist the justices with research and drafting. They also write memos on cases
and discuss opinions with their justices. Although they are instructed to keep
all of this to themselves, the clerks operate a kind of informal communica-
tions system, carrying messages and sharing information from one justice
to another. Frankfurter, who had no children, was a surrogate father to his
law clerks. Indeed, even before he joined the Court and could select his own
clerks, he provided them to Justice Brandeis. Among his own more illustri-
ous clerks were Philip Elman (1941), who as assistant solicitor general had
provided assistance to the appellants' case in *Brown*; Elliot Richardson (1948),
who as President Richard Nixon's attorney general had a key role in the Wa-
tergate affair; and a dozen future law school deans and chaired professors.
Frankfurter had already selected William Coleman, an African American
Harvard Law graduate and a future civil rights litigator, as a clerk for the
1948–49 term. In that capacity Coleman helped draft a memo on Thurgood
Marshall's first *Briggs* brief. It conformed to what the justice would have to say

5. Paul G. Kauper, "Segregation in Public Education—The Decline of *Plessy v. Ferguson*,"
Michigan Law Review 52 (1954): 1158; Robben W. Fleming, "Tribute to Paul Kauper," *Michigan
Law Review* 73 (1974): 3; Marshall Becker, "Note: Constitutional Law—School Segregation Re-
vived," *Nebraska Law Review* 35 (1955): 134.

when the case came to the Court. Bickel was a Frankfurter clerk in the 1952–53 term, during which he corresponded with Coleman about the memo.[6]

It was natural, then, that in 1953, Frankfurter had asked Bickel to perform a task of some difficulty and great importance in connection with *Brown*. During the previous term of the Court, when he was Frankfurter's clerk, Bickel had written a memo for the justice on the case. In it, he urged that the Court exercise a very cautious view of desegregating schools, a jurisprudence of restraint that he and Frankfurter shared. The two men had come from similar backgrounds, and there was an unspoken trust between them. Bickel was, like Frankfurter, Jewish and foreign born, and, like the justice, had starred at Harvard Law. Now, Frankfurter entrusted Bickel with searching the historical record for evidence that the framers of the Fourteenth Amendment had or had not contemplated segregated education, the first of the five questions that the Court had directed to counsel following the first hearing on *Brown*.[7]

Today, one would associate the task with the jurisprudence of "originalism." That is, one way to determine how to interpret constitutional language is to try to find how its original authors intended it to be interpreted. John Davis had argued, along with others in the segregationist legal camp, that the world of the Fourteenth Amendment was not only content with segregation in education, it was widely practiced at the time. Which in turn would suggest that the authors of the Fourteenth Amendment did not expect it to be applied to education. Bickel's research concluded that the legislative record—the debates over the amendment in Congress—was "inconclusive," a finding that Chief Justice Warren repeated in his opinion.[8]

6. On law clerks in this period, and Frankfurter's in particular, see Todd C. Peppers, *Courtiers of the Marble Palace: The Rise and Influence of the Supreme Court Law Clerk* (Palo Alto, CA: Stanford University Press, 2006), 4, 5, 55, 104–5; and Artemas Ward and David L. Weiden, *Sorcerers' Apprentice: 100 Years of Law Clerks at the United States Supreme Court* (New York: New York University Press, 2006), 41; William T. Coleman Jr., *Counsel for the Situation: Shaping the Law to Realize America's Promise* (Washington, DC: Brookings Institution, 2010), 77–81, 84.

7. Lawrence Gelder, "A Legal Conservative," *New York Times*, November 8, 1974, 42.

8. 347 U.S. at 489 (Warren, C.J.); the study later published as Alexander M. Bickel, "The Original Understanding and the Segregation Decision," *Harvard Law Review* 69 (1955): 4–5: "The original understanding forms the starting link in the chain of continuity which is the source of the Court's authority," but finding that understanding is an act of historical scholarship and never easy. On the never-easy part, see Laura Kalman, "Border Patrol: Reflections on the Turn to History in Legal Scholarship," *Fordham Law Review* 66 (1997): 87–124. Similar difficulties apply to the "public meaning" version of originalism. See Jack Rakove, "Joe the Ploughman Reads the Constitution; or, The Poverty of Public Meaning Originalism," *San Diego Law Review* 48 (2011): 575–600. Both Kalman and Rakove are historians, one notes.

Bickel thought that *Brown* was correctly decided but would later write that the Court should use its powers of review and rejection of state and federal enactments sparingly. Judicial review was not a substitute for the passive virtues of letting a democratic society arrive at equal justice on its own. "Coherent, stable—and *morally supportable* government is possible only on the basis of consent," Bickel wrote in 1962 (italics in original). Whether that consent included the willingness of the losing party in litigation to accept the results and work with the court and the winning party to ameliorate the harm, or was the far narrower notion that courts should follow the election returns, Bickel never quite explained in his highly influential career as a Yale Law School professor. But it was clear to him that the failure of compliance for twenty years lay in part on the Court's failure to go beyond simple fiat. "The effectiveness of Brown as law largely depends on the will and the resources that are brought to its administration, and these are in control not of the Court, but of political institutions in the states and in Washington." *Brown* thus had suffered the fate that Justice Holmes had warned of in the early twentieth-century voting rights cases—if the Court could not effectuate its decisions in a recalcitrant state or region, it should not issue them. The authority of the Court itself was at stake when it overreached itself, no matter how desirable the outcome might seem to some people, or to history itself. Judicial self-preservation in a political system that rarely forgave overreaching was not a matter to be taken lightly.[9]

✴

Nor was it so taken by those members of the legal academy most directly affected by desegregation litigation. In these years, race relations were not a popular subject for southern law professors—most seemed to support cordial relations between the races, but only a few said aloud that *Brown* was rightly

9. Alexander Bickel, *The Least Dangerous Branch: The Supreme Court at the Bar of Politics* (New Haven, CT: Yale University Press, 1962), 20; Bickel, *The Supreme Court and the Idea of Progress* (New Haven, CT: Yale University Press, 1978), 92; Giles v. Harris, 189 U.S. 475, 485, 488 (1903) (Holmes, J.): "In determining whether a court of equity can take jurisdiction, one of the first questions is what it can do to enforce any order that it may make. This is alleged to be the conspiracy of a state, although the state is not and could not be made a party to the bill. . . . The circuit court has no constitutional power to control its action by any direct means. And if we leave the state out of consideration, the court has as little practical power to deal with the people of the state in a body. . . . Unless we are prepared to supervise the voting in that state by officers of the court, it seems to us that all that the plaintiff could get from equity would be an empty form." On the political question doctrine to which Holmes referred and both Frankfurter and Bickel bowed, see Rachel E. Barkow, "The Rise and Fall of the Political Question Doctrine," in *The Political Question Doctrine and the Supreme Court of the United States*, ed. Nada Mourtada-Sabbah and Bruce M. Cain (Lanham, MD: Rowman and Littlefield, 2007), 33.

decided and had to be obeyed. In general, according to the recollections of southern academics who taught in the 1950s, there was a studied, if pregnant, silence on racial issues. True, a few spoke out. Teaching law and sociology at Tougaloo College, lecturing on race relations at nearby Millsaps College, and publishing widely, émigré professor Ernst Borinski defended *Brown* and risked the scrutiny of the Mississippi State Sovereignty Commission. Borinski would not back down, but Millsaps did. Between 1958 and 1962, William P. Murphy, a law professor at the University of Mississippi, reminded readers of his essays that states' rights was interred with the dead of the Civil War. He conceded that obedience to *Brown* would present problems for the state (indeed its Citizens Committee was already waging a cold war against desegregation), but bow the state must. For his defense of the Court and its authority, he was hounded out of his teaching post.[10]

More often, southern law professors defended segregation. At the University of Georgia, opponents of desegregation could count on the support of law school dean J. Alton Hosch and his ally law professor Robert McWhorter. With history professor E. Merton Coulter, whose histories of slavery and reconstruction were filled with racist innuendo, they unanimously recommended that black candidate Horace Ward, qualified save for his race, not be admitted to the law school. Ward's appeal was later represented by Donald Hollowell and Constance Baker Motley, and the case came before federal judge Frank Hooper. The state delayed as much as it could until Ward attended Northwestern School of Law and received his law degree there. Much-respected University of North Carolina law professor Frederick Bays McCall was certain that black law students could get just as adequate an education at the all-black North Carolina College as at UNC's law school, and did not think that segregation of law students by race was such a bad idea. In this, he was backed by his dean and members of the North Carolina State Bar. Even louder voices were those like I. Beverly Lake of Wake Forest University School of Law, who frequently proclaimed his aversion to ever mixing the races in the schools. He even ran for the North Carolina governorship on a platform of rabid segregationism, part of the "southern way of life," though he did not advocate

10. Rosen and Mosnier, *Julius Chambers*, 27–28; Pierre Hugo, "The Silence of the Southern Academic in the Segregationist South," *South African Historical Journal* 38 (1998): 183–99; Ernst Borinski, "The Emerging Case Law in the Segregation Decisions of the Supreme Court of May 17, 1954, and May 31, 1955: Its Crystallization and Trends," *University of Pittsburgh Law Review* 17 (1956): 430; John Dittmer, *Local People: The Struggle for Civil Rights in Mississippi* (Urbana: University of Illinois Press, 1994), 61–62; Charles W. Eagles, *The Price of Defiance: James Meredith and the Integration of Ole Miss* (Chapel Hill: University of North Carolina Press, 2009), 188–94.

closing the public schools in preference to ending segregation. He lost, "hand-ily," to racial moderate (though only by comparison) Terry Sanford.[11]

*

North of state-imposed segregation, other legal scholars were freer to express their opinions. Their dilemma was to discover on what principle or principles might *Brown* rest that secured it from the fate of *Plessy*, that is, from the argu-ment that contemporary mores and politics rather than sound constitutionalism motivated the Court. Perhaps the most influential of these academics was Her-bert Wechsler, a chaired professor at Columbia Law School when *Brown* was announced. Wechsler was hardly a newcomer to the federal scene, having served in the U.S. Attorney General's office during World War II (where he helped ad-minister the forced relocation of Japanese Americans). In other matters a leader in legal reform—he was engaged in the drafting project that would lead to the American Law Institute's Model Penal Code and was the director of the insti-tute during one of its most productive periods—Wechsler was hardly a defender of Jim Crow. But he voiced some doubts about how the Court had justified its holding in *Brown*. It seemed to lack the neutral principles on which all judicial review must rest. Wechsler's 1959 Holmes Lecture at Harvard Law School, and the article in its *Law Review* that followed, became the basis for the next two generations of commentary on judicial review. Although seen by many within the legal academy as the long-awaited answer to the excesses of earlier academic writings (in particular, Legal Realism's reduction of judicial decisions to the level of ordinary decision making), the lectures and the article had a much wider audience and a much greater impact than any earlier academic piece.[12]

Wechsler thought judicial review was necessary to "preserve the govern-mental plan." It was a duty that the Constitution imposed on the high court, not an unconstitutional aggrandizement of power. That power included the deci-sion of whether the Court or some other agency of federal or state government was best placed to interpret a statute or even void it. Wechsler thus brushed aside the political question issue. The only issue for him was the "problem of

11. Robert A. Pratt, *We Shall Not Be Moved: The Desegregation of the University of Georgia* (Athens: University of Georgia Press, 2005), 12; Gwen W. Wood, *A Unique and Fortuitous Com-bination: An Administrative History of the University of Georgia Law School* (Athens: University of Georgia Press, 1998), 102–3; Tom Eamon, *The Making of a Southern Democracy: North Carolina Politics from Kerr Scott to Pat McCrory* (Chapel Hill: University of North Carolina Press, 2014), 61, 63, 66.

12. Henry J. Friendly, "In Praise of Herbert Wechsler," *Columbia Law Review* 78 (1978): 974–81; Kent Greenawalt, "The Enduring Significance of Neutral Principles," *Columbia Law Review* 78 (1978): 982–1021.

criteria" for exercising that discretion. It must not rest on a simple exercise of power or the desire to reach a particular conclusion on a favored issue, that is, be results oriented. Instead, judicial review must entail "neutral principles . . . by standards that transcend the case at hand." The results of this somewhat nebulous if high-sounding rule of reason were invariably self-limiting for the Court. For example, to his thinking, there was no need to read the Bill of Rights to require states to provide counsel to defendants too poor to pay for a lawyer nor to constrain the common-law rules of search and seizure by requiring police to warn arrestees of their rights (both rights that the Warren Court would shortly affirm for defendants in state criminal proceedings).[13]

How did this criteria apply, or not apply, to *Brown*? Wechsler would have preferred to see the Fourteenth Amendment as a pledge of a special value, rather than as a "finite rule of law." Thus, "a principled decision . . . is one that rests on reasons with respect to all the issues in the case, reasons that in their generality and their neutrality transcend any immediate result that is involved." It was and should be the rationale the Court offers, not the end result the Court wants, that justifies the exercise of judicial review. This was not exactly an end-does-not-justify-the-means test, but something akin to it.[14]

Did *Brown* then match that standard? Did the "value choices" in it rest on the reasoned principles Wechsler required? The answer was, not really. The decision was right and would endure, insofar as "its reasoning accorded import to the nature of the educational process." By placing education, and its importance in modern America, at the center of the opinion, Warren almost had made it a neutral principle—that is, education was not just important to the black children denied access to white schools, it was important to every American child. It was this—the contemporary importance of education— that allowed the Court to go beyond old cases and old social traditions, a clear reference to Davis's argument about segregation in late nineteenth-century America and precedents like *Plessy*. Wechsler was not so sure that the Court's decisions on less critical social and cultural meeting places like beaches and parks, "which no one is obliged to use," stood at the same level as *Brown*, however. For "judicial restraint" preserved judicial review on the rare occasions when the latter was necessary, since "the Court ought to be cautious to impose a choice of values on the other branches or a state." Only those decisions that passed "the hardest test" of principled reasoning, like *Brown*, answered his skepticism. Only they "have the best chance of making

---

13. Herbert Wechsler, "Toward Neutral Principles of Constitutional Law," *Harvard Law Review* 73 (1959): 5, 9, 11, 16, 17, 18.

14. Wechsler, "Neutral Principles," 19.

an enduring contribution to the quality of our society of any that I know in recent years." Was the quality of endurance then the test of reasoned elaboration, or did it supplant Wechsler's call for such a test? The essay was as intriguing in its incompleteness as it was certain to attract attention.[15]

Wechsler closed his piece with an aside, though it was something of a blockbuster. What if the majority of black parents had opposed integration? He did not say they opposed the end of state-mandated segregation, that would have been too hyperbolic a hyperbole, but what if black parents in the main thought that their children would receive a better education if all-black schools were funded as fully as segregated white schools? What if the case were not about discrimination but simply about educational opportunity? He meant his hypothetical as a teaching tool, I would hope, a way to get his readers to think about the necessity of reaching for neutrality, but it resonated with one older strand of thinking in the LDF itself.[16]

Wechsler's point was that the decision rested on general principles, not special pleading for a special interest group, but his closing hypothetical roused the fury of *Brown* defenders in the academy, in particular those who had been instrumental in aiding the LDF in bringing the case, Charles L. Black Jr. of Yale Law School and Louis Pollak of the University of Pennsylvania Law School. For Black, the Fourteenth Amendment was unequivocal in its historical purpose: preventing states from discriminating against blacks. Moreover, his own experience growing up in segregated Texas taught him that "reasoned" elaboration had nothing to do with equality or inequality—the social facts, and the harms, of racial discrimination were so obvious that even a Columbia Law professor born, bred, and educated in New York City should understand what they were (Black and Wechsler had been colleagues only three years earlier). That was more than a little unfair to Wechsler, who shortly thereafter was arguing for ministers whose advertisement criticized Alabama officials in the case *New York Times v. Sullivan* (1964). Basing his argument on neutral principles of freedom of the press rather than racial discrimination, Wechsler saved them, and the newspaper in which they published an advertisement condemning the treatment of civil rights demonstrators in Birmingham, from having to pay ruinous Alabama defamation awards.[17]

15. Wechsler, "Neutral Principles," 20, 22, 25, 27.

16. Tushnet, *The NAACP's Legal Strategy*, 81.

17. Wechsler, "Neutral Principles," 34; Black, "The Lawfulness of the Segregation Decision," 423, 424; New York Times v. Sullivan, 376 U.S. 364 (1964); Kermit L. Hall and Melvin Urofsky, *New York Times v. Sullivan: Civil Rights, Libel Law, and the Free Press* (Lawrence: University Press of Kansas, 2011), 100–104.

Pollak accepted Wechsler's ideal of neutrality in principled decision making, but rejected Wechsler's application of it, in particular the notion that the Court did not act in principled fashion in its desegregation decisions. Pollak's style was as dispassionate and layered as Black's was passionate and direct, for "one who essays to tinker with constitutional theory may not properly take refuge in the likelihood of less-than-constitutional solutions to bail him out of following the limits of his logic." And that was Wechsler's failing. For he had imposed a strict separation of public and private interests that his own call for neutral principles assaulted. In case after case, defendants were able to escape from judgment, despite evidence of racial discrimination, by simply replacing agents of the state with private individuals. It was an old shell game, going back to the *Civil Rights Cases* (1883)—no state action, no federal remedy. But Wechsler's sophistry had elided the most vital of all principles: that cases like *Brown* were never neutral. They rested on amendments to the Constitution that were meant to lift up the fallen, help the oppressed, and keep faith with those for whom the Court was the only recourse for justice. In real life, in real time, there was no neutrality, one reason why Wechsler's theorem was never more than just that—theory.[18]

✳

If Wechsler's musing did not dictate the results in any particular case, the idea that legal process—protecting the integrity of the Court and insuring that its decisions would meet the test of time—had a following among legal academics. The key notion was that whatever decisions the Court made, they should not depart from well-understood procedural rules. The Court had to husband its store of respect within the democratic system so that it could police the boundaries between federal and state governments and the branches of government. The so-called legal process school gained its most important momentum from and because of the civil rights decisions, although the academics who founded and promoted the ideas did not always concede the connection. Nevertheless, legal process by implication asked whether the civil rights decisions were merely reflections of the liberality of Warren, Douglas, Black and other jurists. Were they, in this sense, political? Or did they further the democratic ideal of American governance albeit outside of the democratically elected branches?

In 1958 Henry M. Hart Jr. and Albert M. Sacks of Harvard Law School had prepared a tentative edition of a casebook for their classes, the collection of

18. Louis Pollak, "Racial Discrimination and Judicial Integrity: A Reply to Professor Wechsler," *University of Pennsylvania Law Review* 108 (1959): 1, 17, 31.

cases, comments, and notes on the interpretation of legislation entitled "The Legal Process," which was widely circulated in elite law schools. It argued strongly for a public-law approach to litigation, beginning with the study of legislation. Until the 1930s, legislation was a relatively neglected subject in the law school curriculum, the emphasis instead on the traditional common-law subjects of contract, tort, property, and procedure. Frankfurter introduced courses on administrative law and later legislation, which Hart assumed in 1942. From the materials he distributed to his classes came the first version of "The Legal Process." After Hart's experience with wartime price management, he developed new enthusiasm for the legislation materials, and working with newly hired Professor Sacks, a former student, the materials emphasized the effect of law on the community and deference to the findings of legislative bodies. All of this was taking place while the school cases were making their way to the high court, and the two Harvard professors could hardly have been unaware of the parallels between the LDF arguments and their own conclusions about the function of law. Central to the latter was the "community of interest" among people affected by law, not just the parties to a case. This, naturally, came from a legislative-oriented view of law rather than a judicial view. In addition, process—following the existing rules for making law—was paramount. This did not mean an obsessive adherence to precedent, for Hart and Sacks were not writing about adjudicative process. They were thinking in terms of legislative process, in particular, the central importance of statutory interpretation in a legal world increasingly strewn with complex legislative acts.[19]

As it happened, Hart had briefly collaborated with visiting Columbia Law professor Wechsler in 1954, and Wechsler was influenced by "The Legal Process" materials, in particular, what became a section on "reasoned elaboration" of the law. One cannot determine in which direction the influence for this section went, but it clearly found its way into Wechsler's idea of principled neutrality. The continuing influence of the materials, finally distributed, still ran contemporaneously with the civil rights campaign. In later years, legal academics like Robert Bork and John Hart Ely would turn to "The Legal Process" as a kind of manual of use, although by this time *Brown* had achieved sacrosanct standing in the constitutional canon. Indeed, to call

19. Henry M. Hart Jr. and Albert M. Sacks, "The Legal Process" (Harvard Law School, 1958), 110, 715; William N. Eskridge Jr. and Philip P. Frickey, "The Making of 'The Legal Process,'" *Harvard Law Review* 107 (1994): 2031–55; William N. Eskridge Jr., "Nino's Nightmare: Legal Process Theory as a Jurisprudence of Toggling between Facts and Norms," *Saint Louis Law Journal* 57 (2013): 866.

Brown "a beloved legal and political icon," as the editor of a collection of these afterthoughts has written, surely collapses the story a little too much.[20]

Alexander Bickel was not done with Wechsler, his former colleague at Columbia and someone whose views he did not entirely share. In *The Least Dangerous Branch*, Bickel summarized Wechsler's view of judicial review. To a non-academic, it may seem redundant at best and a little arrogant at worst for one scholar to summarize what another scholar had already painstakingly explained, but legal academics restate one another's arguments all the time. The restatement may be fair and full or a cleverly disguised refutation. Bickel's was a little bit of both. He changed Wechsler's principle of neutrality to one of judicial disinterestedness—that is, for Wechsler's fulsome version of judicial review to be acceptable, the judges must "stand aside from the party politics of the day." Wechsler had not said this—it was historically and practically impossible, as he knew from his own experience in government. But Bickel now had a straw man to knock down, for if neutrality of this sort was an "indispensable elaboration of any general justification of judicial review as a process for the injection into representative government," then such neutrality was truly impossible. Representative government in America was quintessentially political—the very thing that the justices could not be when exercising judicial review. Indeed, setting aside the logical trap that Bickel's rephrasing of Wechsler's neutral principles had sprung, how could one expect the justices, all of whom had political careers before they rose to the high court, to ever be truly neutral in a case of great moment, much less elevating their decisions above "the concerns of the moment."[21]

For Bickel, the way out of the (self-imposed) puzzle of neutral principles was "an intellectually coherent statement of the reason for a result which in like cases will produce a like result, whether or not it is immediately agreeable or expedient." In other words, neutral principles cannot be result-oriented. Wechsler had said as much. But the logical conundrum Bickel raised in relation to Wechsler's definition of neutrality applied to Bickel's own—in a representative government, most policy was result-oriented. Thus the practice of judicial review by courts of appeal was as likely to lead to unpopular decisions as to well-received ones. Bickel concluded that the only way that the Court

20. Hart and Sacks, "The Legal Process," 168–71; Eskridge and Frickey, "The Making of 'The Legal Process,'" 2047; Michael J. Perry, *The Constitution in the Courts: Law or Politics?* (New York: Oxford University Press, 1966), 4 (Bork and legal process school); John Hart Ely, *Democracy and Distrust: A Theory of Judicial Review* (Cambridge, MA: Harvard University Press, 1981), 74–75; Jack M. Balkin, "*Brown* as Icon," in *What Brown Should Have Said*, ed. Balkin, 3.
21. Bickel, *Least Dangerous Branch*, 50, 51.

could avoid eroding its store of esteem in the public mind was to avoid judicial review as much as possible. When it did reverse state or federal legislation or court decisions on constitutional grounds, the result should be unpopular. "If it sometimes hurts, nothing is better proof of [neutral principles'] validity. Given the nature of a free society and the ultimate consensual basis of all its effective law, there can be but very few such principles." What Bickel did not see was the circularity of his attempt to domesticate Wechsler's formula and apply it to *Brown*. For *Brown* fit his requirements if and only if there was "ultimate consensus" on it. Thus the passage of time, not any particular constitutional logic, proved Bickel right about *Brown*'s neutrality.[22]

Bickel's articles and books had become part of the national conversation on civil rights in the 1960s and apparently remain so. His skepticism about the impact and the desirability of judicial intervention in areas he thought best left to the democratically elected branches is close to orthodoxy among legal academics. His contributions to the *New Republic* gained him the reputation as a true "man of letters," and, in George Will's words, many intellectuals saw Bickel as "the keenest public philosopher of our time." Two of the most influential constitutional theorists of the next generation, Daniel A. Farber and Suzanna Sherry, summed it up: "We would be delighted if someone would like to compare us to the late Alexander Bickel."[23]

*

Well, not so fast, perhaps. Risa Goluboff has suggested, "As *Brown* came under attack both within and without the academy, legal scholars spent considerable effort analyzing and justifying the Court's decision in the case. As is their wont, such scholars [including Goluboff?] not only commented on but refined and systematic the emerging legal doctrine." Supporters of civil rights among the elite constitutional commentators, like Gerald Gunther of Berkeley, urged the courts to go slow. In 1963, Gunther warned against arguments for extensive federal intervention that smacked of "disingenuousness, cynicism and trickery as to constitutional principles." Harvard Law School's Paul

---

22. Bickel, *Least Dangerous Branch*, 59. In other words, popular understanding of constitutional legitimacy has a feedback loop, and decisions like *Brown* influence popular views. See Jack M. Balkin, *Living Originalism* (Cambridge, MA: Harvard University Press, 2011), 88, 116.

23. On Bickel: Maurice J. Holland, "American Liberals and Judicial Activism: Alexander Bickel's Appeal from the New to the Old," *Indiana Law Journal* 51 (1976): 1025–26; George F. Will, *The Pursuit of Happiness and Other Sobering Thoughts* (New York: Harper and Row, 1978), 52; Daniel A. Farber and Suzanna Sherry, *Judgment Calls: Principle and Politics in Constitutional Adjudication* (New York: Oxford University Press, 2008), 187.

Freund, a Frankfurter acolyte, was similarly concerned that "any decision overruling the *Civil Rights Cases* has implications for judicial power and duty that transcend the immediate controversy." In an essay for the *University of Pennsylvania Law Review* in 1964, Freund explained, "It is not a matter of lack of sympathy for the moral claims asserted; the real problem is an institutional one." Judicial activism in civil rights opened "up new areas of direct constitutional relations which will call for judicial creativity and innovation on a formidable scale." For Raoul Berger, whose career spanned years of government service and teaching at UC Berkeley and Harvard Law School, *Brown* was a perfect example of judicial overreach. The Court had tortured the meaning of the Fourteenth Amendment by ignoring the intent of its framers. "There is positive evidence that there was no design to impose segregation on the States. Segregated schools were deeply entrenched in the North." If this conclusion seems familiar, it was. John W. Davis had reached it a quarter century earlier. But Berger did not quote Davis. He relied on his own historical foray into the *Congressional Globe* and other primary sources, redoing Bickel's, Alfred Kelly's, and other contemporaries' research. He found that the proof that states were left to their own devices in matters of education was "overwhelming." Others, like Frankfurter's acolyte Philip Kurland, were still unhappy with the Court's legerdemain. In 1979, reviewing *Brown* and its subsequent cases, he wrote, "It was the beginning of many things. Not least of which was the self-licensing of the Court to recreate the equal protection clause in its own image." Frank Goodman agreed with Kurland about the opinion, but opined that the decision was a good one. The Court had failed to define the constitutional wrong and did not provide a viable remedy. In later essays, Robert Bork and Lino Graglia made similar complaints about the overreach of the Court's Fourteenth Amendment jurisprudence in the area of civil rights.[24]

For a different reason, Goluboff also was not happy with the limitations of *Brown*. It did not go far enough. For to her, it only "reinforced the aspect of *Brown* most at odds with the labor-infused civil rights of the 1940s." The "lost promise" of the war on Jim Crow was a redistribution of wealth, and the LDF did not go there after *Brown*. One might make the same criticism of

24. Goluboff, *Lost Promise*, 263; Gunther and Freud quoted in Schmidt, *Sit-Ins*, 158, 160; Paul A. Freund, "New Vistas in Constitutional Law," *University of Pennsylvania Law Review* 112 (1964): 644; Raoul Berger, *Government by Judiciary: The Transformation of the Fourteenth Amendment* (Cambridge, MA: Harvard University Press, 1977), 151, 244; Philip Kurland, "*Brown v. Board of Education* Was the Beginning," *Washington University Law Quarterly* (1979): 313; Frank I. Goodman, "The Desegregation Dilemma: A Vote for Voluntarism," *Washington University Law Quarterly* (1979): 407; Bork, *Tempting of America*, 75–78; Lino Graglia, "'Interpreting' the Constitution: Posner on Bork," *Stanford Law Review* 44 (1992): 1037.

the radical Republicans' efforts in Reconstruction and the New Deal Democrats. After all, courts tend to protect existing property rights rather than over-
turning them.[25]

As Goluboff's troubling tale demonstrates, the academic discourse on
civil rights lawyering continues today. There is a kind of dirge-like tonality
to some of it, a pervasive disappointment that lawyering did not bring the
millennium of racial equality. Almost predictably, it reflected the diminished
hopes of a new generation of social liberals. The idea that litigation would
bring the end of racism was never part of the LDF strategy, but for academics
who grew up with the race riots of the 1960s, civil rights lawyering seemed
to have changed little. "As it happened, however, many large expectations of
the mid-1960s turned out to be too grand to be achieved," Gerald Rosenberg
wrote in his powerful indictment of the civil rights campaign's reputation.
He was sympathetic to its goals, but skeptical of its achievements. Courts,
he found, citing *Brown*, were not effective agents of social reform. Little
change followed the Court's decisions, and that in turn weakened the impact
of judicial management of desegregation. Michael Klarman agreed that the
Brown decision had relatively little direct impact on racial attitudes, and it
was only when Congress added its weight to civil rights reform that desegregation moved with more than deliberate speed. James T. Patterson's study
of the impact of the decision in *Brown* disappointed him and convinced him
that "large generalizations about the impact of desegregation on interracial
understanding in schools could not stand careful scrutiny."[26]

✳

In recent years, law professors have returned to the scene of the crime, the
Supreme Court briefs and oral argument of 1952–54, to examine whether the
naysayers have the last word. Their assay features historical forays, but insofar
as the law professors may try to rewrite history by returning to the Fourteenth
Amendment's first days, they engage in the kind of source mining that Bickel
warned against and Chief Justice Warren rejected in *Brown*. Undeterred by
Bickel's prudence and Warren's larger vision, these modern law professors
find that Warren was "less than candid" in his treatment of the historical evidence, while others insist that the evidence shows that a "substantial majority
of political leaders who supported the [Fourteenth] Amendment" agreed that

25. Goluboff, *Lost Promise*, 408.

26. Gerald N. Rosenberg, *The Hollow Hope: Can Courts Bring about Social Change?* (Chicago: University of Chicago Press, 1991), 70–71; Klarman, *Jim Crow*, 385–400; Patterson, *Brown*,
xxi, 187.

segregation did in fact violate it. That conclusion, based on evidence from the period between ratification in 1868 and the passage of the Civil Rights Act of 1875, is rejected by other law professors, citing evidence from actual practice in period before and during the debates in Congress. What drives this immensely detailed and often passionate discourse is not, however, the need to get right with history, it is the need to defend or bash the doctrine of originalism. For if the iconic *Brown* cannot be defended on originalist grounds, then originalism itself must be flawed. But if *Brown* can rest on the original understanding of the Fourteenth Amendment, then originalism itself is legitimated. Alas, all of this academic sound and fury pointed to the very problem that Judge Edwards identified. The focus on the doctrine of originalism to which the historical research was directed left the real achievement of civil rights lawyering and the equally hard-fought, if finally incomplete, efforts of anti–civil rights lawyering in historical limbo.[27]

The hypothetical method favored in law school pedagogy is also present in academic re-lawyering on desegregation, particularly in a remarkable book entitled *What* Brown v. Board of Education *Should Have Said*. The work is remarkable not only for the quality of its contributors, a stellar array of law professors, but for the project itself. Who but law professors (and perhaps theologians) would undertake to perfect the past? The editor, Jack Balkin, conceded, "*Brown* has come to mean different things to different people." Most important for the project of the book, *Brown* has become a "sort of Rorschach test for politicians and legal theorists." Thus, "writing an opinion like *Brown* is not simply a matter of declaring what the law is or should be. It also involves making prudential judgments about the likely effect of the opinion." Hence the inclusion of politicians in the taking of the Rorschach test. Note however what was missing from this conventional assessment of the significance of *Brown*. It was not, the editor/law professor implies, a Rorschach test for lawyers. The omission is itself a significant one, along the lines of Judge Edwards's thesis. Civil rights litigators know exactly what *Brown* means, how far it went, and how far its advocates have yet to go. For lawyers who represent

27. In a nutshell, originalism is the proposition that interpretation of the text of the Constitution should rest on the original intent or understanding of those who wrote that text. For the disputes over history, see, e.g., Michael J. Klarman, "An Interpretive History of Modern Equal Protection," *Michigan Law Review* 90 (1991): 252; Michael W. McConnell, "Originalism and the Desegregation Decisions," 953 (defending originalism); Michael J. Klarman, "*Brown*, Originalism, and Constitutional Theory: A Response to Professor McConnell," *Virginia Law Review* 81 (1995): 1883ff. (attacking originalism); McConnell, "The Originalist Justification for *Brown*: A Reply to Professor Klarman," *Virginia Law Review* 81 (1995): 1937, 1950 (defending originalism); Calabresi and Perl, "Originalism and *Brown v. Board of Education*," 440 (defending originalism).

the other side, the same is true—they know precisely the limitations of *Brown* and its progeny.[28]

Balkin donned the robes of chief justice of this alternative-reality Supreme Court to find that the Constitution speaks "to generations long after those who drafted it." Surely this is true, else it would not remain the fundamental law of the land. But what does it say to those future generations? "We must regard the grand phrases of due process and equal protection as promises that we have made to ourselves as a people. . . . They are promises that cannot always be carried out fully in their own era; but they are promises that we nevertheless pledge ourselves to . . . so that someday they may [be] redeemed by future generations." In code, this is the living Constitution that works its way pure to greater equality for all. Elsewhere Balkin called it "framework originalism," but in practice it is the living Constitution, not any varietal of originalism. He followed the doctrine with an admonition: "[Courts] must not allow school boards to facilitate the creation of new school districts and school district boundaries that effectively shut out most racial minorities."[29]

Bruce Ackerman's "concurring opinion" (the contributors wrote as fictive associate justices, and all contributed essays in the form of opinions on the case—making it resemble *Dred Scott* more than *Brown*) was even more confident that history and doctrine together dictated that "the democratic republic contemplated by our Reconstruction Constitution cannot survive under modern conditions without all Americans receiving an education worthy of free and equal citizens." The contortions in this single sentence are themselves remarkable. The democratic republic of the Republicans who wrote the Reconstruction Amendments survived for many years with large portions of the country having little access to education, much less a "worthy" one, whatever that means. Thus the necessity of adding the qualifier "under modern conditions." But the framers of those three amendments did not live under modern conditions. Hence the qualifier is not only misplaced, it is misleading. Again, it is theory, not history and not practice, that drove Professor Ackerman's concurrence.[30]

Frank Michelman, concurring in part and in the judgment, made explicit what Balkin and Ackerman assumed, "The legal principle that decides these cases is one of equality of membership in the civil community." The members

28. Balkin, "*Brown* as Icon," 8. The hypothetical or contrary-to-fact method poses alternatives to actual outcomes and asks students to figure out the consequences.

29. Jack M. Balkin, "Judgment of the Court," in *What* Brown *Should Have Said*, ed. Balkin, 81, 89; Balkin, *Living Originalism*, 3–4.

30. Bruce Ackerman, "Concurrence," in *What* Brown *Should Have Said*, ed. Balkin, 116.

of that community were individuals, not states. The Fourteenth Amendment put paid to the states' rights argument of opponents of desegregation. Michelman had hit the doctrinal nail on the head. He rejected the historical argument, that is, the argument that *Brown* was good originalist jurisprudence of any type. Here he and his fellow contributor Michael McConnell disagreed. McConnell warned against his fellow justices writing as though "the members of this Court are especially blessed with moral foresight. . . . We are not philosopher kings." Cass Sunstein was similarly cautious in his reading of the powers of the Court, the meaning of the Constitution, and the likelihood of compliance. Instead, Sunstein was concerned that "offering adventurous interpretations of Constitution provisions on which the parties [i.e., the actual litigants] do not rely."[31]

Derrick Bell alone dissented. He thought *Brown* "provides petitioners with no more than a semblance of the racial equality that they and theirs have sought for so long." What was more, the decision "while viewed as a triumph by Negro petitioners and the class they represent, will be condemned by many whites as a breach of the compact. Their predictable outraged resistance will undermine and eventually negate judicial enforcement efforts, while political support for the Court's decision, like virtually every other racial rights measure adopted basically to serve white interests, once those interests have been served, will become irrelevant." Setting aside the cynical implication that a white men's Court in a white men's world had found segregation unconstitutional primarily to serve white interests, were one to make the hypothetical realm of the law professors into the real world of 1952, what would have followed had Justice Bell carried a majority of the Court with him? For the sake of sounding like a prophet in the wilderness of racism, he would have delayed, and perhaps destroyed, the prospect of desegregation for years. How might Thurgood Marshall, Robert Carter, and the other litigators of the LDF have regarded this fellow African American, whose cry for a fuller justice would have given the victory to the enemies of civil rights?[32]

Lest a reader conclude that legal academics were the dour cynics of the Civil Rights Era, a few shining exceptions belong here. Call them the friends of Owen Fiss. Fiss taught at Yale Law School for many years, and there knew and now celebrates that friendship in *Pillars of Justice*. Among the heroes of the memoir are government officials like John Doar and Burke Marshall, the

31. Frank I. Michelman, "Concurring in Part and Concurring in the Judgment," in ibid., 124, 125; Michael W. McConnell, "Concurring in the Judgment," in ibid., 158, 159; Cass R. Sunstein, "Concurring in the Judgment," in ibid., 174.

32. Bell, "Dissenting," in ibid., 185, 186.

latter a legal academic after his government service; former Supreme Court justices like Thurgood Marshall and William Brennan (both of whom hired Fiss as their law clerk); and former colleagues like Yale Law School's Robert Cover and Arthur Leff and Harvard Law School's Morton Horwitz. For all of them, Fiss has nothing but praise; these are elegiac portraits. There is no question on whose side of the civil rights question Fiss stands. For him, segregation was an everyday act of violence. All of the men in Fiss's *Pillars of Justice* shared a vision of what law could do, but what strikes the reader is how many of these liberal thinkers, particularly Robert Cover and Burke Marshall, focused on the limits of what law, lawyering, and courts could do. Cover, after all, had gone South to join in the Freedom Summers that Marshall watched from D.C.—they both knew firsthand what Jim Crow violence was. They also understood the "complicity" of the courts and the political caution of an executive branch dependent on southern votes. The real heroes of the story were the lawyers' clients, "who put themselves and their families out in front of their communities and the society in which they lived." As Burke Marshall recalled of 1963, "Well at the time that President Kennedy was deciding about introducing the bill that he introduced in June of 1963, he sought Mr. Johnson's advice. We wouldn't do that. I mean, I wouldn't have done that; that would have been the President that would have had to go to the Vice President. But at that time he did, and in fact he asked me to talk to Mr. Johnson at that time in June or late May of 1963 about the legislation, and I had a long conversation with him." Burke "only turned to the courts when necessary," according to his Yale Law School colleague Fiss. From evidence like this, law professor Judith Resnik concluded, "Judges are never enough to give law meaning," but a student of desegregation might add that, for a time, it was all that opponents of Jim Crow had.[33]

The academic discourse on *Brown* and civil rights jurisprudence had a side effect that the legal academics, and other intellectuals, might not have fully realized. On its face, twentieth-century legal scholarship was like the law itself—hard for laymen to penetrate much less understand. Even the legal academy's

33. Owen Fiss, *The Law as It Could Be* (New York: New York University Press, 2003), 147; Fiss, *Pillars of Justice*, 67 (Marshall view of courts), 76 (Marshall quoted); Robert M. Cover, *Justice Accused: Antislavery and the Judicial Process* (New Haven, CT: Yale University Press, 1977) (limitations judges placed on themselves); Burke Marshall oral history, Johnson Presidential Library, October 28, 1968, 1–5; Judith Resnik, "Living Their Legal Commitments," *Yale Journal of Law and the Humanities* 17 (2005): 52–53.

infatuation with Legal Realism, with its focus on the everyday practices of ordinary people who find themselves enmeshed in law, did not move legal scholarship to center stage in American intellectual life. Indeed, the borrowing of social science methods by the Legal Realists in the academy added another opaque layer to the law professors' writing. Now all that has changed. Even critics of public intellectuals' performance like judge, law professor, and public intellectual Richard Posner concede that law professors can now be found within the ranks of public pundits. Law professors from the leading law schools are routinely elected to the American Academy of Arts and Sciences.[34]

Why? I have a suggestion as tentative as Judge Posner's list. When law professors started writing about civil rights, they focused on matters that were central to public policy, politics, and public opinion. General readers understood the substance of the law professors' arguments, even if the precise formulations of those arguments remained highly abstract. That focus, in turn, made these law professors' work more important to other intellectuals and to the intellectual discourse of the day. Wechsler had broken the ice, and I think he knew it. He intended his work to be widely read outside the legal academy as well as in it. He had already caused controversy with the draft of the Model Penal Code for the American Law Institute. In it, he called for reforms in abortion law, capital punishment, sentencing, and other contemporary topics. He knew that law professors could have an impact on politics and current affairs like criminal justice if they wrote on those topics, for "no one will question its importance in society." Although in the 1950s expertise was under attack (all those "eggheads" beware), law professors' expertise in areas of law was somewhat isolated from the anti-intellectualism of the day.[35]

34. Richard Posner, *Public Intellectuals: A Study of Decline* (Cambridge, MA: Harvard University Press, 2001), 112–21, 125–27; Arthur Austin, "The Law Academy and the Public Intellectual," *Roger Williams University Law Review* 8 (2003): 263–66; 43 percent of Yale Law School's faculty, 33 percent of Harvard Law School's faculty, and over one-fourth of other leading law schools' faculty are members of the AAAS: Brian Leiter, August 14, 2017, http://leiterlawschool.typepad.com/leiter/faculty_news/. On the law professors' arcane lexicons in earlier times: N. E. H. Hull, *Roscoe Pound and Karl Llewellyn: Searching for an American Jurisprudence* (Chicago: University of Chicago Press, 1997), 97–105 (Pound and Wesley N. Hohfeld on analytical methods), 173–222 (Pound and Llewellyn on how to define Legal Realism). On impenetrable social science legalism: John Henry Schlegel, *American Legal Realism and Empirical Social Science* (Chapel Hill: University of North Carolina Press, 1995), 65–66 (Walter Wheeler Cook's search for a perfect terminology), 143–45 (novel terminology's allure to the law professors), 259 (on intellectual history as intelligible history).

35. Lewis B. Schwartz, "The Wechslerian Revolution in Criminal Law and Administration," *Columbia Law Review* 78 (1978): 1163–66; Markus Dubber, *An Introduction to the Model Penal Code* (New York: Oxford University Press, 2015), 10–12; Herbert Wechsler, "The Challenge of a

Return next to the essays in Balkin's edition. The subtitle is *The Nation's Top Legal Experts Rewrite America's Landmark Civil Rights Decision*. In other words, the reason to buy and read the book is the clout of the legal experts. Who are they? Law professors. All of them had written previously on civil rights. The introduction explains that the book's larger purpose is not just a discourse on doctrine, but to inform general readers' understanding of "the role of courts in a democracy." For *Brown* had been and remained the "center" of a "continuing debate over the role of law in reshaping society." Balkin had no need to elaborate who was listening to that debate—by the new millennium it was clear that the audience was far larger than the legal academy. All the essays were lucid, written for educated lay readers, not for other law professors (although they have both overt and implied criticisms of one another that the non-initiate may miss).[36]

Trade presses now routinely publish books by law professors who joined in the civil rights discourse later, writing on history, political science, policy studies as well as law. Law professors routinely publish op-ed pieces in major venues, are interviewed on NPR and other news outlets, and have their own blog sites visited by thousands, especially when civil rights questions become major public issues. For example, writing for the Bloomberg News Service, Harvard Law professor Noah Feldman has logged over 1,000 and counting entries. Richard Posner's blog site, co-edited with economist Gary Becker, had nearly 4,000 followers on Facebook, and the blog had over 100,000 hits on Google. Lists, like comparisons, are odious, and I am sure that any list of the constitutional law and history experts in academia whose works have gone platinum would omit someone. But the footnotes of the present book would have been incomplete without frequent recourse to many of these superb scholars.

A last proof, by counterexample this time. Why isn't Herbert Wechsler's name engraved in the pantheon of law-school public intellectuals? Of course, it may be because he never wrote a book for a general audience. But that is not why he would be a counterexample of my thesis. The real reason is that he did not really write on civil rights. His Holmes Lecture and his article certainly spurred debate among civil rights–inclined legal academics, but his real topic was judicial review, not civil rights. His comments on civil rights were almost (if not quite) asides and applications of his doctrine, and that never appeals to general audiences.

Model Penal Code," *Harvard Law Review* 65 (1952): 1098; Richard Hofstadter, *Anti-Intellectualism in American Life* (New York: Knopf, 1962), 3 (1950s a time when anti-intellectualism flowered), 10 (the case against the expert).

36. Balkin, "Preface," in *What Brown Should Have Said*, ed. Balkin, xi.

Politics or Law?
Legacies of Lawyering in the Civil Rights Era

Practicing lawyers have always played a part in the political life of the nation, from Alexander Hamilton, Gouverneur Morris, and their peers at the Continental Congress, through the presidencies of John Adams, Thomas Jefferson, Andrew Jackson, John Quincy Adams, James Buchanan, and Abraham Lincoln, all trained counsel, to William Jefferson Clinton and Barack Obama. Lawyers like John Quincy Adams, Henry Clay, John C. Calhoun, Daniel Webster, and Charles Sumner dominated our national legislature. The list could continue for many pages. History—and historians—rarely sees these luminaries as litigators, but rather as politicians. As a consequence, as Daniel A. Farber and Suzanna Sherry wrote recently, "Critics sometimes argue that as currently practiced, constitutional law is just a charade whereby judges conceal their political views." The same could be said of the politics of past decisions like *Marbury v. Madison* (1803), *Dred Scott v. Sandford* (1857), *Plessy v. Ferguson* (1896), and *Lochner v. New York* (1904). In the context of civil rights lawyering, however, the connection between politics and constitutional lawmaking is natural and not quite so censurable. The civil rights school cases raised both legal and political questions of the greatest moment. The litigation certainly fits into a political narrative as well as a legal one.[1]

Nevertheless, any political narrative of civil rights lawyering should not rest on the naive assumption that the courts are merely political institutions, lawyers are but political actors, and the civil rights cases merely represent special interest lawyering. To be sure, it was this kind of assumption that so worried Alexander Bickel, Herbert Wechsler, and others that they engaged in what Louis Pollak called theoretical constitutional tinkering. For if so

---

1. Farber and Sherry, *Judgment Calls*, 3.

important and far-reaching a decision as *Brown* could be fully described as a triumph of a liberal political moment, as the William Rehnquist 1952 memo warned, then no decision by any court would stand the test of time. The losers could always hope (as their successors in fact do) that a new era with new justices and new political alignments would undo what prior generations of lawyers and judges had accomplished. Heraclitus's philosophy would be triumphant: nothing was certain or lasting.

For most of *Brown*'s contemporary legal opponents, the decision seemed merely political, a victory of North over South, the federal over the state governments, radicals over conservatives, and blacks over whites. Whether or not this argument was colorable, historians have not given high marks to lawyers for the segregation side. Yet as advocates for their clients, they did well, holding off true integration for generations. Their political careers did not suffer for being on the losing side of constitutional history either. Quite the opposite was true. Among those featured in the pages above, the members of the Southern Caucus were reelected. They are still honored in their locales. Their names grace buildings and libraries in university settings. Some later held federal judicial office, despite their anti–civil rights stance. Price Daniel went on to a career of distinction in federal service. Richard Ervin, John Patterson, LeRoy Collins, and J. Lindsay Almond became governors, fulfilling their political aims. The federal judges who dragged their feet, like John Parker, remained in black robes and retired with pensions and honors intact, although jurists like Clement F. Haynsworth and G. Harrold Carswell, and doubters like Robert Bork—all of whom had expressed little sympathy for civil rights cases in their courts—suffered later in their careers.

By contrast, the black-robed heroes of the history books—judges like Frank Johnson, Elbert Tuttle, and John Minor Wisdom, and justices like Earl Warren—occupied larger niches in the pantheon of American constitutional jurisprudence than those who thwarted civil rights, but that is because, in the end, so much of the reputations of history's figures depend on the judgment of historians. Historians have been kind to the civil rights lawyers, especially Thurgood Marshall, Robert Carter, Spottswood Robinson, and Constance Baker Motley. Whatever one says now of the lasting value of their efforts to end Jim Crow, those efforts were certainly Herculean.

With the aid of hindsight, Derrick Bell was right: *Brown* and later civil rights decisions had as much impact on national politics as on the law. White massive resistance led in time to a shift in political allegiances, the so-called Republican Southern Strategy formed in part by Strom Thurmond, a leader in the pro-segregationist camp. The white South is no longer Democratic— indeed parts of that electorate are as solidly Republican as they had been

Democratic in years prior to *Brown*. Bell's *And We Are Not Saved* was a power-ful indictment of the shortcomings of the civil rights movement. In education, the damage that forced desegregation had done to the children themselves, to their black teachers, and to the parents, when "all the black school-age children were gone," was, like the children in Bell's imaginative essay, invis-ible to those who celebrated *Brown* as if it had wrought all good things. But if one can argue that Bell's disappointment was "something real," it is in the long view of history misplaced. *Brown* stands as a rock-like sentinel in the narrative of the liberalization of American politics. It launched a debate, not only among academics, but among policy makers and educators, about what equality meant and how it could be best achieved. It is a meta-narrative we tell ourselves, part of the end of slavery and the triumph of civil rights, a self-congratulatory motif, even if in many parts of the country, public schools are as segregated as they were before *Brown*. Two-nation politics still directly in-fluence the legislative gerrymandering of state and national electoral districts and presidential contests. We are not color-blind, and perhaps we never will be, and, even more important, calls for a color-blind constitutionalism may obscure hidden inequities, but one look at the train stations, movie theaters, athletic fields, hotels and motels and restaurants, and all the public accom-modations whose integration Professor Wechsler once upon a time doubted belonged under *Brown*'s penumbras, and who can doubt that Jim Crow is dead if not quite buried.[2]

If the legal issue is not state-mandated segregation but federally spon-sored integration, the narrative shifts dramatically. For a time it seemed that with the Civil Rights Act of 1964 and the Voting Rights Act of 1965, Congress and the federal courts would work together to create a national legal regime of actual equality. Localities and local interests, as well as some state govern-ments, resisted. Over time the federal courts stepped away from integration as a bridge too far for judicial decrees to cross. As national politics in the 1980s and 1990s became more wary of federal government as a whole and govern-ment initiatives like affirmative action in particular, federal commitment to goals beyond color-blindness fell away. In a sense, it was the replay of the last years of Reconstruction, followed by the victory of southern redemption— the story that the parties in *Brown* briefed, albeit with different results.

2. Derrick Bell, *And We Are Not Saved: The Elusive Quest for Racial Justice* (New York: Basic Books, 1987), 102; Martha Minow, *In* Brown's *Wake: Legacies of America's Educational Landmark* (New York: Oxford University Press, 2012), 2, 5, 10; Reva Siegel, "Discrimination in the Eyes of the Law: How 'Color-Blindness' Discourse Disrupts and Rationalizes Social Stratification," *California Law Review* 88 (2000): 79.

Public interest litigation of the school cases sort cannot help but have political repercussions. After all, as much as they may try to hold themselves out
from partisanship, courts are still institutions in a political system. The courts'
inputs and outputs, to use the language of the political scientists, touch other
branches of government. In our democratic republic, the fact that the federal
judiciary is not elected makes the entire process suspect. Alexander Bickel
called this "the countermajoritarian dilemma." For this reason, "such things
[as desegregation] cannot be made to happen in a day." For although strata-
gems of pupil placement and the like were perverse, they were still emblem-
atic of a "tangle" of intractable facts. Southern lawyers opposing *Brown* raised
both of these arguments—that in the South, where the weight of the decision
fell most dramatically, a majority rejected court-mandated desegregation
and in any case implementation required arrangements hard to "unscramble
overnight."[3]

For lawyers, the inevitable and necessary political aspect to civil rights
cases meant that they had to be waged in the public area as much as in the
courtroom. Thurgood Marshall understood this. His manner in court was
well suited to a wider stage. Folksy, plainspoken, morally committed, his language in the pleadings and the oral argument, as well as the press conferences
he held, made the political case for his cause.

By contrast, because at least in court and Congress they could not engage
in openly racist rhetoric, the anti–civil rights lawyers lost the public relations
battle. Making subtle points about federalism, the Constitution, precedent,
and the like simply did not resonate with the media or the larger public. The
underlying message was well understood by their constituents, as the correspondence of men like Richard Russell demonstrated, but that private language stayed private. Thus when Russell, two years after *Brown* II, addressed
the graduation at Mercer University in Macon, Georgia, he talked in code
about desegregation. "Today we hear a great clamor for many changes . . . in
our social order and system of government. . . . [T]hey are largely old theories
which have been tried and discarded." Such changes "place in the hands of a
few men the power to determine the way of life which they deem most ad-
vantageous to 170 million individual citizens." The proposals that these men
imposed on the South "propose to do justice to a minority . . . but . . . actually
do injustice to a majority." Mercer had not integrated, and Russell's audience
of white students and their parents knew just who the "few men" and the
"minority" to whom he referred were and what the "changes" meant. But the

3. Alexander Bickel, *The Least Dangerous Branch: The Supreme Court at the Bar of Politics*,
2nd ed. (New Haven, CT: Yale University Press, 1986), 16, 249.

coded language only worked in friendly southern audiences. Russell was not asked to give graduation addresses outside of the South.[4]

In much of his career, Russell had been a progressive Democrat. He favored public improvements for the poor, improved public education, and other reforms. Were it not for his racial views and his efforts to stymie civil rights legislation, he might have been regarded as modern. The same was true of other southern politicians, for example, John Patterson of Alabama, a lawyer whose efforts to elevate the poor of his state ran athwart his die-hard segregationism, but who in later years supported integration and, in 2008, the candidacy of Barack Obama.[5]

There was a final consequence of civil rights lawyering in the political sphere that concerns the checks-and-balances system. Separation of powers among the executive, legislative, and judicial branches of government has always presumed that the judiciary is and was to be the weakest of the three branches. It does not have the sword or the purse, and relies on the assistance of the other branches and the compliance of the parties before it to accomplish its goals. When the executive and the legislative are not cooperative, and parties to litigations drag their feet, courts may seem to be impotent. That, certainly, is why Justice Frankfurter urged caution on the Court in *Brown*. But if his concern was warranted, and local officials did not hurry to obey the courts in the desegregation cases, in the end the courts participated in a profound shift in the politics of both South and North. In this sense, civil rights lawyering's greatest impact lay in the elevation of the role and status of the courts. In the public eye, they became as visible a source of authority as the other branches of government. The "Impeach Earl Warren" signs that appeared throughout the recalcitrant South bore ironic witness to this rising salience of the courts, if not increased respect. At the time, who else was as important in political life as this one sitting judge, save perhaps President Lyndon Johnson?[6]

Assuming one can set aside the politics of and around the cases, at least for the sake of argument, the constitutional story of civil rights lawyering

4. Richard Russell, draft Commencement Speech at Mercer University, June 3, 1957, Russell Collection, Russell Library, University of Georgia, box 27, folio 1. A review of all his speeches post-1956 does not reveal any to audiences outside of the South. Russell Collection, Subgroup C, Series III.

5. Compare, e.g., Howard, *Patterson for Alabama*, 90–139 with 222.

6. Charles H. Franklin and Liane C. Kosaki, "Media Knowledge and Public Evaluations of the Supreme Court," in *Contemplating Courts*, ed. Lee J. Epstein (Washington, DC: CQ Press, 1995), 352–75; Jim Newton, *And Justice for All: Earl Warren and the Nation He Made* (New York: Penguin, 2007), 386.

would seem to be a triumph for the civil rights bar. *Plessy* no longer stands, *Cumming v. Richmond Country* (1899) no longer stands, *Berea College v. Kentucky* (1908) no longer stands, and *Gong Lum v. Rice* (1927) no longer stands. It is clear that they will never be resuscitated. Children will never be forced to attend public school or barred from attending one on the basis of perceived race or color. But will people never be denied equal protection because of their color? Here the triumphal account of civil rights lawyering runs into a contrary reality. Stop-and-frisk and the summary deportation of suspected undocumented aliens suggests that color still matters to law enforcement officials. Profiling is one proof that the Constitution does not always reach down to the ground. In this sense, *Plessy*, with its demeaning and disfiguring classification by color, is still permissible law enforcement, if not good law.[7]

The legal narrative does not end with color, however. Civil rights lawyering on both sides of the aisle forced the Court to reexamine the jurisprudence of federalism. While Congress provided special proceedings, actually safeguards, that such action would require a three-judge panel, and the Court, in a series of cases, told those panels to avoid striking down state criminal laws whenever possible, it was a step that realigned the boundaries of federalism. Historians of the courts and the Constitution recognize that those boundaries have been shifting since they were created in 1787. The Judiciary Act of 1789, in the course of fashioning a system of inferior federal trial courts, was solicitous of state courts' jurisdiction, but over time gave to federal courts more and more jurisdiction over matters that had been reserved to the states and their courts. The Reconstruction Amendments and the jurisprudence of Substantive Due Process shifted the boundaries still further. By reinvigorating the Equal Protection Clause of the Fourteenth Amendment, the Warren Court moved the boundary once again. In later years, the Court retreated

---

7. Cumming v. Richmond County, 175 U.S. 528, 545 (1899) (Harlan, J.) ("the education of the people in schools maintained by state taxation is a matter belonging to the respective states, and any interference on the part of Federal authority with the management of such schools cannot be justified except in the case of a clear and unmistakable disregard of rights secured by the supreme law of the land"); Berea College v. Kentucky, 211 U.S. 45, 55 (1908) (Brewer, J.) ("That the legislature of Kentucky desired to separate the teaching of white and colored children may be conceded," and Berea College violated that law by allowing whites and blacks to matriculate); Gong Lum v. Rice, 275 U.S. 78, 85 (1927) (Taft, C.J.) ("The case then reduces itself to the question whether a state can be said to afford to a child of Chinese ancestry born in this country, and a citizen of the United States, equal protection of the laws by giving her the opportunity for a common school education in a school which receives only colored children of the brown, yellow or black races," and Mississippi could). But see Mark V. Tushnet, "Litigation Campaigns and the Search for Constitutional Rules," *Journal of Appellate Practice and Process* 6 (2004): 101–11 (various new procedural rules limited effectiveness of litigation campaigns like civil rights).

from the high-water mark of the Warren years. So-called New Federalism jurisprudence in the 1980s and 1990s shifted the boundary back to give a little more space to the states and their courts, but in the long history of federalism, the impact of *Brown* and the school cases is undeniable.

Although primarily a constitutional matter, federalism always had political repercussions. It may be that working lawyers did not always focus on this issue. Judges tried to avoid it. The very self-imposed constitutional constraint that the Court would not entertain political questions—leaving these to the elected branches of government, policing the boundaries of federalism—was revisited in the "watershed" reappointment cases. These and later decisions on campaign finance and the 2000 presidential election showed that the Court was willing to set aside its own prudential doctrines regarding political questions.[8]

Civil rights lawyering could not have been effective without a strong version of judicial review. That doctrine—a prudential assertion that the courts had the authority to strike down legislation that conflicted, in the opinion of the majority of the Court, with the Constitution—had its own history. The common complaint about the Court's exercise of judicial review is that the justices assume the role of legislators, and the Court become a miniature Congress. This, I think, is unfair and misleading. While it may be true in other cases, in the desegregation cases, judicial review was an example of public interest lawyering by the justices. The Court could have viewed the graduate school cases and the school cases as political and declined to decide them, deferring to legislatures, or finding some other prudential way of avoiding stepping into what had been a local or state matter. The Court did not, even when led by Chief Justice Vinson, opt for this self-denying role. Instead, the justices became advocates of a certain cause—the cause of an oppressed minority. Whether this was a role contemplated much less assigned the Court by the framers is a matter for others to debate. The historian's job is to see what happened, not to make constitutional judgments.

Civil rights lawyering required familiarity with the conventional principles of equity. In *Brown* II, the justices asked the district court judges to exercise their powers as chancellors to insure that all parties fulfilled the

8. Reapportionment cases and "political question": Lackland H. Bloom Jr., *Do Great Cases Make Bad Law?* (New York: Oxford University Press, 2014), 20, 235–53; campaign finance jurisprudence and "political question": Peter Kobrak, *Cozy Politics: Political Parties, Campaign Finance, and Compromised Governance* (Boulder, CO: Lynne Rienner, 2002), 227; Bush v. Gore (2000) and the "political question": Richard Posner, *Breaking the Deadlock: The 2000 Election, the Constitution, and the Courts* (Princeton, NJ: Princeton University Press, 2001), 4, 182–83.

mandate of the Court. Once a separate body of precepts heard in a different kind of court, in 1938 the Federal Rules of Civil Procedure joined equity and law in a single "complaint" whose call for a remedy included traditional equitable remedies like the injunction. Unlike law courts, which dealt with things and provided damages, courts of equity dealt with persons. Thus the injunction is a command to do something or to stop doing something. Most commonly seen in private nuisance cases, injunctions could be deployed in a far wider, public arena. The rub was that parties before the court had to have "clean hands," that is, equity presumed good-faith performance on all sides. Southern pupil placement and step-by-step plans were more often than not products of bad faith, attempts to subvert the decrees of the district courts. In assuming good faith, district courts allowed refractory school districts to delay compliance for decades. But the Court's use of equitable remedies had a side effect that Warren might not have anticipated. It made the equitable remedy the tool of choice for all manner of political reformers seeking to win political aims through litigation. Thus the injunction became a vital part of electoral reform in the redistricting cases and environment causes in the pollution cases.[9]

In the courtroom, the halls of Congress, the public arena, and the classroom, civil rights lawyering transformed a nation. If it did not end racism, it offered victims of racism the hope of recourse. It opened doors for African American litigators. It forced opponents of civil rights to recognize that past regimes of state-sponsored inequality must be abandoned. It elevated judges and judging to full partnership in the checks-and-balances system of republican self-government. It moved legal scholarship into center stage in American intellectual life. Its penumbras reached far and wide.

9. On equity and civil rights: Peter Charles Hoffer, *The Law's Conscience: Equitable Constitutionalism in America* (Durham: University of North Carolina Press, 1990), 180–98; on equity and redistricting: Gordon Silverstein, *Law's Allure: How Law Shapes, Constrains, Saves, and Kills Politics* (New York: Cambridge University Press, 2009), 61–62; Charles Bullock, *Redistricting: The Most Political Activity in America* (Lanham, MD: Rowman and Littlefield, 2010), 33–36.

Index

abolitionism, 165

Ackerman, Bruce: on *Brown*, 184

Alabama, segregation in, 98

"all deliberate speed," 126, 134

Almond, J. Lindsay, 3; and *Davis v. Prince Edward County*, 59; and LDF, 95; and segregation, 129

American Revolution, vii, 1

Bailey v. Alabama (1911), 20–21

Balkin, Jack: on *Brown*, 183–84

Becker, Marshall: and *Brown*, 169

Bell, Derrick: on *Brown*, 185, 190–91

Berger, Raoul: on desegregation, 181

Bickel, Alexander: and desegregation, 172; and Fourteenth Amendment, 70; and freedom of association, 157; and Herbert Wechsler, 179–80; and originalism, 171; as public intellectual, 180; and reargument in *Brown*, 69, 171; and Reconstruction, 70

Black, Charles L., Jr.: and *Brown*, 170, 176

Black, Hugo, 42; and *Sweatt v. Painter*, 42

black litigants, and Jim Crow, 15–16

Blocker v. Manhasset (1961), 147–48

Bolling v. Sharpe (1954), 83

Boston, segregation in, 154–55

Bowers, Claude, 77

"Brandeis brief," 31

Briggs v. Elliott (1951), 24, 55–58, 60–69

Browder v. Gale (1956), 135

Brown, Henry Billings: in *Plessy v. Ferguson*, 17–18

Brown v. Board of Education (1954), 54–55, 81–84

Brown v. Board of Education II (1955), 87, 93–94, 122

Brownell, Herbert, 80; and *Briggs v. Elliott*, 81

Bryan, Albert V., 143

Buchanan v. Warley (1917), 22

burden of proof, 12

Burton, Harold, 46; and *Sweatt v. Painter*, 46

Byrd, Harry, 97; and segregation, 103, 129; and "Southern Manifesto," 103

Byrnes, James, 52; in *Briggs v. Elliott*, 12

Calhoun, John C.: and states' rights, 90

Cameron, Benjamin F.: and segregation, 140

Cardozo, Benjamin: on judging, 123

Carswell, G. Harrold: and segregation, 140

Carter, Jimmy: and judicial appointments, 142

Carter, Robert L., 10, 28; and *Davis v. Prince Edward County*, 59; and *Sweatt v. Painter*, 40

Chambers, Julius, 10

checks and balances, 109, 193

Civil Rights Act of 1875, 16, 75, 77, 112

Civil Rights Act of 1957, 145

Civil Rights Act of 1964, 145–47

Civil Rights Cases (1883), 16, 75, 76, 112

Civil War, vii, 1

Clark, Kenneth, 59

Clark, Tom C., 46; and *Sweatt v. Painter*, 46

"clean hands" doctrine, 115

Coleman, James P.: and segregation, 100

Coleman, William, 170

Collins, LeRoy: and segregation, 100

"community of interest," 178

Constitution (U.S.), as living document, 67

Cooper v. Aaron (1958), 134

Coulter, E. Merton, 173

Cover, Robert, 186

Crawford v. Los Angeles (1982), 158

Cumming v. Richmond (1899), 30, 37

Daniel, Price, 3; and "Southern Manifesto," 110–11; and *Sweatt v. Painter*, 34, 35, 41, 50

Davidson, T. Whitfield: and segregation, 10

Davis, John W., 66; and *Briggs v. Elliott*, 12, 65–67, 77–79; and expert witnesses, 67–68; as solicitor general, 23

Davis v. Prince Edward County (1952), 58–59

de facto segregation, 65, 147–48, 151

Detroit, segregation in, 153–54

DeVane, Dozier Adolphus, 139; and James Meredith cases, 139–40

Dillard v. Charlottesville (1962), 143–44

Dixon v. Alabama (1961), 148–49

Dobie, Armistead Mason, 60; and *Briggs v. Elliott*, 61

Douglas, William O., 44–45; and *Sweatt v. Painter*, 45

Dred Scott v. Sandford (1857), 14, 65, 71

Due Process Clause, 22, 23

Durham, William J., 33; and *Sweatt v. Painter*, 33, 39–41

Eastland, James, 101; and Harland confirmation, 101; and Motley confirmation, 143; and "Southern Manifesto," 101

Edwards, Harry T.: on law schools, 168–69

Eisenhower, Dwight D.: judicial appointments of, 52–53; and segregation, 52–53

Eleventh Circuit (Court of Appeals), 134

Equal Protection Clause, 36, 48–49, 62

equitable remedies, 195–96

Ervin, Richard, 88, 91; brief for Florida in *Brown II*, 88–93; and implementation, 88; and segregation, 88

Ervin, Sam, 106; and limits on judiciary, 10; and "Southern Manifesto," 102

expert witnesses, 59, 62

Fairman, Charles: and "Southern Manifesto," 119–20

federal judges: attitudes of, 25; desegregation of, 140–43; and implementation, 87, 123; local experience of, 26, 56; and managing remedies, 156–57; and resistance to desegregation, 124–29

federalism, 194. *See also* states' rights

Fifteenth Amendment, 15

Fifth Circuit (Court of Appeals), 129–30

Finger, John, 152

Fiss, Owen, 168; on civil rights, 185–86

Fitzhugh, George, 92

Flowers, Richmond, 9

footnote 11 (to *Brown v. Board*), 83–84

"Founding Fathers," 109

Fourteenth Amendment, 15, 110. *See also* Equal Protection Clause

Fourth Circuit (Court of Appeals), 129

Frankfurter, Felix, 42; and *Briggs v. Elliott*, 63, 67, 74, 76; and implementation, 64, 79–80; and law clerks, 170; and *Sweatt v. Painter*, 43, 47

Franklin v. South Carolina (1910), 19

freedom of association doctrine, 157–59

Freund, Paul: on desegregation, 181

"Fugitive" literary movement, 164

Garrity, W. Arthur: and desegregation in Boston, 154

George, Walter: and "Southern Manifesto," 107–8

Goluboff, Risa: on limits of desegregation, 181–82

Gong Lum v. Rice (1927), 37

Goodman, Frank: on desegregation, 181

Green v. New Kent County (1968), 134

Greenberg, Jack, 28

Greenhill, Joseph: and *Sweatt v. Painter*, 34–35, 39, 41

Grooms, Harlan H., 53

Guinn v. United States (1915), 23

Gunther, Gerald: on desegregation, 180

Hall v. West (1964), 128

Hand, W. Brevard: and originalism, 161–62

Harlan, John Marshall, I: and *Civil Rights Cases*, 16; and *Plessy v. Ferguson*, 18

Harlan, John Marshall, II, 99; and *NAACP v. Alabama*, 99–100

Hart, Henry M., Jr., 177–78

Hastie, William H., 27

Haynsworth, Clement, 143

Higginbotham, A. Leon, 142

Hill, J. Lister: and Civil Rights Act of 1964, 145

historical neutrality, 8

Hodges v. United States (1906), 29

Hollowell, Donald, 11, 173

Hooper, Frank A., 127; and segregation in Atlanta, 126–28

Houston, Charles Hamilton, 4, 24

Hughes, Charles Evans, 21

Hurley v. Irish-American Gay Group (1995), 159

Hutcheson, Charles Sterling, 97

integration, 191–92

Jackson, Robert H., 45; and *Briggs v. Elliott*, 78; and *Sweatt v. Painter*, 45

Jim Crow, 14–24

Johnson, Frank, Jr.: and desegregation, 131

Johnson, Lyndon: and judicial appointments, 142

Johnson v. Virginia (1963), 11–12

judicial review, 195

Kauper, Paul G.: and *Brown*, 169

Keeton, Page: and *Sweatt v. Painter*, 50–51

Kelly, Alfred, 73, 77

Kennedy, John F.: and judicial appointments, 26, 141–42

Killian, Lewis: and segregation in Florida, 89, 91

King, Martin Luther, Jr., 122; and Birmingham Bus Strike, 135
KKK, 69
Klarman, Michael: on limits of desegregation, 182
Kurland, Philip: on desegregation, 181

Lake, I. Beverly: on segregation, 173–74
law professors, 167–69; and civil rights, 4, 173; and opposition to desegregation, 173–74; as public intellectuals, 186–88
law schools, 5, 167–69
lawyering: as big business, 4; corporate model of, 2; and politics, 9, 189–96; public interest model of, 2, 6, 28, 192
LDF (Legal and Educational Defense Fund), 2, 28; and charges of ethical misconduct, 94–98; and local lawyers, 29; and school segregation, 30; and segregation, 122. See also Marshall, Thurgood
legal pedagogy, 8
"legal process school," 177–79
Lieb, Joseph Patrick: and resistance to desegregation, 125–26
Little Rock, AR, desegregation in, 132–34
local experience of educators, 62
Los Angeles, segregation in, 157–58
"Lost Cause," 117
Lynne, Seybourn, 27; and Browder v. Gayle, 136

Marshall, Burke, 167, 186; on civil rights, 1, 186
Marshall, Thurgood, 24, 28; and Briggs v. Elliott, 12, 61–65, 76; on Court of Appeals, 142; and implementation, 64, 79–80; and LDF, 4; and "school cases," 53; as solicitor general, 142; on U.S. Supreme Court, 142
Mays, David J.: and segregation in Virginia, 95
McClendon, James Wooten, 36; and Sweatt v. Painter, 36–39
McCree, Wade, Jr., 141–42
McLaurin v. Oklahoma (1950), 31
McMillan, James B., 151, 152; and Swann v. Charlotte-Mecklenburg, 152–53
Meese, Edwin, III: and originalism, 160–61
Michelman, Frank: on Brown, 184–85
Milliken v. Bradley (1974), 153–54
Minton, Sherman, 46–47
Mize, Sidney, 138; and James Meredith cases, 138–39; and "sit-ns," 137–38
Morgan v. Hennigan (1974), 154–55
Morton, L. Clure: and segregation in Nashville, 154
Motley, Constance Baker, 126, 142–43

NAACP, 2, 19–20
NAACP v. Alabama (1958), 99–100
NAACP v. Button (1963), 97–98
Nabrit, James, Jr., 33
Nashville, segregation in, 154

Necessary and Proper Clause, 78
"neutral principles," 175–76, 177
New Deal, vii
New York Times v. Sullivan (1964), 176
"nullification," 90, 104, 117

"Old Constitution," 6–7
originalism, 160–61, 183, 185
outside agitators, 68, 114

Parker, John J.: and Briggs v. Elliott, 55–58, 63; and segregation, 9–10
Parks, Rosa, 135
Parsons, James, 141
Patterson, James T.: on limits of desegregation, 182
Patterson, John, 3; and Dixon v. Alabama, 148–49; and segregation, 100
peonage, 20
Plessy v. Ferguson (1896), 7, 16–17, 37, 49, 84, 111, 136
"political question" doctrine, 174–75, 179
Pollak, Louis H.: on Brown, 170, 176–77
Posner, Richard: on judging, 124
Powell, Lewis: and segregation, 158
precedent, 7, 37, 110, 111
public law, 5

race: of lawyers, 8; and school segregation, 38
race war, 86
racial discrimination, 69, 79; in employment, 30; and law, 166; in South, 107–8, 118
Rankin, J. Lee, 81; and Briggs v. Elliott, 81
Reconstruction amendments, vii
Redding, Louis, 59; and Gebhart v. Belton, 59
redemption, of the South, 15, 116
Reed, Stanley Forman, 42; and Briggs v. Elliott, 69, 76–77; and Sweatt v. Painter, 42, 47
Rehnquist, William, 70; and Plessy v. Ferguson, 71; and segregation, 70
resegregation, 144, 165
Rives, Richard T., 136; and Browder v. Gayle, 135
Roberts v. City of Boston (1849), 113
Robinson, Spottswood, 29; and Briggs v. Elliott, 73–75; and Davis v. Prince Edward County, 58–59
Rosenberg, Gerald: on limits of desegregation, 182
Roth, Stephen, 153; and Milliken v. Bradley, 153–54
Russell, Richard, 3, 193; and Civil Rights Act of 1964, 146–47; and desegregation, 192; as legalist, 106; and "Southern Manifesto," 102, 105, 111–12, 119

secession, 107, 117
seditious libel, 140
segregation, in the North, 147–48
segregation, in Reconstruction Era, 113
Seitz, Collins, 59; and Gebhart v. Belton, 59–60

Sellers, Grover, 33–34
"separate but equal," 54, 62, 82
separation of powers, 101, 110
Sipuel v. Board of Regents (1947), 31
"sit-ins," 137–38, 149–50
Sobeloff, Simon: and desegregation, 140–41
social science experts, 31, 39, 63, 68
"sociological jurisprudence," 83–84, 92
sociology of law, 7
sociology of the South, 92, 114
Soper, Morris: and LDF misconduct cases, 96–97
Souter, David: and freedom of association, 159
South: conservatism of, 7, 163–64; legalism in,
    165; as a minority, 116, 118; and resistance to
    desegregation, 86–87; traditions of, 92–93, 114,
    163–64; uniqueness of, 164
southern attorneys general, 94
Southern Caucus, 105, 107, 119, 146
"Southern Manifesto": 101–21, 163; constitutional-
    ism in, 109; legal force of, 108–9, 120; racism
    in, 106
"Stanley Plan," 95
stare decisis, 80
states' rights, 90, 112
Stennis, John, 102, 106; and "Southern Manifesto,"
    102, 106
Stephens, Alexander, 106
Storey, Moorfield, 19–20, 22
Strauder v. West Virginia (1880), 76
Swann v. Charlotte-Mecklenburg (1970), 152–53
Sweatt, Heman Marion, 32–33
Sweatt v. Painter (1950), 32–51

Taney, Roger: in *Dred Scott v. Sandford*, 14
Thirteenth Amendment, 15

Thurmond, Strom, 3, 104; and "Southern Mani-
    festo," 102, 104, 105
Timmerman, George Bell: and *Briggs v. Elliott*,
    55–56, 57; and segregation, 124–25
Truman, Harry S.: and Fair Deal, 27; judicial ap-
    pointments of, 26
Tuttle, Elbert, 131; and *Brown v. Board*, 131; and
    Civil Rights Act of 1964, 132

University of Michigan Law School, 5

Vandiver, Ernest: and segregation, 100
Vinson, Fred, 42; and *Briggs v. Elliott*, 63; and
    Sweatt v. Painter, 42, 47, 48–49
Virginia, segregation in, 95

Wallace, George: and segregation, 100
Wallace v. Jaffree (1982), 161–62
Ward, Horace, 127, 173
Waring, J. Waties, 57–58; and *Briggs v. Elliott*, 58
Warren, Earl, 72; and *Briggs v. Elliott*, 73; and
    Brown v. Board, 82–84; on education, 83;
    and implementation, 87; and segregation, 73;
    and unanimous Court, 85–86
Wechsler, Herbert, 170; on *Brown*, 174–75; on judi-
    cial review, 174–75; as public intellectual, 187
West, Elmer Gordon, 128–29
"white flight," 65, 144, 154–55
whiteness, 118
Wisdom, John Minor, 128; and James Meredith
    cases, 138–39
Woods, Henry: and Little Rock cases, 156–57
Wright, J. Skelly, 130; and segregation, 130

Zavatt, Joseph: and *Blocker v. Manhasset*, 147–48